Young Playwrights' Theater

Write to Dream

A Collection of Plays by the Students of Young Playwrights' Theater
And the Tools to Turn *Anyone* into a Young Playwright

Featuring plays by

Kenrry Alvarado	Cecilia Jenkins	Miranda Pomroy
Cassidy Boomsma	Julie Kashmanian	Sophie ReVeal
Breena Bradford	Shawn Lee	Mayra Rivera
Sam Burris	Elaine Qi Ling Li	Mariana Pavón Sánchez
Cameron Byrd	Zainep Mahmoud	Nora Spellane
Chris Chio	Shannon Marshall	Antawan Taylor
Kamilia Epps	Paul McCoyer	Edwin Ventura
Kyrtham Franco	Engedasew Menkir	Sheila Walcott
Ann Gill	Laila Parada-Worby	Amber Faith Walton
Pete Hall	Josh Perles	Julia Winkler

Young Playwrights' Theater Publishing
Washington, DC

Cover Photo: ©iStockphoto.com/KLH49
Interior Photos: Liza Harbison
Cover and Text Design: Liza Harbison

Library of Congress Cataloging-in-Publication Data
Young Playwrights' Theater
Write to dream: a collection of plays by the students of Young Playwrights' Theater and the tools to turn anyone into a young playwright / Young Playwrights' Theater
p.cm.
2012921498

ISBN 978-0615728032

Young Playwrights' Theater (YPT) is the only professional theater in Washington, DC dedicated entirely to arts education. Our mission is to teach students to express themselves clearly and creatively through the art of playwriting. Through interactive in-school and after-school programs, YPT activates student learning and inspires students to understand the power of language and realize their potential as both individuals and artists. By publicly presenting and discussing student-written work, YPT promotes community dialogue and respect for young artists.

This book is dedicated to the many members of the YPT family - past, present and future. To our staff, board, teaching artists, actors, directors, designers, partners, donors, funders, collaborators, audience members and – most importantly – our students and alumni. This book is for you.

Preface by Karen Zacarías
Founding Artistic Director

When I was ten years old, my family moved from Mexico to the United States. Different country, different customs, different language. I was bewildered and lonely. After school, some boys taunted me and I stood slack-jawed and said...nothing. On the way home, I developed a come-back. I heard the dialogue in my mind. I wondered about the boys and invented a story about why they were mean.

That night, I wrote the scene. On paper, I didn't stand mute and scared, but turned and faced my bullies. On paper, the bullies weren't just mean boys, but children with their own past and motivations. I realized that although I was overwhelmed in my everyday world, every word I wrote gave me a new sense of clarity and discovery.

Suddenly, I was not a powerless child but a playwright with a story.

I started Young Playwrights' Theater (YPT) because I will never forget how it feels to be a child with a lot to say and no clear way to express it.

Playwriting is a vital art form that involves building character, navigating conflict, making choices – it is a perfect vessel for teaching young people about literacy, about conflict resolution, about the power of the arts. But more than anything, playwriting helps young people find their voice...and an audience that is listening.

It is with great pride that I present to you the first publication of plays written by YPT students. All of these compelling pieces of theater have had readings, been produced and have already delighted thousands of audience members with their imagination, insight and honesty.

Each one was written by a student in the Washington, DC, Metro area.

Each one reflects a vital story and a unique voice in our community.

May these plays inspire you to write as well.

Write on!

Karen Zacarías
Founding Artistic Director
Young Playwrights' Theater

I first met Karen Zacarías at her kitchen table. She had called me a few days before, told me about the Producing Artistic Director job at YPT and that a mutual friend had suggested we meet. I told her how much I believed in DC students, in their creativity and compassion. She told me about YPT. We talked for hours. It seemed like we had known each other forever. And I knew I had discovered something very special.

On my first day in the office at YPT, I discovered something else: boxes and boxes of plays, handwritten pages of lined notebook paper, written by hundreds and hundreds of DC students. As I read through these plays, I was blown away by the students' creativity, their bravery and brilliance. I was inspired. And I realized we had everything we needed to succeed.

Over the next seven years we would go far, inspired by the bravery and creativity of each and every student.

As I reflect on my time at YPT and everything we accomplished, I think of the students, the staff, teaching artists, artists and board members who made it all possible; the countless donors, volunteers and funders who supported us; and the thousands of plays created by our students. I think of all the mini-miracles and acts of courage I witnessed over the years, of all the progress we made as a company, and I feel blessed to have been a part of it.

We've grown an idea into an organization – a creative impulse into a company. And all this work has been in the service of our students – to ensure that they know that what they have to say truly matters – to all of us.

These plays represent a fraction of what our students created in the first seventeen years of YPT. So as you read and hopefully perform these plays, imagine how much more joy, insight and inspiration would exist in the world if we invited all of our youth to write plays.

And then ask the young people in your lives, "What do you think?" You'll be amazed by the results.

David Snider
Producing Artistic Director
2005-2012

Introduction
Brigitte Pribnow Moore, Executive Director
Nicole Jost, Artistic Director

Young Playwrights' Theater (YPT) dreams of a country – of a world – where the arts are a core part of every student's education. Since 1995, we have pursued this vision in classrooms throughout the Washington, DC, region. Our interactive programming and performances activate student learning, inspire students to understand the power of language and show students the impact and value of their ideas and stories.

Founded by award-winning playwright Karen Zacarías, YPT is the only professional theater in Washington, DC, dedicated entirely to arts education. YPT teaches students to express themselves clearly and creatively through the art of playwriting. Each year, YPT provides free in-school and out-of-school-time programming for students throughout the Washington, DC region, and then shares student-written plays with thousands of audience members through productions and tours featuring local professional artists.

As of the day we publish this book, we have inspired over 10,000 elementary, middle and high school students to dream on paper and express themselves through playwriting. By the time you read this introduction, we will have reached hundreds – perhaps thousands – more. In recent years, we worked with an arts education researcher, Dr. Barry Oreck, to establish assessment tools that clearly demonstrate the positive impact of our arts education model on student learning and development. You will hear directly from Dr. Oreck about this process on page 325. We are working to establish a measurable model for arts learning in classrooms throughout the Washington, DC, region, and – through this book – we are excited to share this model with classrooms and living rooms throughout the United States.

Over the past seventeen years, YPT students have written thousands of amazing original plays. This book contains some of the most exciting scripts from 1995-2012. Every play we've included in these pages has been professionally produced by YPT artists and showcased for a public audience. We chose plays that represent the diversity of our student playwrights. These 30 YPT students and alumni hail from different neighborhoods, attend different schools and have different backgrounds. They represent the full picture of YPT's seventeen-year history, and we could not be more proud to share their words with you.

When YPT comes into the classroom, most of the students we meet have never written a play before. In just twelve short weeks, they gain all the tools they need to write a successful script. Professional teaching artists train students on finding inspiration, creating characters and developing conflict, among other essential playwriting skills. The resulting plays are as unique as the students themselves. Mayra Rivera, an eleventh grader at the time she wrote her play, chose to imagine a romance between a pair of ten-year-olds (page 55). In his fifth-grade year, Paul McCoyer wrote a sophisticated satire of capitalism (page 33). And Kamilia Epps, also an eleventh grader when she wrote her play, found her inspiration in history class (page 105).

YPT does not dictate the content of our students' plays. They write about a wide variety of subjects, from superheroes, to love, to social justice. It is vital to the YPT process that students recognize their playwriting assignment as a creative outlet for whatever they need to get off their chests. For our older students particularly, this can mean grappling with serious and mature themes. To make this collection as user-friendly as possible, we've organized the plays by age appropriateness: All Ages, 13 & Up, or 16 & Up. You'll find exceptional works in all three categories.

As you read, we hope you will be as proud of these evolving writers as we are. It takes great daring to create art, particularly if you are a young person offering up your story for the first time. We believe that all people deserve the opportunity for creative self-expression, and when presented with this opportunity our students never disappoint.

With this publication, we are also sharing our curriculum for the first time. Here you'll get a sense of how we do what we do. If you are a teacher, we encourage you to use the workshops in this book to engage your own students, whether you teach English, history or even math. Although we celebrate and support our students if they choose to pursue playwriting beyond our program, it is not our mission to develop the next great American playwright. Rather, we strive to help every student we encounter enhance his or her literacy skills and self-esteem. All students can benefit from sharpening their critical thinking, communication skills, collaboration and creativity, no matter what career path they pursue. In the curriculum section of this book, you'll find a list of Common Core State Standards addressed by our material, to help you easily integrate these workshops into the school day. You can read more about the growth that we've seen in our students during the program, and how we measure that growth, on page 325.

Your purchase of this book includes a donation to support YPT. We are incredibly grateful for your contribution. As a nonprofit organization, we depend on community members like you to continue our work. Your support will help us realize the visions of even more young playwrights and reach even more students in the classroom.

This book is for everyone. We hope you will read these plays aloud in classrooms across the country, that you will discuss them as a family around the dinner table and read them on your own in quiet moments of inspiration and reflection. If you are a young artist – or just young at heart – we hope these plays inspire you to discover your own voice through playwriting. And, when you do, we hope you will share your plays with us. We can't wait to read what you create.

Brigitte Pribnow Moore
Executive Director

Nicole Jost
Artistic Director

To learn more about YPT, go to **www.yptdc.org**

Table of Contents

Plays for All Ages

Love, Math and Martians Don't Mix

by Cassidy Boomsma (2010)

ABOUT CASSIDY

What grade were you in when you wrote your play? 8th

What school did you attend? Swanson Middle School

Where do you go to school now? Washington Lee High School

What do you like to do for fun? Travel, go to the beach, read and hang out with friends.

Is there anything you'd like to say to the readers of this book?

My main goal in writing this play was to make people laugh, but I think that the deeper anti-bullying message is also very important. We are rooting for the nerds because, let's face it, there is a little nerd in every one of us. So let's all fight those cowardly bullies, Martian style!

Characters:

THADDEUS, mega nerd, 11 years old, high pants, very thick glasses, always has textbooks in his arms

LITTLE LUCY, sweet (not prissy) little 8 year old girl, with a HUGE crush on Thaddeus

BULLY, very big compared to Thaddeus, mean, in middle school

SCENE 1: _In the library._

(THADDEUS is sitting at a table. There are many textbooks, paper—and other supplies. He is hard at work. LITTLE LUCY is hiding behind a shelf of books, looking longingly at THADDEUS, giggling and twirling her curls.)

THADDEUS: Hello...my name is Thaddeus the fourth. I am commonly referred to as Thaddeus. And I am well...uhh...very intellectually gifted. One day in the future I am going to have the occupation of a rocket scientist. I'm also the youngest individual in my algebra class as well as all my other advanced classes. By about, uhh...3 years. My favorite place in the whole world is this library, and I never leave home without three textbooks, six folders, two sharpened #2 pencils and a calculator...You never know when you'll have extra time to study.

LITTLE LUCY: _(Talking to herself)_ Oh Thaddeus, why don't you ever notice me? You're always studying and we can never play like we used to. I'm very sad and it's all <u>your</u> fault!

(LUCY looks around and starts making paper airplanes and throwing them at THADDEUS.)

THADDEUS: *(Whisper shouting)* LUCY—stop it. Can't you see that we are in a LIBRARY? When you are in a library it is customary to be SILENT! Now stop your chattering and leave me be.

LUCY: Don't you wanna go to the park?

THADDEUS: I veto that idea. I don't engage myself in useless and frivolous behavior. Now run off and leave me unaccompanied.

LUCY: But, we would play rocket ship just like we used to. You would be the captain and I could be the lookout for the evil Martians.

THADDEUS: There is no life on Mars—

LUCY: And then we would go to Mars and build a house and explore the rest of the galaxy! We would have to be careful of meteor showers and no gravity and...and what's that thing you always used to tell me to watch for? Oh yeah, black holes.

THADDEUS: I have no time for such impractical and ridiculous entertainment, by pretending we could actually go to Mars. Haven't you matured at all?

(LUCY gets wide eyed then runs off stage.)

THADDEUS: That Lucy, she is so maddening. She is always pestering me to play with her. She is a constant distraction from my studies. I don't know what I'm going to do about her. I am aware of the fact that I'm being a bit awful, but it doesn't seem to get in her head that I have better activities to take part in in any other way.

SCENE 2:

(LUCY is by herself playing on a playground, she has a flower in her hand and is picking off petals one by one muttering he likes me, he likes me not under her breath. LUCY spots THADDEUS and runs toward him. THADDEUS is carrying many books as usual.)

LUCY: Thaddeus, wait up!

(THADDEUS sees her, rolls his eyes and speeds up. LUCY catches up to him.)

LUCY: Hi Thaddeus.

THADDEUS: What do you want?

(LUCY hands THADDEUS a flower. THADDEUS smells it.)

THADDEUS: Ah, the Gerbera Aurantiaca, from the Genus Gerbera. Commonly referred to as a daisy–

LUCY: Do you want any help carrying your books?

THADDEUS: NO, not from you anyways. You're. So. Annoying. Don't you have any other friends??? All you ever do is follow me around, pester me and attempt to persuade me to engage in...in...RECREATION. Now, if it's all right with you, I have an algebra final to take!
(THADDEUS storms off, in the midst of his stomping he drops his calculator and math homework, LUCY rushes over to pick them up.)
LUCY: Thaddeus—
THADDEUS: *(Without turning around)* WHAT???
(LUCY holds up the calculator but thinks better of it.)
LUCY: Never mind.
THADDEUS: UGH.
(THADDEUS stomps off stage.)
LUCY: Thaddeus doesn't appreciate me at all, he thinks I'm annoying; well he's annoying, so there. I hate him, that's right I do...
(She seems to be trying to convince herself.)
LUCY: I hate him, yeah; he's...he's...
(She looks lovingly in the direction that THADDEUS left.)
LUCY: He's STUPID! AND. I. HATE. HIM!
(She throws the calculator on the ground and steps on it and jumps on it and destroys it. Then she picks it up [it's destroyed] and examines it.)
LUCY: HA!
(She sticks her tongue out and drops it on the ground.)
LUCY: Now for the homework!
(She winces as she begins to rip up the homework.)
LUCY: I hate you, I hate you, I hate you.
(She throws it on the ground and stomps and jumps on it. She looks down at what she's done, starts crying, and rushes off the stage after THADDEUS.)

SCENE 3:
(THADDEUS is in the hallway looking shocked and muttering to himself. He just failed his algebra final because he didn't have a calculator. BULLY comes onstage.)
BULLY: Helloooooooooooooo THA-DE-US. You're stupid you're only 11 years old. You're stupid. Gimme your lunch money.
THADDEUS: I d-d-don't have a-any.
BULLY: Oh yeah??
(BULLY pushes THADDEUS.)
THADDEUS: Aahh. Fine here you go here you go here you go.
BULLY: That's what I thought, hey aren't you the dumb guy that forgot a

calculator?? HA!!! I can NOT believe you didn't bring a calculator!! Mr. Burberry only said that you had to about 10,000,000 times!! Plus that was the final exam of the semester. Did that get into your baby brain??? You TOTALLY failed! Hahahahaaaa. Now are you stupid or are you stupid? That wasn't very "intellectually gifted" of you!! HELLOOO??? I asked you a question! You dimwitted duck! You brainless bird! You stupid snail! You weird walrus! You strange snake! You peculiar penguin!

THADDEUS: I...guess that would make...me...stupid.

BULLY: You got that right! Hahahaha you think you're so smart, but you can't even. Remember. A....CALCULATOR.

(BULLY is almost in hysterics.)

THADDEUS: Well umm...I was in possession of an HP 50g Graphing calculator, my parents bought it for me for the umm test.

BULLY: Hahaha what a joke. Your PARENTS bought it for you??? Ha, what a baby. Not to mention your math homework, didn't you understand that that assignment counts as a PROJECT GRADE? Did that get in through that thick SKULL of yours?!? Or maybe it was just reflected off those thick GLASSES!

THADDEUS: Yes umm well I must have dropped it at the park...Maybe an automobile or a stroller ran over it because when I went to retrieve it, it, it, was well...demolished, along with my math project that took about a <u>month</u>. OH the TRAGEDY!!

BULLY: Oh you're so lame, Lameeooooooooo.

(BULLY pushes THADDEUS again. LUCY rushes onstage, and runs up to THADDEUS.)

LUCY: Thaddeus I am soooo, soooo sorry! I tore up your math homework, and broke your calculator. I feel very bad. Very very bad. I'm a very bad girl I am so sorry. I am so sorry. I don't know what I was thinking. I was just so mad at you. I didn't mean to, I mean I did, but now I wish I didn't. Oh Thaddeus.

(THADDEUS is very angry.)

THADDEUS: Lucy! I can't...fathom why? You...of all people...would do...that.

LUCY: I'm so sorry. I'm so sorry. Sorry, sorry, sorry.

BULLY: Who's your girlfriend THADDEUS??

THADDEUS: She's NOT my girlfriend, and I never want to see her again.

(LUCY gasps.)

BULLY: Oh my god you guys are so stupid.

LUCY: Thaddeus is NOT stupid.

(BULLY pushes both of them.)

LUCY: You bully!! You MONSTER!!

(LUCY unleashes a series of very advanced karate moves.)

LUCY: You stay AWAY from Thaddeus. Hi-ya, take that you ogre, you you, evil MARTIAN. Hi-ya Hi-ya.

(BULLY runs away.)

THADDEUS: Wow, Lucy, that was...amazing.

LUCY: Thank you.

THADDEUS: It was really brave of you to stand up to Joe like that.

LUCY: Thank you. He was really just an evil Martian. I had to protect...the ummm, captain.

(They look awkwardly at each other.)

THADDEUS: Ummm, why'd you do it?

LUCY: Do what?

THADDEUS: You know.

LUCY: Ohhhh. Well I was really mad that you didn't pay attention to me at all and well I guess I just had a umm, temper tantrum.

THADDEUS: Well thank you for apologizing, and of course, thank you for umm...protecting...me. And, I'm sorry too for being so hostile and mean. I guess I was just forgetting that you just wanted to do stuff like we did in the past.

LUCY: Friends?

THADDEUS: Forever.

(THADDEUS holds out his hand, but LUCY runs up and hugs him.)

LUCY: So I guess you have to go the library.

THADDEUS: Not until we go the park and play rocket ship. We've got to go beat up some more evil Martians.

End of Play

Magnet Dude

by Kyrtham Franco (2006)

ABOUT KYRTHAM

What grade were you in when you wrote your play? 6th

What school did you attend? Capital City Public Charter School

Where do you go to school now? Springbrook High School

What do you like to do for fun? Spend time with family and friends.

Is there anything you'd like to say to the readers of this book? Let your imagination run free and you might accomplish something you didn't expect. I know this because it happened to me when I wrote this play.

Characters:

MAGNET DUDE, superhero

EVIL GENIUS, world's worst villain

HOSTAGE, a millionaire

JOHN, Magnet Dude's friend – a scientist

POLICE

SCENE 1: MAGNET DUDE'S and EVIL GENIUS'S monologues.
(MAGNET DUDE speaks to himself or to the audience – he does not realize that EVIL GENIUS – the worst villain in the world – is hiding and listening. The audience knows EVIL GENIUS is there, but MAGNET DUDE does not.)

MAGNET DUDE: Oh my God, it is so hard being a Super Hero! I mean you don't even get paid and you gotta fight any villain that causes trouble. In order to do that, you gotta lift weights and I HATE lifting weights! I mean think about it – your arms get sore and your legs get sore and you don't get enough sleep because you are always out saving people and the world. Worst of all, if anyone finds out my secret weakness I would be in serious trouble. Even if a one year old found out that metal weakens me – that if somebody throws metal on me I fall and can't get up – it would be terrible. And imagine if some evil villain found my secret out... The world would not be safe. This is so much pressure!!... But there is no way anyone could find out my secret – it is impossible... Lifting all these weights has really worn me out – I am going to take a nap. *(Leaves)*

EVIL GENIUS: *(Coming out of hiding)* Mu ha ha ha... I shall destroy the world and nobody will be able to stop me! I will be invincible. Now that I

7

know Magnet Dude's secret weakness I will be able to squish him like a cockroach – the days of him beating me and stopping me are over!! I will kidnap a very rich woman and force her to give me all her money. Then I will use that money to buy a bomb! Then I WILL DOMINATE THE WHOLE WORLD!! My evil plans are looking good. *(Leaves)*

SCENE 2: *The Villain's Evil Lair.*
(EVIL GENIUS drags in a HOSTAGE covered in chains… In flies MAGNET DUDE.)
MAGNET DUDE: Give me back the hostage you villain. It's not her you want.
EVIL GENIUS: Oh, but she is what I want! I know your weakness, Magnet Dude. You will never stop me.
MAGNET DUDE: For your information, I do not have any weaknesses and I will stop you, no matter what!
EVIL GENIUS: Ha, ha, ha, in your dreams! Magnet Dude, you are just a weak, good for nothing superhero.
MAGNET DUDE: You will eat your words, you dirty villain! You shall pay for all the evil things you have done.
EVIL GENIUS: I am the Ultimate Villain! I will crush you like a bug. You will suffer. You will beg for me to stop.
MAGNET DUDE: Enough trash talking!
(MAGNET DUDE flies up into the air, the villain throws a bunch of metal stuff at him – MAGNET DUDE falls.)
MAGNET DUDE: Let me out of here!
EVIL GENIUS: Ha, ha – I told you I knew your weakness! And you thought it was such a secret from the world! Are you ready to feel my wrath?!
MAGNET DUDE: Let me go! You are going to be dead when I get out of here.
EVIL GENIUS: Never! I will never let you escape. I am not that dumb. *(To the HOSTAGE)* Now, give me your money or I will kill your husband and daughter! I don't have much time. I need to buy bomb supplies.
(HOSTAGE gives him money) Thank you very much, I shall be gone. I have to go to my laboratory to set up plans for the bomb. *(He leaves.)*
HOSTAGE: Please, Magnet Dude, save my husband and daughter!
MAGNET DUDE: Oh yeah, how dumb can I get? With my magnetic force, I can break these chains.
(He does.)
MAGNET DUDE: *(To the HOSTAGE)* I shall break you out of your chains too.
(He does and they escape.)

SCENE 3: At MAGNET DUDE'S friend's Scientific Lab...

MAGNET DUDE: John, buddy, I need your help. The villain, Evil Genius, knows my weakness. She threw metal at me and it was too heavy and unbalanced me. I need a suit that will stop her.

JOHN: So you want a suit that will stop metal from sticking to you. Hmmm. It will cost you like five hundred thousand dollars. I am broke.

MAGNET DUDE: Are you crazy? Where are you going to get that much money?

JOHN: All right – four hundred thousand dollars. Take it or leave it.

MAGNET DUDE: The evil villain is going to blow up the country with her bomb. Do you want to be destroyed?

JOHN: All right, sheesh... can't you take a joke? The suit will be done tonight. Come at 8:00pm. It will be ready and don't make me wait!!

MAGNET DUDE: Thank you, thank you, thank you! I'll be back at 8:00. (Flies up and away...)

JOHN: I had better get to work – this is going to be harder than I thought!

(JOHN begins to work. MAGNET DUDE is outside...)

MAGNET DUDE: Evil Genius' metal made me so weak – I need to rest before I go after her again. I will just take a nap.

(Time passes – MAGNET DUDE is sleeping and JOHN is working on the suit...)

MAGNET DUDE: (Waking and looking at his watch) It's 8:00! I had better get back there!

(He flies to the laboratory...)

JOHN: Oh, there you are. Here it is. Do you like it?

MAGNET DUDE: I love it! Does this thing really work?

JOHN: Of course it works. Whenever that villain throws metal at you the metal will now instantly reflect back to him.

MAGNET DUDE: Awesome! I gotta see if it works! Bye! (Flies up and out to the villain's lair...)

SCENE 4: At EVIL GENIUS'S lair.

MAGNET DUDE: (Landing at villain's lair) Evil Genius, you shall be stopped and destroyed!

EVIL GENIUS: I can't believe you escaped. And now you are back for more? Don't you get it? I will always squash you!

MAGNET DUDE: Don't you get it? This time it's different. Do you notice anything different about me?

EVIL GENIUS: Oh, that ugly suit? That won't change anything. Ready to suffer???

MAGNET DUDE: Bring it on!!!

(Villain throws metal at MAGNET DUDE and it goes back on the villain.)

EVIL GENIUS: NOOOOOOOOOOOOOOOOOOO!

MAGNET DUDE: *(Hearing sirens)* It's the police – coming to take you to jail.

POLICE: *(Entering and putting EVIL GENIUS in handcuffs)* Thank you, Magnet Dude for catching the villain. You have been a great help. Now we don't have to worry about the world being blown up by this evil villain's bomb.

MAGNET DUDE: You are welcome. I have a feeling you are gonna be in jail for a long time!

EVIL GENIUS: I hate you Magnet Dude! *(Is taken away)*

MAGNET DUDE: *(To the audience)* You are welcome, citizens – you are not going to be blown up. With me around, you will always be safe!

(Flies off with music playing)

End of Play

The Day After Bob Said, "Yeah, Right"

by Ann Gill (2010)

<u>ABOUT ANN</u>

What grade were you in when you wrote your play? 6th

What school did you attend? Maya Angelou Public Charter School Campus

Where do you go to school now? Benjamin Banneker Senior High School

What do you like to do for fun? I like to draw, play drums, read and hang out with my friends.

Is there anything you'd like to say to the readers of this book?

I would like them to be inspired and use their imaginations. Do your best during everything because you might just write a play that gets turned into a staged play. Express yourself as well as take the risk.

Characters:

BOB

MOM

GARRY, Bob's friend

CUSTOMER

MANAGER

BOB: I rock the wheels! I can't wait until the skate off tomorrow. It's going to be awesome! Other than that I'm starving. I hardly ate today. My mom refused to make me breakfast, so I just had toast, just really, really, dark. I could've made cereal, or something else. Psych, all I know is that I know how to make toast, or cereal. Then, I thought about that, why didn't I have both? Well, whatever. I need some R&R. I wonder what's Mom cookin'.

MOM: I'm so tired! I've been working all day with these patients. Especially Mr. Vandurant. That man gives me the creeps. Ew. Just thinking about the left eye staring at the wall. Oh, and don't get me started with that right eye staring me down like I've done a crime. I just want to get home and rest. Oh, right, I can't because I have another big little baby at home. Well, I can't blame him because I've been treating him like a kid all 22 years. What should I do?

SCENE 1:

BOB: Hey Mom, what's in the bag?

MOM: Don't worry about it, I just need some help.

BOB: I'm sorry, I can't help right now because I'm watching my favorite show. You're good.

MOM: Bob, don't make me—

BOB: You're being too loud. I can't hear. *(Turns up the TV)*

MOM: I'm tired of all this being lazy and being selfish.

BOB: What?! I can't hear you!

MOM: Bob, you better stop this or else.

BOB: What, what?!

MOM: I'm not kidding. I need some help around here, not a big –

BOB: OK, cool!

MOM: Uhhh! Bob, I'm going to kick you out until you figure out what to do with yourself.

BOB: Yeah right. Whatever.

MOM: OK.

(MOM goes up to BOB'S room and packs his stuff, then throws it out the door.)

BOB: What are you doing?

MOM: I know what you're doing.

BOB: What?

MOM: Leaving.

BOB: *(Shocked)* What is this?

MOM: This is you leaving.

BOB: What?

(MOM pushes him out the door.)

SCENE 2:

(BOB goes to his friend GARRY'S house.)

BOB: What's up, dude?

GARRY: Nothing.

BOB: So I was just going to ask you a little question.

GARRY: What?

BOB: Well, can I stay here, because my mother kicked me out.

GARRY: Why?

BOB: Well, she was talking about me being selfish or something like that.

GARRY: Oh, OK. Maybe she is right. I mean—

BOB: Wait. What? Come on dude. I didn't come here to see another clone of my mother.

GARRY: I'm just trying to tell you the truth. I mean you're 22, you need to start doing something. Other than graduating from high school. Get a job.

BOB: Tell me you didn't say that.

GARRY: Um I think I did.

BOB: Whatever. How do I do that anyway.

GARRY: I'll get you a job where I work.

SCENE 3:

(BOB is at the job.)

CUSTOMER: Can I have a turkey sandwich with fries and a milkshake?

BOB: *(Whispering)* Wow you should hold up on the fries for your age.

CUSTOMER: Excuse me?

BOB: Oh nothing.

(BOB drops the lettuce on the floor and puts it in her sandwich.)

CUSTOMER: Oh no, I'm not paying for that.

BOB: Why, oh no you're paying for that.

CUSTOMER: Is that a threat? Oh you're lucky I didn't bring my boxing gloves.

(BOB backs up.)

CUSTOMER: Where's the manager?

MANAGER: What's the problem?

CUSTOMER: This rude boy dropped my lettuce and put it in the sandwich. He also threatened me to pay for it.

MANAGER: Is this true Bob?

BOB: Well...yes.

CUSTOMER: *(Hits him with her purse)* Hah!

MANAGER: You're fired.

SCENE 4:

GARRY: I can't believe you got fired on the first day.

BOB: I don't want to talk about it. It's complicated.

GARRY: Maybe you should apologize to your mother.

BOB: Why? She was the one being mean. She was calling me names.

GARRY: Well, she has a reason. You're rude and selfish to her and you don't even know it.

BOB: Oh.

GARRY: What do you like to do?

BOB: Skateboard.

GARRY: Why don't you work at the skate park?

BOB: Well that's not a bad idea!

GARRY: Just tell your mother you apologize and tell her that you're getting a job at the skate park.

BOB: OK fine, but that's not going to be easy.

GARRY: OK then go.

BOB: OK I'm gonna go.

GARRY: Bye.

BOB: Bye.

SCENE 5:

(BOB knocks on the door)

BOB: Hi mom.

MOM: What are you doing here?

BOB: Don't I get a hi?

MOM: Hi Bob.

BOB: Hi. I just came to apologize about –

MOM: What?! I didn't quite understand that.

BOB: I just came to apologize! For being such a nut. I didn't realize I was selfish. I'm different now. I even got a job at the skate park.

MOM: I'm proud of you.

BOB: But all of this wasn't my fault. You were –

MOM: I know, I know. I was still treating you like a baby. But I'm gonna change too. I'm still proud of you.

End of Play

Friendship: The Wonka Wonka Cool Girls Club

by Cecelia Jenkins (1999)

ABOUT CECELIA

What grade were you in when you wrote your play? 6th

What school did you attend? Hardy Middle School

What do you do now? I have a B.A. in Communications and I am a New Media Artist/Writer.

What do you like to do for fun? Connecting with people, exploring new places, continuously immersing myself in all things creative.

Is there anything you'd like to say to the readers of this book? Nothing is impossible. All things good or bad can influence your art. Use your surroundings to create great things.

Characters:
CAT
CAT'S DAD
SHELLY
ANNE MARIE

SCENE 1: At home.
(CAT is seen preparing for school. She is visibly upset, slamming doors, checking her appearance and finally sinking into a chair crying. DAD enters.)

DAD: Okay, okay. Let's get a move on here. Chop chop. We're already running late. I've got to be in court by 8:30 this morning. *(Notices her crying)* Cat, honey, what's wrong?

CAT: Oh...nothing.

DAD: What do you mean nothing? I can see something's bothering you. What is it, Pumpkin?

CAT: Do I have to go to school today?

DAD: What kind of talk is that? You know you have to go to school. Did something happen I should know about?

CAT: No. It's nothing, Dad. Nothing you'd understand anyway.

DAD: Well okay, if you say so. So smile. Stop biting your lips and let's get out of here. Hurry, hurry...unless you want to walk.

CAT: I'm coming, I'm coming.

DAD: Come on, Cat, you're going to make me late! *(They leave)*

SCENE 2: At school.

SHELLY: Hi, Cat.

CAT: Oh, hi, Shelly.

SHELLY: What's up with you, Cat? Ever since we started seventh grade, you act like you don't want to be friends anymore.

CAT: What do you mean?

SHELLY: I mean, I say hi to you and you say "Oh hi Shelly," like I'm the last person in the world you want to talk to.

CAT: It's not that. I just feel like nobody likes me but you; like I don't have any friends.

(ANNE MARIE enters surrounded by other kids; she is clearly the center of attention.)

CAT: Hi, Anne Marie.

ANNE MARIE: Cat! Hi! Ooh cool shoes.

CAT: Thanks.

SHELLY: Hi, Anne Marie.

ANNE MARIE: Oh. Hello, Shirley.

SHELLY: It's Shelly.

ANNE MARIE: Whatever. Hey, guys, guess what? I'm starting a new club and it's called the Wonka Wonka Cool Girls Club.

CAT: Cool.

ANNE MARIE:

Wonka wonka Wonka wonka

Wonka wonka girls are the best

Double-U, round the O, N-K-A and go, girl go!

Wonka wonka

Wonka wonka

SHELLY: Can I join?

ANNE MARIE: No. Cat can join if she wants to, but not you.

SHELLY: Why not?

ANNE MARIE: Because it's a club for girls.

SHELLY: I'm a girl.

ANNE MARIE: Yeah, but I heard that late at night when you go to sleep, you take your hair off. Your brother even said so. I don't know what you are underneath.

SHELLY: I can't believe you said that.

CAT: Ignore her, Shelly, she doesn't know what she's talking about.

ANNE MARIE: (pulls CAT aside) Are you going to hang out with her for the rest of your life? You know you want to be in the Wonka Wonka Cool Girls Club.

CAT: I don't know. The name of your club is so stupid.

ANNE MARIE: Well, think about it. My mother is going to take the whole club to Kings Dominion for my birthday.

SCENE 3: *Later that day at home.*
(CAT answers the phone.)

CAT: Hello?

ANNE MARIE: Hi, this is Anne Marie from school.

CAT: Anne Marie! How did you get my phone number?

ANNE MARIE: My mother has the Parents' Association contact sheet. Look, I still want to know if you want to be in my club.

CAT: Let me guess: you mean the Wonka Wonka Cool Girls Club?

ANNE MARIE: Yeah. It's gonna be so cool. We're all gonna get red shirts that say W.W.C.G.C. on one side and have our pictures on the back. And if everybody puts in $5.00 every month for dues, we can have a pizza party every month. And, and, and my mother said she would take us all to Disney World for my birthday...

CAT: I thought you said Kings Dominion.

ANNE MARIE: Well, one or the other. It's gonna be so much fun and so cool. What do you say?

CAT: What about Shelly?

ANNE MARIE: I don't want her, I only want cool girls like you. What is Shelly anyway, your mother or something? Do you have to have her do everything you do?

CAT: Well....I guess not.

ANNE MARIE: Okay then. Do you want to join or not?

CAT: I guess so. Okay.

ANNE MARIE: Cool! We're going to meet on the playground in the morning before school and at lunch we're all going to sit together.

CAT: Okay.

ANNE MARIE: Oh, and if you have a red shirt, wear it. Bye! See you tomorrow!

CAT: Bye. *(DAD enters)* Wonka wonka, wonka wonka...

DAD: Well, somebody's sure in a better mood than this morning. What happened?

CAT: Nothing much: I just got asked to join the coolest club at school!

Wonka wonka, wonka wonka.

DAD: I don't know what you're talking about but I sure am glad to see you happy again.

CAT and DAD: Wonka wonka, wonka wonka.

SCENE 4: *A week later at school, Cat is wearing a red shirt.*

CAT: Hi, Shelly! Hey, how come you're not talking to me? Shelly?

SHELLY: I hate you! How come you are in that club and I'm not?

CAT: It's only been for one day. And it's not my fault. Come on, you and I have been friends since kindergarten.

SHELLY: Well, you wouldn't hardly know it now that you've got your new friend Anne Marie.

CAT: You're still my friend. Let's have lunch together.

SHELLY: I hate this pizza.

CAT: Stop complaining. You hate everything and you're acting like a dumb-dumb because first you said you hate me, now you are eating pizza with me. *(ANNE MARIE enters)* Hi, Anne Marie.

ANNE MARIE: Hi, Cat. Who's that you're sitting with?

SHELLY: I hate you.

ANNE MARIE: How did I know you were going to say that?

CAT: I just thought I'd sit with Shelly today.

ANNE MARIE: Humph. Come on. It's time for the Wonka Wonka Cool Girls meeting. Are you in or not?

SHELLY: Yeah, Cat. Are you one of those stupid Wonka Wonka girls or not?

CAT: It's not stupid, it's very cool. Come on, Anne Marie. I'd rather be in the Wonka Wonka Girls Club than be Shelly's friend.

SCENE 5: *On the playground.*

ANNE MARIE: Welcome to the Wonka Wonka Cool Persons Club. The meeting will now come to order.

CAT: Where's everybody else?

ANNE MARIE: Oh, I decided I don't want any of those stupid girls. They're not cool at all, and besides, who needs them? Right? Right?

CAT: I guess.

ANNE MARIE: Anyway, I changed the name to "Cool Persons" in case we want to get a cool boy to join.

CAT: Okay.

ANNE MARIE: Now, let's get down to business. To get into the Wonka

Wonka Cool Persons Club, you have to do my homework for a week, eat a lemon and — best of all — call the teacher a cow.

CAT: What?! I don't think that is fair at all! Would you do those things?

ANNE MARIE: I don't have to do. But either you do it, or you're out.

CAT: No!

ANNE MARIE: That's it, you are out of the Wonka Wonka Cool Persons Club.

CAT: Fine! I would not be in the Wonka Wonka Cool Persons Club if it were the last club in the world.

ANNE MARIE: Fine!

CAT: Fine! *(Leaves)*

ANNE MARIE: Fine! Hey, Shelly!

SHELLY: Why are you talking to me?

ANNE MARIE: You know about my club, right? Well, I want you to be in it.

SHELLY: The Wonka Wonka Cool Girls Club?

ANNE MARIE: Yes. Only now it's the Wonka Wonka Cool Persons Club.

SHELLY: Is Cat in the club?

ANNE MARIE: Yeah, that's actually why I'm inviting you; because Cat wants me to be your friend. She talks about you at every meeting.

SHELLY: Wait…You're lying.

ANNE MARIE: I am not.

SHELLY: Yes, you are. I know you're not telling the truth because Cat just got in the club today.

ANNE MARIE: Well, so what? Do you want to be a Wonka Wonka girl or not?

SHELLY: Okay I'll join your stupid club anyway. It's lonely eating pizza all alone.

ANNE MARIE: All right! We can have the first meeting of the Wonka Wonka Cool Persons Club right now.

SHELLY: But what about the other members? Shouldn't Cat be here?

ANNE MARIE: Sorry, she did not follow my rules so I kicked her out of the club.

SHELLY: What?! Well, if Cat is out, I'm out.

ANNE MARIE: You can't do that! You can't just quit! Come back here please! I need somebody to be in my club.

SHELLY: You're pitiful.

(SHELLY leaves.)

ANNE MARIE: Well, nevermind then! I didn't really want you in my club anyway, I just wanted somebody to do my homework.

SCENE 6: *The next day at school.*

SHELLY: Can I eat with you, Cat?

CAT: Sure, but I heard that you were in Anne Marie's club.

SHELLY: I could not last a second in the Wonka Wonka Cool Girls Club, I
mean the—

SHELLY and CAT: Wonka Wonka Cool PERSONS Club. *(They laugh)*

CAT: Do you want some pizza?

SHELLY: Thanks!!

CAT: Anytime!

SHELLY: You know Cat, we should make our own club.

CAT: Yeah, great idea. But what will we call it?

SHELLY: The Pizza Friends Clubs.

CAT: I like that.

SHELLY: Let's be friends forever.

CAT: Yeah! Friends forever.

CAT and SHELLY:

Pizza pizza

pizza pizza

Pizza pizza friends are the best!

End of Play

Polished

by Julie Kashmanian (2011)

ABOUT JULIE

What grade were you in when you wrote your play? 8th

What school did you attend? H-B Woodlawn Secondary Program

Where do you go to school now? H-B Woodlawn Secondary Program

What do you like to do for fun? I like to act, sing, dance, read, write, crochet, sew, draw, listen to show tunes and make costumes.

Is there anything you'd like to say to the readers of this book? I think that it's really important that kids are given the chance to express themselves. Too often kids' opinions are not acknowledged enough, and through programs like YPT, they can have the chance to let their creative voices be heard.

Characters:

JO, thirteen, semi-obnoxious and very outspoken and annoying, Leah's sister

LEAH, thirteen, rather a stereotypical girly-girl, skeptical, Jo's sister

MOM, their mother

SCENE: *A small, roughly 10 by 4 foot bathroom. A girl is standing in front of the mirror, painting her nails. Another girl is standing outside the bathroom, tapping her foot impatiently.*

JO: *(Grumbling to herself)* The bathroom is busy. Again. Just like it always is. Obviously. I know what she's doing in there: painting her nails, just like usual. She probably hasn't even finished one hand yet. No, she probably hasn't even done one *finger*. Half a finger, maybe. At the most. Now she's probably flapping it around like crazy, like a nail-drying psycho. Then she'll do, like, ten different coats. Then she'll decide she doesn't like it and redo them. *(Raising her voice)* And some of us have more important things to do in there!

LEAH: *(Rolls her eyes and starts talking to herself, still painting her nails)* Oh, gimme a break. She's always complaining about everything I do. Well, news flash, pal, you're not my top pick for a sister either. And this is just as important as whatever she wants to do. If I had nails that looked like hers — I mean, has she ever *seen* a file? — I'd either end my misery quick or come begging on my knees to me for help. Not that I

21

would help her. Not after all the grief she gives me.

JO: Leah, open up!

LEAH: Wait a minute!

JO: I've waited, like, a million hours already. Let me in!

LEAH: You have not. Just let me finish.

JO: *(Sighs, pulls a bobby pin from her hair and starts fiddling with the bathroom lock)* If you're going to be like that…

LEAH: What're you…*(Lock clicks)* Hey!

JO: It worked! Thank you, WikiHow!

(JO opens the door and enters.)

LEAH: Get out!

JO: It's *my* turn in here! *You* get out!

LEAH: No way! I haven't even finished yet!

JO: *(Looks at her hand)* I was right! You did only one nail!

LEAH: Get out, Jo!

JO: Can't make me!

LEAH: Ugh! *(Takes a deep breath)* What do you even have to do in here? Oh, ew, don't tell me if it's something gross.

JO: I have to wash my hair.

LEAH: Oh…fine, but don't take too long.

JO: *(Raises an eyebrow)* You're actually letting me use the bathroom? This is a milestone, Leah.

LEAH: Be quiet. I just don't want Mom to get ticked at me.

JO: Your ulterior motives just warm my heart. *(Starts to pantomime washing her hair in the sink)* And anyway, isn't Mom going to get ticked off anyway when she finds out you're painting your nails?

LEAH: *(Looks out the door)* Shut the door. I don't want her to see me.

JO: So she did tell you not to!

LEAH: Yeah, but that's only 'cause she's all paranoid about nail polish.

JO: Why?

LEAH: She thinks the "fumes" are bad for you. Bogus, right?

JO: *(In an annoying singsong)* But she told you not to…

LEAH: Oh, be quiet. And shut the door!

JO: *(Shuts the door)* I can't be held responsible if you get in trouble.

(Several moments pass as both the sisters continue. Suddenly, JO wrinkles her nose.)

JO: Ugh, that stuff stinks.

LEAH: Well, I put the fan on after I finish.

JO: Put it on now. It's giving me a headache.

LEAH: *(Sniffs)* I don't smell anything.

JO: I guess you're immune to the "fumes." But turn it on, it stinks!

LEAH: *(Pantomimes pressing a button. Nothing happens. Presses it again.)* It's not working.

JO: Oh, come on! *(Tries it herself)* Argh, no way! *(Pinches nose)* I can't wash my hair like this!

LEAH: Stop being a wimp.

JO: *(Whines)* I'm not! I'm getting out of here. *(Tries door knob)* What the heck, it's stuck!

LEAH: What? Did it lock itself or something?

JO: Aw, come on! I need to get out of here. I'm calling Mom.

(JO inhales, preparing to yell.)

LEAH: No! She'll get mad at me! Just wait until I finish!

JO: No way, I have to get out of here!

LEAH: Please, she'll kick my butt! Just wait until I'm done. I only have a couple more nails to do.

JO: Oh...fine, but hurry up! I'm dying here!

(A few moments pass. JO holds her forehead.)

JO: Ugh, I'm getting dizzy. I think I'm going to be sick. Ugh. Man, I'm going to throw up. *(An expression of horror goes across her face.)* The fumes, Leah! The fumes!

LEAH: What are you talking about?

JO: The fumes from the nail polish! The fumes Mom was talking about! They're going to poison us to death in here! *We're going to die!*

LEAH: Calm down, crazy. There aren't any "fumes." Mom was just being paranoid.

JO: There *are* fumes, Leah! We have to get out of here! It'll be like when you hear about those people who let the gas run on the stove, only we'll die from nail polish! *(Frantically tries to open the door)* Help me!

LEAH: *(A note of doubt in her voice)* We'll be fine.

JO: Come on, Leah! Don't just stand there! We're going to die! *(Covers mouth)* We have to stop breathing in these fumes! If only I had a gas mask right now!

LEAH: I'm feeling kind of dizzy too...*(Gasps for air)* I'm choking! You're right, Jo!

JO: Never mind! We have to turn on the fan, or open the door! Hurry! Mom!

LEAH: No, I'll get in trouble!

JO: It's better than dying! *Mom!*

LEAH: Ohh...*Mom!*

(They continue shouting, growing more and more frantic, falling over each other as they repeatedly re-try the doorknob and the fan button.)

JO: I'm...choking...can't....breathe...

LEAH: Everything's going black...I can't see!

JO: *(Coughing)* Hang in there, man! We have to live!

LEAH: I can't make it!

JO: *(Sobbing)* Why does it have to end this way? Why?

LEAH: *Mom! Help us!*

JO: *(Feebly)* Mom...help...

LEAH: This is the end, sis.

JO: *(Crying)* I'm sorry I was such a bad sister!

LEAH: Me too!

JO: Bye bye, world...

(All is silent for a moment. Then the door clicks open.)

MOM: What's wrong?

JO: Mom...? I'm...alive?

MOM: What stinks in here?

LEAH: *(Gasps)* We survived!

MOM: Leah, were you painting your nails?

LEAH: I'll never do it again!

MOM: What...?

LEAH: You were right, Mom. The horror...the unspeakable horror...

MOM: What are you talking about?

BOTH: The fumes, Mom. The fumes.

MOM: Yeah?

LEAH: Um, we almost died because of them?

MOM: *(Chuckles)* You guys are such drama queens.

JO: *(Angry)* They almost killed us!

MOM: Um, sure. You know, I just meant that it smells really bad. Just being in the bathroom with some nail polish for a few minutes isn't going to kill you.

LEAH: What?

MOM: But I did tell you not to do it anymore, Leah.

JO: I was the one doing it, Mom. Leah just came in to wash her hair.

MOM: And I suppose that's how you got wet hair and Leah got her nails painted.

JO: Um...yeah?

MOM: I'm not mad at you guys. In fact, keep up the niceness! This is the first time you guys are actually being civil towards one another.

JO: Phew!

LEAH: And so we both survived, in possibly the strangest near-death experience ever recorded. I don't take up as much time in the bathroom anymore. After that, I'd never paint my nails again. Maybe it can't kill you, but then again, who knows? Better to be safe than sorry, eh?

JO: Despite being an *incredibly* embarrassing experience, I'm sort of almost glad it happened. Because, y'know, we lived, and also 'cause after that we didn't really mind each other so much. Well, that was a bad word choice, let me rephrase that: after that we didn't really get into fights anymore. There were a few, but after that we became...friends. Like, buddy friends. Pals. Mom didn't have to remind us to be "civil." It was like someone had given the fingernail of our friendship a much-needed manicure; like someone had filed away all the jagged edges and annoying little uneven parts and painted it with cherry-red perfection. Kinda like everything had been...polished.

End of Play

Frozen Cactus

by Shawn Lee (2011)

> <u>ABOUT SHAWN</u>
>
> **What grade were you in when you wrote your play?** 9th
> **What school did you attend?** Ballou Senior High School
> **Where do you go to school now?** Ballou Senior High School
> **What do you like to do for fun?** Play sports.
> **Is there anything you'd like to say to the readers of this book?** I just want to say that anything is possible no matter what. If you can think of it, it's possible.

Characters:

KENNY, 22 years old, optimistic, gamer
MOTHER NATURE, arrogant, sassy
CREATOR, forgiving, omniscient

SCENE 1: Kenny's house. Fans and air conditioners running full blast, a video game system, a TV, a couch with a safety blanket on it, a vase and a lamp. (KENNY is sinking into the couch playing a racing game, and sweating. His phone rings, and he pauses the game before picking it up.)

KENNY: Hey. Wassup? Can you believe how hot it is today? Yeah! The job that Mother Nature is doing right now is horrible! I think she doesn't like us! I think she hates New Mexico! It's never been this hot, ever! And I've been here all my life! Maybe I will...anyway...what're you doing?...Oh cool. Alright well, I'm just playing the game, trying to stay out of the heat. What?...I can't hear you...

(The air conditioners and fans stop, the TV goes static. KENNY gets up to see what is wrong with the TV. The TV is turned off, and the game system has stopped.)

KENNY: Ugh! I forgot to save!

(The door is blown open by the wind. MOTHER NATURE walks in.)

KENNY: Who're you?

MOTHER NATURE: Well, Mother Nature, of course!

(KENNY laughs in her face.)

KENNY: Well, if you are Mother Nature, I have a few words to say to you.

MOTHER NATURE: Oh do you?

KENNY: Why doesn't it snow here?

MOTHER NATURE: Because it's too close to the equator!

KENNY: Oh really? Or is it just because you don't want it to?

MOTHER NATURE: Look, who do you think you're talking to? I'm just doing my job.

KENNY: Your job!? Your job isn't to torture innocent people!

MOTHER NATURE: No! It's to control the weather!

KENNY: That's exactly what I don't like.

MOTHER NATURE: Why don't you get that I have someone to listen to? I just can't make everyone's wishes come true!

KENNY: You're just like any normal person, just with weird clothes and powers! Why can't you treat everybody the same just like you treat yourself!?

MOTHER NATURE: Why am I even talking to you—I'm the one with the powers, you're not. Just because I used to be human doesn't mean that I have to listen to your ideas now! We're two completely different people! I have everything and you have nothing!

(MOTHER NATURE leaves and the door closes behind her. Thunder after she storms out.)

SCENE 2: Later that night. A really foggy place, and a giant chair.

(MOTHER NATURE walks into the space. THE CREATOR is sitting on the chair.)

MOTHER NATURE: ("Best friends") Hey...

CREATOR: Why?

MOTHER NATURE: Why what?

CREATOR: Why don't you get it? Why do you think that you're better than everybody else?

MOTHER NATURE: Well that's not the way I think. I'm a nice person to everybody, right?

CREATOR: Not from what I've just heard.

MOTHER NATURE: What're you talking about?

CREATOR: You and that boy were just arguing. You told him that you have everything and he has nothing.

MOTHER NATURE: You didn't hear what he said to me!

CREATOR: Either way, you just can't go around to anybody — I have to punish you for that.

MOTHER NATURE: But he treats me with no respect! You can't do this! I am Mother Nature! The Ruler of All Weather!

CREATOR: But you're still normal — you're just a girl from Cincinnati with a magic necklace! I could've chosen anybody for this role, but I chose you. I chose you because you had potential, you seemed like you could make a difference in the world, but now I'm starting to regret that. I'm going to take your powers away, until you understand that you're just like everybody else.

MOTHER NATURE: Wait, no! You can't!

CREATOR: I can and I will!

(THE CREATOR takes the necklace off of her, and sends her back to Earth.)

CREATOR: One down, one to go.

(KENNY, asleep, wakes up in the space.)

KENNY: What the—? Where am I?

CREATOR: Hello Kenny.

KENNY: Hello, Weird-Guy-Who-Knows-My-Name. Who are you?

CREATOR: The Creator.

(KENNY laughs in his face.)

KENNY: WHAT!?

CREATOR: You really have to stop doing that. But seriously, I am the Creator.

KENNY: Well anyway, how do you know my name, Mr. Creator?

CREATOR: I know everything about you.

KENNY: No you don't.

CREATOR: Your name is Kenny Rogers. You're 22, you've slept with a special blanket since you were four. You don't like heat, and you control the weather.

KENNY: Wrong! I don't control the weather. That's Mother Nature.

CREATOR: Not anymore. Take this necklace.

(He hands him the necklace.)

CREATOR: It gives you the powers to control the weather, and do anything using the weather. You can use the wind to send you across the world in two seconds. You can use heatstroke to make yourself look like other people. You would never need a costume, or a car, or a plane. BUT: you can't tell anybody. And you can't make it snow in New Mexico.

KENNY: Oh my God! Okay...I guess.

CREATOR: Oh, one more thing, you can't ever tell Mother Nature.

(KENNY wakes up in his house, with his blanket.)

SCENE 3:

(MOTHER NATURE wakes up on a street, without her powers.)

MOTHER NATURE: I can't believe that he took away my powers just because of a silly argument. There are a lot of other things that are worse. Like the earthquake in D.C. or the tsunami in Asia. *(Pause)* Ugh...why is it so hot in here? Wait...so if it was that boy who made my powers get taken away then he might be able to help me get them back. So I'll go apologize just to get my powers back. But I don't want to see him again. He reminds me so much of my childhood bully, Father Time. But I do want my powers back. And after I get them back I will make his town the worse.

(She finds a bus station. She sits down waiting for the bus. It's not abandoned, but empty. She doesn't see anybody. Then, out of the blue, KENNY enters/appears. MOTHER NATURE doesn't notice him and he sits down so he's back to back with her.)

KENNY: Wooooph! I think this is the hottest it's ever been! Don't you think so?

(MOTHER NATURE turns around and sees KENNY, gives him a look.)

MOTHER NATURE: Don't I know you from somewhere?

KENNY: No, I don't know what you're talking about. I never met you before.

MOTHER NATURE: Yeah I have. You are...that Kenny kid.

KENNY: Kenny? My name is...Lester.

(MOTHER NATURE puts her face in her hands. KENNY exits.)

MOTHER NATURE: I'm sorry, I thought you were someone else. I must be seeing things, I guess.

(She looks up—KENNY is gone.)

KENNY'S VOICE: *(Over the intercom)* Last bus ride to Truth or Consequences, New Mexico, is boarding and leaves in five minutes, in Bus Wing X!

MOTHER NATURE: Wing X? What wing am I in? Wing B! No!

(MOTHER NATURE gets up and runs to the bus. When she gets on the bus, the bus driver is KENNY.)

MOTHER NATURE: *(Rushed)* Hi how're you doing? *(She sits down. Turns back.)* Wait, what? This can't be the same person. I don't know why but everyone looks like that brat Kenny.

(The bus pulls away. The bus swerves back and forth.)

MOTHER NATURE: What are you, blind?

KENNY: Oh I'm sorry, I guess, I must be having heatstroke or something.

(A few moments later, the bus jerks to a stop.)

KENNY: *(Announcing to the bus)* I'm sorry, but apparently the heat has melted the tires, and we cannot go any further.

MOTHER NATURE: Oh my God, but I have to get to Kenny's house.

(KENNY goes out to the tire with a manual. He flips through, looks through a toolbox and keeps trying random tools: screwdriver...)

KENNY: No. *(...wrench...)* No.

(MOTHER NATURE leaves the bus and confronts KENNY.)

MOTHER NATURE: Look, I see what you're trying to do here. You are that Kenny kid! You're trying to sabotage me from getting my powers back! I don't know how you know it but you keep finding ways to show up everywhere at once!

KENNY: Look lady, I don't know who Kenny is or what you're talking about.

(He shows her his driver's license, with a different name.)

KENNY: I'm just doing my job.

(MOTHER NATURE thinks to herself.)

MOTHER NATURE: Yeah, you're right. I'm sorry. Oh, I still have to get to Kenny's house....I don't have time to watch you sit around and fix a tire!

(MOTHER NATURE starts walking. She gets a good distance away, and then out of nowhere the bus zooms past her. It's hot, and she tries to chase the bus but stops after a little bit. She can't catch it. She keeps walking. She hears thunder. Clouds come out of nowhere, and it starts pouring down rain.)

MOTHER NATURE: Why is it raining, in the middle the desert? Okay! I get it! I messed up! I'm going to apologize now, and only apologize! I changed my ways! I've learned my lesson for the final time. I know I was selfish with the weather, I know I make choices but I don't think of the effect they have on people. I'm sorry for Katrina, that day my dog ran away. The D.C. earthquake, I dropped my groceries...wait, what? Katrina happened just because my dog ran away? The D.C. earthquake happened just because I dropped my groceries? I was so selfish...it will never happen again. I will never take out my feelings on everybody through the weather.

(It stops raining. Out of the blue the sun comes back out. A bus pulls up. The CREATOR is driving the bus.)

CREATOR: I'm glad you see things from other people's point of view now.

SCENE 4: *Kenny's house.*
(MOTHER NATURE knocks on the door. KENNY answers it. KENNY looks at her kind of like "oh, I know what's going to happen next" type face. A "you can apologize now" type of face.)
MOTHER NATURE: Are you okay?
KENNY: Yeah I'm fine. What do you want?
MOTHER NATURE: Well, I want to apologize for earlier. I've learned my lesson. I've changed my ways.
KENNY: Why are you apologizing?
MOTHER NATURE: My life hasn't been that great lately. For some reason, everyone that I've seen looked like you.
KENNY: Oh really? That's weird. That's a first, I've never had anybody say that to me. And you say you've changed your ways?
MOTHER NATURE: Yeah! I thought you heard me the first time! I've seen what I've done, and it hasn't been too well.
KENNY: I forgive you. I guess.
(KENNY takes off her necklace from around his neck. MOTHER NATURE gasps.)
MOTHER NATURE: Wait so the whole time—
KENNY: Yup.
(KENNY gives her the necklace.)
MOTHER NATURE: *(Suddenly threatening)* I'm going to make you...no. I've changed my ways.
(It starts snowing. KENNY walks her to the door of his house. When he opens it, he realizes that it's snowing.)
KENNY: Snow!
(He's suddenly like a little kid in a candy store, he gets so excited he starts running around.)

End of Play

Money, Money, Money

by Paul McCoyer (2010)

ABOUT PAUL

What grade were you in when you wrote your play? 5th

What school did you attend? Bancroft Elementary School

Where do you go to school now? Deal Middle School

What do you like to do for fun? Write and film videos, read books and ride my bicycle.

Is there anything you'd like to say to the readers of this book? A writer can be inspired about things that annoy him/her, in addition to things they like. For example: when somebody is stubborn or lazy, or when your teachers give you too much homework, things like that. I was recently inspired to write a video script about the five most annoying things my little brother does. Inspiration isn't always about what you like.

Characters:

NARRATOR

JACK

RONALDO

PEOPLE, customers at the lemonade stand

LADY

MAN

SCENE 1:

NARRATOR: Once there were two friends. Their names were Jack and Ronaldo. They had one big thing in common: they loved to make money.

(Exit stage left. JACK and RONALDO enter stage right.)

JACK: ...and then, after we know people like the lemonade, we <u>reduce</u> the price to 75¢ per cup!

RONALDO: Why would we want to reduce the price? We'd make less money!

JACK: But more people will buy the lemonade if the price is lower. Then we'll get those movie tickets faster!

RONALDO: Oh, I get it now!

JACK: Let's get making this lemonade.

(Curtain closes as JACK and RONALDO gather materials, opens 15 seconds

later. Table set up with sign reading "Lemonade 75¢", apparently outside, selling lemonade.)

JACK: Lemonade! Get your lemonade!

RONALDO: Only 75¢!

(PEOPLE gather, buy lemonade, and eventually all leave.)

RONALDO: OK, so we've got $3.00 now. *($3 in $1 bills on the table)* I get the extra dollar, because I sold the most lemonade.

JACK: I should get it! I decided to sell the lemonade for 75¢!

RONALDO: Let's flip a coin. I'm heads!

JACK: Fine then. *(Flips coin)* Man! I was going to say heads!

RONALDO: Take your stupid dollar then! And we're not friends anymore!

(End of Scene 1, curtain closes)

SCENE 2:

(Curtain opens, NARRATOR enters.)

NARRATOR: So now Jack and Ronaldo were competing for the business that would make the most money.

(Exit stage right as RONALDO enters stage right.)

RONALDO: I should start a lawn mowing business!

(Exits briefly, re-enters with lawn mower. Goes to side of stage, says to imaginary person:)

RONALDO: Would you like me to mow your lawn for just $15?

LADY: Sure!

(RONALDO begins pushing lawn mower around stage, begins panting, then stops, very tired.)

RONALDO: It sure isn't as good without Jack.

(Curtain closes, RONALDO exits behind curtain, JACK enters, and curtain opens. To imaginary person, just as RONALDO did:)

JACK: Would you like me to rake leaves for you for only $10?

MAN: Of course!

(RONALDO peeks at JACK from side of stage, visible to audience.)

RONALDO: Hmph! That wise guy. Trying to get more people to pay him by lowering the price! I've seen that one before. Well, two can play that game. Hee hee hee!

(JACK has been raking the entire time. Curtain closes.)

SCENE 3:

NARRATOR: Looks like both of these two have got their businesses started.

Who do you think will make more money? Jack and Ronaldo each
have a few tricks up their sleeves. We'll see what happens.
(JACK and RONALDO stop in front of each other.)
JACK and RONALDO: Oh. Uh, hi.
*(They pass each other, begin putting up signs, Jack's says "Jack's Lawn Care
Service, Only $10!" with picture of Jack's face, Ronaldo's says "Ronaldo's Lawn
Care Service, Only $9.50!" with picture of Ronaldo's face. When they get close to
each other, JACK puts up one of his signs, RONALDO puts one of his on top.)*
JACK: Hey, you can't do that!
RONALDO: Why not?
JACK: It's just not fair!
RONALDO: So what? I don't care!
JACK: *(Sighs angrily)* I'm going home. *(Exits.)*
RONALDO: *(Look around nervously)* Hee hee hee!
*(Takes black marker out of pocket, begins drawing on Jack's signs, adding extra 0's
to "$10" and drawing mustaches on pictures of Jack).*
RONALDO: Wait. If I made more businesses, I could make even more
  money! I'm going straight home to get started!
(Curtain closes, scene changes to Ronaldo's bedroom.)

SCENE 4:
*(RONALDO is at his desk, drawing an ad for Ronaldo's Dog Walking Service.
Also in front of him are ads for lawn care, babysitting and car washing. Four
phones are also sitting on the desk.)*
RONALDO: *(Finishing ad)* There! That's all of them! Wait 'til Jack sees –
(Phone rings, interrupting him.)
RONALDO: My first customer! *(Picks up phone)* Hello? You have reached–
  (Pauses) Oh, sorry, no, this is not the pizza shop. But would you like to
  have your lawn mowed by Ronaldo Industries? *(Pauses)* Oh, alright, I
  understand, you need your pizza. Goodbye.
(Hangs up and sighs. Phone rings.)
RONALDO: My first customer! *(Answers phone)* Hello? You have reached
  Ronaldo Industries. What is it you require? *(Pauses)* Does your child
  take naps? *(Another phone rings)* Let me check that...Ronaldo Industries.
  What is it you require? How big is your car? A bus? *(Counts)* That'll be
  $20. Let me check that... *(Another phone rings)* Ronaldo Industries. What
  is it you require? Exactly how vicious is your dog? Uh...okay...let me
  check that... *(Phone rings)* Ronaldo Industries. What is it you require?

Do you have roses? With thorns? How about maple trees? Because I'm allergic...Let me check that...

(Puts one phone down, checks through more papers, picks up phone again, upside down.)

RONALDO: Yes I can clean your baby Saturday at 12:15. *(In another phone)* I can babysit your bus at 2:20. *(In another phone)* I can rake your dog at 1:30 on Saturday. Um, I mean, mow your car. No, no, no — wash your leaves — right? Oh, yes, yes, walk your dog, that's right. Thank you. Goodbye! *(Talks in other phone)* Yes, I can walk your lawn at 3:15. I'll just have to be very, very careful...Because I'm allergic. Goodbye! *(Hangs up both phones)* Phew! I'm glad that's over. At least I'll be making more money than Jack. He won't even—

(Phone rings, RONALDO puts his head down on the table, sighs exasperatedly.)

SCENE 5:

JACK: Oh, well, time to do some more.

(Gathers lots of lawn tools, awkwardly holding them. Walks towards the door, ready to leave.)

JACK: Hey, the mail's here. *(Goes through envelopes)* Bills, bills, bills...Hey, something for me!

(Opens envelope, reading aloud, still awkwardly holding lawn tools.)

JACK: Dear Mr. Jack Meyer,

It is our great pleasure to inform you that we are representing Mr. and Mrs. Houston, former customers of your lawn care service. We demand a full refund of $5.25 for services not rendered last Saturday afternoon. *(Stops reading for a moment)* What? *(Drops tools, continues reading)* Mr. and Mrs. Houston expected their lawn to be mowed, and instead found their prize rose bushes crudely destroyed and tools scattered across their lawn. Please refund the $5.25 immediately. We will happily collect our minimum fee of $5.00 separately. With our warmest regards,

Fred Scoff and Todd Smirk

JACK: Oh, no!!! This is a major setback! Where's a good friend when you need him? *(Pauses)* Wait, what's the point of not being friends? I haven't gotten anywhere. I'll go ask Ronaldo if he wants to be friends again.

(Curtain closes briefly, opens to JACK and RONALDO both onstage.)

RONALDO: So, um, how has your business been going?

JACK: Not very well. Two of my customers demanded refunds.

RONALDO: Things haven't been going well for me either. Listen — I was just wondering—

JACK: *(Interrupting RONALDO)* Do you want to be friends again?

RONALDO: Of course!

(They exit as NARRATOR enters.)

NARRATOR: Being friends again really helped. Those two really made a lot of money together!

JACK: ...23, 24, 25! We've got $25!!! That's just enough for two movie tickets. The extra dollar goes to me.

RONALDO: You got it last time!

(NARRATOR enters, JACK and RONALDO begin to move their mouths silently, apparently still arguing.)

NARRATOR: Here we go again!

JACK: You know what? Let's not argue over this. Just take the dollar.

RONALDO: Thanks!

NARRATOR: Phew!

(Curtain)

NARRATOR: *(Not visible to audience)* 20 years later...

(Two grown men enter, apparently JACK and RONALDO, dressed in suits, ties and sunglasses.)

JACK: Hey, Ronaldo, remember that time in the 5th grade when we fought over the dollar bill?

RONALDO: Oh, yeah, I'd forgotten all about that. And look at us now! We're rich! I could lose $100 and practically not care!

JACK: That was so stupid of us, fighting over $1.

RONALDO: You know, we should write a play about that fight...We'd make a lot of money...

(JACK and RONALDO exit. Curtain.)

End of Play

Mr. Pig
by Miranda Pomroy (2011)

ABOUT MIRANDA

What grade were you in when you wrote your play? 4th
What school did you attend? Watkins Elementary School
Where do you go to school now? Stuart Hobson Middle School
What do you like to do for fun? Crafting and writing.
Is there anything you'd like to say to the readers of this book? YPT was really fun!

Characters:
MR. PIG, a super-absorber that accidentally got created with acid, boastful.
MASON, nine years old, very bold
ADAM, ten years old, smart and anxious, loves cheese
MS. KELLOGG, 4th grade science teacher, likes control
MS. MELLOUK, 4th grade ELA teacher, team teaches with Ms. Kellogg
MS. JONES, 4th grade math/ELA teacher, she's a diva
MS. THOMPSON, 4th grade math/ELA teacher, very strict
FACTORY WORKER 1, Eugene, bossy
FACTORY WORKER 2, Jim, likes green
FACTORY WORKER 3, Carl, diva

SCENE 1: At the super-absorber factory, on a regular day.
FACTORY WORKER 1: First load ready! (_Points to a conveyor-belt looking object_)
FACTORY WORKER 2: Thanks Jim! (_Brings to the conveyor-belt a wagon-shaped item_)
(_A machine is now pressing the absorbers into actual animal shapes. FACTORY WORKER 2 leaves the wagon for FACTORY WORKER 3. FACTORY WORKER 3 places the super-absorbers from the conveyor-belt into the wagon object, but stops to stare at one suspiciously._)
FACTORY WORKER 3: I guess I'm just losing my marbles! (_Tosses the absorber behind his back into the wagon_) Oh well! (_Shrugs shoulders and gets back to his job. Does not look back for the super-absorber._)

SCENE 2: In MS. KELLOGG'S classroom. Everyone has super-absorbers and water. Two large tables and a couple of chairs at each table. MASON and ADAM are in one group. The other students are in the other group.

39

MS. KELLOGG: Since we've studied the scientific method, we're going to do a little science experiment ourselves. *(Class cheers.)* Wait, you don't even know what the experiment is! It could be anything, like EATING YOUR VEGETABLES! *(Class gasps but shortly after cheers and laughs.)* Anyway, our little project has nothing to with eating veggies, because it is on polymers, super-absorbers, and grow-a-creatures! They are all the same thing! But the name that they are most commonly used with is super-absorbers. *(Two hands shoot up.)* Now before you guys rally me with questions, I am going to tell you what a polymer really is. *(Their hands go down.)* You guys can think of it as a diaper, which is in fact a polymer. What it does is it soaks in the water, and the other stuff, *(Class laughs)* and then it gets bigger, and bigger, and bigger, until it's really big! But not huge. If it was bigger than your desks, then that would have taken some serious science magic! Impossible! I don't want to tell you anymore, because I might spoil the video! But first, let's conduct the experiment. Now place your super-absorbers into the water. *(Everyone places their super-absorbers into water. Someone splashes in the water.)* Wait, wait, wait! Don't do that! *(Looks at watch)* Oh no! I completely lost track of time. We'll have to do the video another time. Class dismissed!

(Class exits normally, maybe even a little slowly. Then class does normal routine fast, representing the two days of science class in a fast forward motion. Two days later.)

ADAM: Look at that size, our pig is huge!

MS. KELLOGG: *(Mumbling)* And it's been huge for a while.

SCENE 3: *Night.*

MS. THOMPSON: Over there! The boy's bathroom! *(Points to the boys' bathroom. Putting a shovel in air.)* I'm going in ladies!

MS. JONES: *(Blows whistle)* Teachers huh!

(All teachers except MS. JONES go "huh!" MS. JONES snaps like a diva, waving her finger.)

MS. JONES: No way I'm going in that restroom!

MS. KELLOGG: *(In mad voice)* If one goes in, we ALL go in! *(Puts on lab coat)*

MS. MELLOUK: Wow we are ready!

(Suddenly superhero theme music turns on and an unseen voice comes on saying, "Ms. Kellogg with the lab coat, Ms. Mellouk with the finger pointer, Ms. Thompson with the shovel, and Ms. Jones with the whistle! Together they create,

THE 4TH GRADE TEACHERS!")

MS. JONES: I'm glad that finally turned on!

(Teachers nod. They walk into the restroom.)

MS. THOMPSON: Where is that dag on pig!?!

MS. JONES: Ladies look over there! *(Pointing to the toilet)* The toilet to your left!

(All teachers whip their heads to see the toilet.)

MS. KELLOGG: He gets stronger when with water! Stop him!

(The PIG turns around to see everyone staring at him.)

MR. PIG: AGGRAMAKA!

(He starts running towards MS. JONES. MS. JONES screams and they all run out.)

MS. JONES: *(While running)* I told you we shouldn't have gone to the boy's bathroom! The worst things happen in there – trust me!

(The PIG jumps out of the toilet and starts to chase the teachers. They exit.)

SCENE 4: Science class, MS. KELLOGG has a torn lab coat on.

MS. KELLOGG: *(Drowsy voice)* And now we will cancel science class. Stayed up soooooo late, sorry class!

MASON: *(MASON whispers to ADAM)* I don't know what's been wrong with the 4th grade teachers, and why OUR super-absorber pig is so huge, but I'll be willing to find out! Are you with me?

ADAM: *(Whispering)* But, but, but what if we get in trouble?

MASON: Oh, Adam, shut up!

SCENE 5: Night. All the fourth grade teachers are huddled up. MASON and ADAM are spying on them.

ADAM: Mason, Mason I snuck some cheese and random juices out of the fridge!

MASON: Be quiet! *(MASON elbows ADAM.)* Wait, what are you wearing?!

ADAM: You said to wear something orange!

MASON: No! I said to wear BLACK! How did you get ORANGE out of BLACK?

ADAM: My mother did say I have a problem with listening to directions.

(MASON shrugs his shoulders and nods, looking annoyed.)

ADAM: *(Whispering)* I was guessing we needed some weapons so I loaded 3 marshmallow guns for us!

MASON: Oh Adam, just be quiet!

MS. KELLOGG: I've got it!

TEACHERS: *(Say in unison)* What, what?

MS. KELLOGG: If we make sure he doesn't get any water, he won't grow...

MS. MELLOUK: You're right he'll shrink!

MS. KELLOGG: Block off <u>all</u> water sources!

(All teachers but MS. KELLOGG exit and block off water sources. The teachers come back panting.)

MS. MELLOUK: We blocked off all water sources, Captain!

(The PIG walks by casually, drinking a mug of water. The mug says "I ♥ Bacon." The teachers stop to stare. Their jaws drop. MASON and ADAM come in.)

MASON: Step away teachers, Mason is coming in!

(All teachers look at MS. KELLOGG for permission, MS. KELLOGG nods.)

MS. KELLOGG: Step aside.

(All teachers step aside but MS. KELLOGG. MASON hands MS. KELLOGG a marshmallow gun and they all shoot at the PIG.)

MS. JONES: Wow! What's happening?

ADAM: *(Still shooting)* I read on the internet that pigs hate marshmallows!

MS. THOMPSON: He's shrinking! Amazing!

MR. PIG: AGGGRROOGGAAAA!

ADAM: *(Bragging voice)* Thank you, thank you very much.

MASON and the TEACHERS: Shut up Adam!

End of Play

Ally in Blunder Land

by Sophie ReVeal (2008)

ABOUT SOPHIE

What grade were you in when you wrote your play? 4th

What school did you attend? Francis Scott Key Elementary

Where do you go to school now? Washington Latin Public Charter School

What do you like to do for fun? Play soccer, read and write.

Is there anything you'd like to say to the readers of this book? If you want to be a writer, just start writing. You can never be too old or too young to come up with great ideas.

Characters:

ALLY

MARIO, her brother

MARGRET, lady in the bleachers

EARLY RABBIT

TWEEDLE SMART

TWEEDLE SMEE

BUTTERFLY

CHECKERED CAT

MAD HATTER

DORMOUSE

APRIL BUNNY

CARDS

QUEEN OF DIAMONDS

GUARD(S)

SOCCER PLAYERS

COACH

MAGICIAN

SCENE 1: *Down the rabbit hole.*

(ALLY runs onto stage dressed for soccer wearing a white jersey with a red diamond on it and black shorts. She is frantically searching in her backpack. She tosses it to her brother, MARIO.)

ALLY: Mario, help me find my blue soccer socks.

MARIO: *(Looking in her bag for the socks)* You know Ally — we all know you're the star of everything. Can you just calm down?

ALLY: No. I have to improve my skills in advanced math, soccer, juggling and pottery.

MARIO: You're already fine in those, and come on, it's *advanced* math. Ally, today is my birthday and we're gonna have a magician.

ALLY: Yeah, I know. Whatever. Where did you put my cleats? The soccer game is about to start and coach wants them on.

MARGRET: *(Lady in the bleachers)* You're wasting time! Get your cleats on and *score me a goal. Yah!*

ALLY: Sorry Margret give me a sec.

MARGRET: Fine but hurry up the game is about to start! And after the game get me my regular — a double, half-caf, no whip, skim, vanilla cappuccino and you know how I like them.

ALLY: Yes Ma'am *(Leaves to find MARIO practicing his dribbling)* Sorry every week I have to do chores for Margret.

MARIO: And she is…

ALLY: One of Mom's friends from law school. She always calls me "the child I never had." It's so annoying.

MARIO: Oh. *(Looking away. Looks back to change subject)* You can play for the first half but then you're coming to my party, right?

ALLY: Well, uh — hey, did you see me dribbling? Let me show you.

(He starts dribbling and accidentally hits her ball into the woods.)

ALLY: Right into the woods. Thanks! *(Goes to get the ball. Under her breath)* Great job… *(Talking to herself)* Where is that dumb ball?

EARLY RABBIT: *(Wanders onto stage – holding ball – looks at a ball, sighs)* SIGH, I'm early, so so early, always early. *(Looks at watch – sighs)* Yep, still too early.

ALLY: *(Staring at RABBIT in shock)* Uhhhhhhh, Talking Rabbit? Over here? Um, well, that's my ball.

EARLY RABBIT: *(Sighs, looks at watch, sighs, shakes his head again)* I'm going to be early. Hole.

(Disappears down a deep hole while holding soccer ball)

ALLY: What the? Talking Rabbit? You took my BALL DOWN YOUR *(Runs up and looks into hole)* VERY VERY VERY DEEP HOLE?!?!?! Oh well, we have plenty of balls. You'd have to be crazy to jump down there. How deep is that anyway. Like a mile?*(ALLY turns around to walk away. Ball flies out of the hole; hits her on the back of head, she loses her balance and falls back into hole.)*

AHHHHHHHHHHHHHHHHHHHHHHHHHHHHHHHH! *(Falling)* I'm

falling, still falling, still falling. How can I still be falling? How deep is this hole? (Cross her arms over chest) Seriously? No really? Seriously? You gotta be kidding me with this falling. This is like crazy falling. Stupid gravity. (Lays down on back – almost like floating) I don't HAVE all afternoon to fall here people, I have a game to play then I have to go and finish my advanced math homework in time to walk Dyno-mite – the world's best dog. Geez, what if I'm falling here forever? Who's going to walk Dynomite? I know Mario wouldn't because he's mad at me for being such a rock star. This falling has got to stop. (BUMP – she hits bottom – soccer ball rolls and hits her in the head – lays for a minute then props herself up on elbow.)

ALLY: Whoa – what is going on?

(RABBIT wanders slowly by, right in front of ALLY, kicks soccer ball. Pretends to be excited.)

EARLY RABBIT: Oh my gosh Oh my gosh… (Sigh) I'm early. (Kicks ball through small dark passageway and then wanders through himself. ALLY gets up and walks over and looks into passage way.)

ALLY: Ugh — what on earth is this place? (Beside the passage is a small table with a bottle of sports drink, ALLY picks it up.) Sports Drink! Alright! Wait, there's a note on here. Drink me. Drink me? OK no. Not alright. I'm not drinking some random sports drink just sitting around in a mile deep hole. This is 2009. I read the papers. I know better than to take a sports drink from strangers, even if I don't actually see any strangers. This place is strange and that definitely counts. (ALLY turns around and sees a bright, open passageway going the other direction.) That's more like it. I'm going that way. Following rabbits gets you in trouble around here. (Walks offstage through a bright hallway)

SCENE 2: Adventures with Tweedle Smee and Tweedle Smart.
(ALLY walks onstage as if it's a dark and scary woods and leans against a tree.)
ALLY: It's dark in these woods. Maybe if I stay put my coach will find me. (Waits) What am I saying there is no way anyone will find me in this hole! I'll figure this out myself.
TWEEDLE SMART: (Jumps from offstage smiling) Tweedle Smart!
TWEEDLE SMEE: (Jumps from offstage runs next to TWEEDLE SMART bowing and smiling at ALLY) Tweedle Smee!
TWEEDLE SMART: (Whispers in other TWEEDLE'S ear but he lets audience hear) Do you know why she's here?

TWEEDLE SMEE: *(To other TWEEDLE)* Don't ask me, but if the Queen finds out, she's dead.

ALLY: Uh, hello? Can either of you tell me how to get out of here?

TWEEDLE SMART: *(Cutting her off and ignoring her)* Let us tell you a story!

TWEEDLE SMEE: Yes let's begin!

ALLY: *(Getting up trying to leave)* No that's okay I'm fine.

(TWEEDLE SMART links arms with one of her arms and TWEEDLE SMEE does the same thing to the other arm and they drag her back against the tree. ALLY sighs.)

TWEEDLE SMART: The Waffle and the Copier.

(Hits his side against TWEEDLE SMEE)

TWEEDLE SMART: Beep

TWEEDLE SMEE: *(Holding up his pinkie trying to look smart)* Or you can call it the STORY OF the Waffle and the Copier. *(Bumps TWEEDLE SMART back)*

TWEEDLE SMEE: Bop

TWEEDLE SMART: *(Bumps him over to the side again)* Beep

TWEEDLE SMEE: *(Bumps him back again twice moving TWEEDLE SMART over a few steps)* Bop Bop

TWEEDLE SMART: *(Bumps him over to the side again)* Beep

TWEEDLE SMEE: *(Bumps him back again twice moving TWEEDLE SMART over a few steps)* Bop Bop

TWEEDLE SMART: *(Gestures big and goofy)* The time has come!

TWEEDLE SMEE: *(Silly gestures as well)* The Waffle said

TWEEDLE SMART: To talk of many things

TWEEDLE SMEE: *(Looking confused cutting him off)* Wait a minute. *(Pause)* Waffles can't talk.

TWEEDLE SMART: *(Looking over at TWEEDLE SMEE)* Hush up! Where were we oh yes, of shoes—and ships—and sealing wax—of cabbages—and kings

TWEEDLE SMEE: If you let waffles talk well then pancakes will want to talk and *(In French accent)* even *ze crepes.*

TWEEDLE SMART: Would you let me finish, And why the sea is boiling hot—And whether pigs have wings.

ALLY: Uh, if we're finished discussing breakfast food, can you guys tell me how to get out of here or do you know where the Talking Rabbit went with my ball?

TWEEDLE SMEE: Nope not a clue.

TWEEDLE SMART: Ugh, don't mind him he's dumber than a baby's rattle. You know how having a brother is. You have a brother right? Anyway, the Rabbit is supposed to be at the Queen's croquet, but it doesn't start until 3—so you know he's already there. Now, if you would excuse me I have to talk some sense into Tweedle Smee. Don't you agree that waffles can talk? I could have sworn the one this morning said he needed more syrup!

TWEEDLE SMEE: You had cereal for breakfast! More importantly, little girl, *(Looking at ALLY sideways)* however did you manage it?

ALLY: *(Getting very annoyed)* Manage WHAT?

TWEEDLE SMART: Your escape of course.

ALLY: I didn't escape. I fell, and now I am just trying to get out of here.

TWEEDLE SMEE: But what about the uniform?

ALLY: You mean my soccer jersey?

TWEEDLE SMEE: SOCK HER? Who Socked Her? I didn't sock her.

TWEEDLE SMART: I didn't say you did.

TWEEDLE SMEE: Now you're blaming me again!

ALLY: Guys just break it up!

TWEEDLE SMEE: Well I didn't sock anyone!

TWEEDLES: *(Runing away, yelling)* Beep Bop Bop! Beep Bop Bop! Beep Bop Bop!

TWEEDLE SMEE: *(Turns around)* Oh, you could ask the caterpillar on the mushroom!

ALLY: *(Yelling after him)* Caterpillar? Whatever. I guess I'll just go this way. *(Walks down road cautiously)*

SCENE 3: *Advice from a Butterfly.*
(ALLY wanders in the woods and finds the BUTTERFLY.)

ALLY: *(In the dark woods looking around)* Anyone there? *(Echo)* I guess not. *(Echo)*

(ALLY looks scared and keeps walking.)

ALLY: *(Thinking aloud)* What's that light in the distance? *(Walks into light clearance in the woods, sees mushrooms big enough for her to lie across on and still not touch the sides.)* Wow, there *is* a mushroom. I can't believe those guys were right about anything. *(Comes to a mushroom with a BUTTERFLY bigger than her sitting on it.)*

BUTTERFLY: *(Fast voice — chewing gum between each word)* Who are ya— *(Cutting herself off)* Oh. It's you.

ALLY: It's me? Whatever. Can you tell me how to get out of here?

BUTTERFLY: The question should be, what are you doing here in the first place. Does she know you've escaped?

(In between every few words loud chews like she's chewing gum.)

ALLY: Who is *she*? Do you mean my mother? Anyway, I thought you were supposed to be a caterpillar?

BUTTERFLY: Hello? *(Chewing gum constantly)* That story is so dated. I USED to be a caterpillar. We all know what happens to caterpillars — we don't stay caterpillars forever. Didn't you learn the life cycle stuff in kindergarten?

ALLY: Oh right, sorry. Why are you chewing that gum?

BUTTERFLY: *(Chews in between every few words)* Because smoking is bad for you — doncha know?

ALLY: Okaaay. I do know that. But do you know how I could get out of here?

BUTTERFLY: Out of where?

ALLY: Out of here! This place, this country, this crazy land.

BUTTERFLY: Oh, out of Blunderland entirely. You really do want to escape. *(Thinking about it and chewing loudly)* Well I don't know but my mushroom might.

ALLY: Right, you think your mushroom's going to know?

BUTTERFLY: *(Rubbing mushroom)* That's insulting. *(Talking to mushroom)* She didn't mean that Carlisle.

ALLY: The Mushroom is named Carlisle?

BUTTERFLY: *(Looks up at Ally)* Just look, he always has an answer.

ALLY: *(Bends down and looks at the bottom of the mushroom)* Well I do see some writing but it's upside down!

BUTTERFLY: *(Still chewing gum)* Stand on your head, silly. *(Under her breath)* While you still have one.

ALLY: *(Looks up startled, then shrugs)* I'll try… *(Leans over and stands on her hands)* It does say something. It's a poem:
"The Cheshire Cat is where you should go
The Cheshire Cat is wise, you know
Just look for a tree shaped like a 'V'
And don't come back bothering me"

BUTTERFLY: So there you have it. I told you Carlisle knows his stuff.

ALLY: Thanks, I'll go now. And don't worry I'm not coming back.

BUTTERFLY: Good, because this is the only head I've got.

SCENE 4: *Seeing the Cheshire Cat. In a big clearing with one single tree in the middle.*

ALLY: *(Walking up to tree)* Hello. *(Waits for answer)* Cheshire Cat where are you?

CHECKERED CAT: *(Appears lying on the tree propped up on a elbow looking at ALLY)* Ohhh noooo not THAT again. I'm the *Checkered* Cat not the Cheshire Cat. Everybody except for that stupid mushroom knows it's Checkered! What is Cheshire anyway?

ALLY: I think it's some place in England.

CHECKERED CAT: Never mind. See the squares? I'm CHECKERED. CHECKERED! I have never even BEEN to England. *(Starting a new subject)* Hey, we don't like your kind around here — people around here need their heads for things! Heads can be very handy, you know. Actually, hands would be handy too.

ALLY: Okay...Okay I don't want your head. It scares me actually. I have heard you are wise oh — CHECKERED cat — I'm trying to get out of, uh, Blunderland — could you point me in the right direction?

CHECKERED CAT: *(Pointing left paw to the right)* That's a good thought. If you stay here you'll surely lose your head. If you go over there you'll meet the Hatter, but of course he's quite *MAD*. *(Pointing right paw to the left)* If you go that way you'll meet the Queen, but she's *MAD* too: but you would know that more than anyone since we can tell you've been around her. That's why you escaped from home.

ALLY: I didn't escape. I fell. You remind me of someone. I can't quite put my finger on it.

CHECKERED CAT: Now you're starting to sound mad.

ALLY: I know! It's my brother. He always wants me home. I'm always everywhere else in his mind.

CHECKERED CAT: I know.

ALLY: How do you know?

CHECKERED CAT: We're all mad I'm mad, you're mad, everybody's mad!

ALLY: *(Under her breath)* Okay, I'm leaving. But I cannot deal with crazy people right now. What about the Talking Rabbit he's not *MAD* is he?

CHECKERED CAT: The Early Rabbit? Why, he's the maddest of them all!

ALLY: Really? You got to be kidding. He doesn't seem mad to me. Plus he knows where I live. Can you tell me where he is?

CHECKERED CAT: *(Pointing to the right)* He could be over there. *(Arms crossed over each other pointing opposite way)* Or he could be over that way.

ALLY: Um well do you know which way exactly?

CHECKERED CAT: Just follow my pointing paw. *(Disappears)*

ALLY: Yeah, Great idea, follow a paw that's invisible. *(Stomps off angrily—yells over her shoulder)* NOW I AM MAD—JUST ADD ME TO THE LIST. THAT'S RIGHT, I'M MAD – DEAL WITH IT!!!!

<u>SCENE 5:</u> *A mad tea party. A table in the woods covered with fine china. (Walking, ALLY comes to a long table. Sitting at the table are a small man with a huge hat, a bunny rabbit and a Dormouse. ALLY walks up to the table.)*

ALLY: Hello there I'm Ally.

MAD HATTER: *(Loud crazy voice)* No you're not, you're the Ace of Diamonds. And you can't sit here. There's uh, there's no room!!!

APRIL BUNNY: Yes no room, no room!!!

DORMOUSE: *(Sleeping)* Shuuuu

ALLY: It looks like there is room, because well it's a mighty big table and you guys are all crowded at one end. *(Without asking pulls out a chair on the end and sits)* And my name is not Ace it's Ally. I can see how you might be confused because of my soccer jersey.

MAD HATTER: SOCK HER? I'm not going to sock her. You sock her.

APRIL BUNNY: I'm not going to sock her. I need my head.

(Puts hands over his head, moves DORMOUSE hands over his head.)

MAD HATTER: Why, you're not using it? I need my head more. I am a hatter after all.

ALLY: What is it with you guys and your heads!?

APRIL BUNNY: *(Lowering hands)* Yes OK I'll introduce myself I'm the April Bunny NOT the Easter bunny!

MAD HATTER: *(Whispering to ALLY)* People get him confused. *(Speaking louder)* And I am the Mad Hatter!

APRIL BUNNY: Well now that you are sitting would you like some tea?

ALLY: I don't see any tea.

APRIL BUNNY: That's because there isn't any. *(Laughs loudly)*

ALLY: Well that was rude!

APRIL BUNNY: It was just as rude to sit down without asking!

ALLY: I didn't sit down.

MAD HATTER: Well calm down anyway! Look, cute dormouse is waking up.

DORMOUSE: 'Twinkle, twinkle, little ball!
Down the mile long hole you fall;
Little girl will follow too.

To go back up here's what to do:

Twinkle twinkle *(snoooooorrrre)*

ALLY: Wait, what? What?

MAD HATTER: Too late, he's gone to sleep again.

ALLY: Wake him up! Wake him up!

APRIL BUNNY: He only wakes up on Thursday at precisely 5 o'clock.

ALLY: But today's Saturday.

MAD HATTER: Exactly!

DORMOUSE: Shhhhuuuuu hhuuuuuuu hhhhsshuuuu

ALLY: ARGHHHHHHHHHHH! I see now why everyone here is MAD!

MAD HATTER: I would be careful if I were you. Someone at this very table might turn you in. *(Glares at APRIL BUNNY)*

APRIL BUNNY: That's right — spies are everywhere. *(Looking at DORMOUSE)*

MAD HATTER: Good idea. Help me shove him into the tea pot! *(Lifts MOUSE and drops in tea pot)*

ALLY: *(Sneaking away)* The Cheshire...Checkered Cat said something about a Queen. A Queen might know something. At least she can't be crazier than *that. (Runs back into woods)*

SCENE 6: The Queen's croquet ground. A big garden outside the Queen's palace.

ALLY: I've been walking forever! *(Comes into a garden, where it looks like a soccer team is practicing)* Hey, you guys has anyone seen my team? The Diamonds? We play for the city league. Oh, you guys aren't soccer players. You're...playing cards.

(CARDS scatter and run.)

QUEEN OF DIAMONDS: *(Pointing at ALLY)* You! Where have you been? Where is my double, half-caf, no whip, skim, vanilla cappuccino? OFF WITH YOUR HEAD!

ALLY: *(Stalling)* Uhh, yeah, well, uh they put whip cream on it the first time, and I know how you hate that. So, I had to wait while they made another one. And then they ran out of ice and I've got it right here.

QUEEN OF DIAMONDS: Never mind. It's time for the croquet. *(Whispering to GUARD so audience can hear)* She doesn't think we know she's been wandering around AWOL all afternoon. AWOL! You know what that means?

(GUARD draws fingers across his throat.)

QUEEN OF DIAMONDS: Exactly.

ALLY: Croquet is not really my game.

(GUARDS sneaking up behind ALLY — grab her.)

QUEEN OF DIAMONDS: OFF WITH HER HEAD!

ALLY: Hey, what did I do?

QUEEN OF DIAMONDS: You know you've been AWOL all day long. You're supposed to work for me. You've been seen in the forest, the mushroom patch, the rabbit hole. You even went to a tea party.

ALLY: But there wasn't any tea!

QUEEN OF DIAMONDS: No tea? OFF WITH HER HEAD!

(GUARDS close in on ALLY. She walks backwards and trips over her soccer ball and hits her head — everything goes black.)

SCENE 7: *The soccer field.*

(ALLY is lying on the ground, crowded around her are actual SOCCER PLAYERS.)

MARGRET: *(Yelling at her while poking her rapidly)* You are fine, shake it off! You still haven't scored me a goal yet! Get up kid!

ALLY: NOOOOOOOOOOO get away from me. I need my head. I have a math test next week and it counts as half my grade. Stop!!

COACH: Ally, honey, it's okay. When you tried for that header you hit the goal. But you seem to be okay now. You scared us there for a minute.

ALLY: A minute? I've been gone for hours and hours. And I hadn't even started to play soccer yet. I was talking to my brother on the sidelines and then he dribbled the ball into the woods...

COACH: Woah there partner. Your brother's not even here. Your whole family is at his 6th birthday party. We were surprised you chose to play today.

ALLY: What? No no no. That can't be true. Wait, his birthday party was today and I played? What kind of weirdo am I? Oh, it's not even half time yet. Sarah, can you drive me home? Do you mind if I go coach?

MARGRET: You can't leave without my goal. My day can't be complete without telling my friends all about MY star!

ALLY: NO! Find a new star 'cause I quit!

(Gets up with her friend and walks offstage.)

SCENE 8: *Birthday party.*

(ALLY runs in just as the MAGICIAN is getting ready. MARIO runs up and gives ALLY a big hug.)

MARIO: I can't believe you made it. How was your game? Are you winning?

ALLY: I don't know. I don't even really remember playing. I just rushed home for the party.

MARIO: Oh, really. That's why you came? I thought you were just coming to pick up your ball. You left it in the hall.

MAGICIAN: Ally, I'm so glad you made it. We're about to start the magic show. *(Sees the bump on her head)* What happened to you?

ALLY: I don't know. It was all strange and I fell into another world.

MAGICIAN: *(Smiling mysteriously)* Sounds like a big dream you had.

ALLY: It wasn't a dream. I was in this whole other land. And you were there...and you and you. Some of it was very creepy. But it was beautiful too. And all I kept saying is I want to go home. Because there's no place like... *(Smiles and winks at the audience)* But that's another story.

End of Play

Love What!? No!? Me a 10 Year Old?! What? Uh-oh!!

by Mayra Rivera (2007)

ABOUT MAYRA

What grade were you in when you wrote your play? 11th

What school did you attend? Bell Multicultural High School

What do you do now? I am a student at American University, and I work at Kid Power.

What do you like to do for fun? I have recently discovered decoupage, and I like transforming dull and simple stuff into something fun and colorful. In addition, I enjoy taking long walks, reading and watching foreign films.

Is there anything you'd like to say to the readers of this book? I hope you guys can relate to some of the plays in this book. Sometimes we are unable to voice what we feel and we remain silent in hopes that someone else will take the initiative. However, you should not be passive. You should find the confidence within to say what you want. Do not set up an imaginary obstacle that prevents you from speaking up. This is why I wrote this play. Through this play I was able to express my thoughts and parts of myself. Think about it… if not you, then who?

INTRODUCTION:

JACQUELYN: (*From offstage*) SO, YEA, LET'S BEGINNING WITH THE CHARACTERS

*Jacquelyn!

*My Stinky Brian, *cough*

*That girl, Patti

*My momma

*Daniela, which is my little sister

*McDoom's Brother

*Teacher, a teensy role in my play

SCENE 1:

PATTI: (*Dancing around yelling it out loud*) Jackie and Stinky sitting in a tree.
     K-I-S-S-I-N-G. First come love, then comes —

(*JACQUELYN comes*)

JACQUELYN: STOP! I don't like Stinky Brian!!

PATTI: (*Stretching each word*) Yeeeees yoooou doooo!!

JACQUELYN: No, I don't!!!!!

PATTI: I saw you holding hands with him!!!

JACQUELYN: I was helping him to get up!!!!

PATTI: *(Points at the Barbie that JACQUELYN is holding)* Whatever. I know what I saw. But, I'll make a deal with you. Give me your Barbie, and I won't say anything.

JACQUELYN: *(Is shocked at the request)* My....Barbie...? You mean Tammy...No! It is special to me!!!

PATTI: Oki Dokey! *(Yells out!)* STINKY AND JACKIE ARE—

(JACQUELYN covers her mouth.)

JACQUELYN: *(Gives the Barbie to PATTI)* Here! You can have my Barbie. Just take care of her. Make sure you feed her, and read her a book before she goes to sleep.

(JACQUELYN walks sadly towards the swings.)

JACQUELYN: God, what have I done to deserve this? I only went to help Stinky Brian because it was the right thing to do. Now, stupid Patti thinks I like him. God, this sucks. I lost my favorite Barbie, the one my dad gave me before— *(Starts to cry)*

(BRIAN come and sits to the next available swing.)

BRIAN: *(Says in hyper voice)* Hi! Hi! Hi! Hi! Hi!

(JACQUELYN remains quiet.)

BRIAN: *(Looks worried)* Hey! What's wrong?

JACQUELYN: Leave me alone!

BRIAN: No! I want to know what's wrong!!?

JACQUELYN: It is because of you!

BRIAN: Here!

JACQUELYN: It is because I was stupid enough to help you to get up after the McDoom's Brother pushed you in the mud.

BRIAN: Oh! I'm sorry. I didn't want to start stuff.

JACQUELYN: It's whatever.

(BRIAN jumps off the swing and runs to the field until he sees dandelions and picks some out, and runs back to JACQUELYN.)

BRIAN: Here!

(He holds out the flowers for her. JACQUELYN looks up and takes the flower.)

JACQUELYN: Thanks, they look pretty.

BRIAN: I chose the best one.

(JACQUELYN smiles. TEACHER comes out and starts to blow out the whistle.)

JACQUELYN: I guess it's time to go.

BRIAN: Yup! *(Walk to their class together)*

SCENE 2:
(At JACQUELYN'S home, JACQUELYN comes home holding hands with her little sister, DANIELA who is 5 years old.)
JACQUELYN: Mami, we're home!
DANIELA: *¡Si! ¡Si! Mami.*
(JACQUELYN walks to the kitchen.)
JACQUELYN'S MOM: *Hola mi'hijita.* How was school?
JACQUELYN: *(JACQUELYN says quietly)* Bien.
JACQUELYN'S MOM: *Y tu* Barbie, where is it?? You always carry it with you.
JACQUELYN: *(Avoids eye contact with her mom)* I let my friend borrow it.
JACQUELYN'S MOM: Isn't that the doll that your *Papi* gave you before he left
    to— *(JACQUELYN interrupts)*
JACQUELYN: It's okay *Mami. Papi* will always be in our heart.
(DANIELA comes in the kitchen.)
DANIELA: *Mami! Mami!* I draw a picture for you!! *(Holds up a picture of her
    mom, her sister, and herself holding hands.)*
JACQUELYN'S MOM: *¡Ah mi'hijita! Que lindo.* Thank you!
DANIELA: You're welcome.
JACQUELYN'S MOM: I made *pupasa!!!!!!*
JACQUELYN and DANIELA: *(In unison)* Yay!!!

SCENE 3:
*(JACQUELYN walks to school with her little sister; she turns around and sees a
boy walking alone, who happens to smell clean, and realizes that it is STINKY
BRIAN!)*
JACQUELYN: Uh-oh!
DANIELA: What's wrong Jacquelyn??
JACQUELYN: I see Stinky, I mean Brian, but if I walk with him my friends
    will think I go out with him.
(BRIAN catches up with them.)
DANIELA and JACQUELYN: *(In unison)* Huh?
(DANIELA stops and looks at some flowers.)
BRIAN: Hi-Ya!
JACQUELYN: *(Whispers)* Darn!
BRIAN: Huh?
JACQUELYN: Nothing Stink—, I mean Brian.

BRIAN: Oh OK. Hey, I told my mom that you helped me and she baked a cookie for you to thank you for helping me.

JACQUELYN: Huh?

(BRIAN starts looking through his book bag, and takes out a cookie that is broken.)

BRIAN: Oh man! Not again! This was not supposed to happen.

JACQUELYN: It's okay.

BRIAN: Believe me, my mom makes the best cookies! But, I don't know if you want it now that it is broken.

JACQUELYN: It's OK, I'll take it. Tell your mom that I say thanks.

DANIELA: I want a cookie too!!!

JACQUELYN: Um… here take a piece.

DANIELA: Thank you.

BRIAN: You seem like a good sister.

JACQUELYN: Thanks. Hey, why do people call you Stinky?

BRIAN: I don't really know. Do I smell to you?

JACQUELYN: No. You smell good today.

BRIAN: Cool. I guess my mom was right. Oh, man we have to get to school.

DANIELA: Uh-oh! Let's run to school.

BRIAN: Yea!

JACQUELYN: Umm… I don't think that's a good idea.

(DANIELA and BRIAN start running to school.)

JACQUELYN: Shoot!

(Starts to run to catch up with them, BRIAN grabs her hand and run together, while DANIELA is ahead running.)

DANIELA: Yay!! We made it!!!

BRIAN: High five. *(Give each other high five)*

JACQUELYN: Phew! We made it on time!!

BRIAN: So, where are you going?

JACQUELYN: Um… I have to drop off Daniela to her class.

BRIAN: Cool. Can I go with you??

JACQUELYN: Um… I dunno.

BRIAN: It can't possibly hurt?

JACQUELYN: Okay.

(Walks to the class and they happen to run by PATTI.)

PATTI: Oooooo! Jacquelyn you have a boyfriend!

JACQUELYN: He is not my boyfriend. He is my friend.

BRIAN: …yeah. What she said.

PATTI: Yea. Whatever.

(BRIAN notices she's carrying JACQUELYN'S Barbie.)
BRIAN: Hey! Isn't that yours, Jacquelyn??
JACQUELYN: Yeah, that's my Barbie.
BRIAN: Why do you have her doll???
PATTI: Don't worry about it.
(And she walks away; JACQUELYN starts feeling sad and starts walking.)
DANIELA: Bye Sista, me have to go to class.
(JACQUELYN waves.)

SCENE 4:
(BRIAN walks to class alone, and is concerned about JACQUELYN, last night he secretly wrote a love letter to JACQUELYN, but he's not sure whether or not to give it to her.)
BRIAN: Oh, man should I tell her? Or just give her the letter I wrote for her? What if she doesn't like me? What if she thinks I am too ugly or that I am weird? What if she thinks I am dumb for even trying. But...
McDOOM'S BROTHER: Hey Stinky!
(BRIAN walks faster.)
McDOOM'S BROTHER: I said hey!
BRIAN: Leave me alone.
McDOOM'S BROTHER: Where the food at?
(BRIAN ignores them and walks away.)
McDOOM'S BROTHER: Stop!
BRIAN: You can't stop me! *(Starts walking faster)*
McDOOM'S BROTHER: Oh really?
(McDOOM'S BROTHER snatched BRIAN'S book bag, and the love letter happens to fall off the book bag. BRIAN tries to get the letter, but then McDOOM'S BROTHER...)
McDOOM'S BROTHER: Well, well, well...... is this a loooooove letter???
BRIAN: None of your stinky business!!!
McDOOM'S BROTHER: Hmmm? Oh really? *(Starts to read it out loud)* Dear Jacquelyn, My momma says that if I really want something I have to ask politely. So... I want you to be my girlfriend. Can you pretty please be my girlfriend?? Love, Brian
(BRIAN tries to grab the love letter, but he is unable to do so. McDOOM'S BROTHER laughs and runs off with the letter. BRIAN tries to chase him but a teacher stops him.)
TEACHER: Young man, in this school running is not permitted. Go to class

or I am going to call your parents.

BRIAN: OK, I'm going to my class.

(He starts to head off to class.)

SCENE 5: *Lunch time. Children are lining up for lunch.*

(JACQUELYN sees BRIAN entering and she calls him over for him to bus.)

JACQUELYN: Hey Brian! Come over here!!

BRIAN: Umm.. I don't know.

JACQUELYN: Come on!

BRIAN: OK.

(McDOOM'S BROTHER enters also, looks for JACQUELYN, and sees them. He walks toward her.)

BRIAN: Uh-oh.

JACQUELYN: *(She repeats)* Uh-oh — *(Is interrupted)*

McDOOM'S BROTHER: Hey Jacquelyn. You look pretty as always.

JACQUELYN: What do you want from me?

McDOOM'S BROTHER: Me? Um… nothing. But, I know someone who does.

BRIAN: Leave us alone!!

McDOOM'S BROTHER: Why? So you can smooch her?

JACQUELYN: What are you guys talking about?

McDOOM'S BROTHER: Brian wants you to be his girlfriend.

BRIAN: That's not true!!

(JACQUELYN is confused.)

McDOOM'S BROTHER: So, you doubt me?

(Hands the love letter to JACQUELYN, she reads it, while she is reading, BRIAN leaves to the playground and McDOOM'S BROTHER laughs. JACQUELYN starts to run after BRIAN.)

PATTI: Hi Jacquelyn.

JACQUELYN: Bye.

(JACQUELYN is running but PATTI blocks her.)

PATTI: Where you are going?

JACQUELYN: Let me go!

PATTI: Well, if you leave then Tammy is not going to be the same anymore. I will cut her bald, rip her arms out, and make her smell so bad that you can't even imagine!

JACQUELYN: Tammy?

PATTI: Yes, Tammy!

JACQUELYN: Leave her alone!

(BRIAN sees PATTI with JACQUELYN and assumes the worst, he runs back to them.)

BRIAN: Give her doll back!

PATTI: No, it's mine. She let me have it.

JACQUELYN: Don't hurt Tammy.

BRIAN: I said give it back to her. It is not yours.

PATTI: Yes, it is. She gave it to me. She didn't want you —

(JACQUELYN interrupts her.)

JACQUELYN: I didn't want her to tell you that I like you.

PATTI and BRIAN: *(In unison)* What?!

JACQUELYN: I like Brian. And I don't care if he stinks or not.

BRIAN: Really?

JACQUELYN: Yup. And I want to be your girlfriend.

BRIAN: Really?

JACQUELYN: Yup.

(PATTI drops the doll and starts to yell out.)

PATTI: I will never be your friend if you're with him. I will tell the whole world you two are together!

JACQUELYN: I don't want a friend like you anyways.

PATTI: Jackie and Stinky sitting in a tree. K-I-S-S-I-N-G. First comes love then comes…

(BRIAN picks up the doll, and gives it to JACQUELYN. JACQUELYN hugs it and hugs BRIAN. While PATTI is yelling out to the whole world they are going out. BRIAN and JACQUELYN walk together holding hands.)

End of Play

Playwright Profile: Antawan Taylor

When Young Playwrights' Theater came to Antawan Taylor's fifth grade class at Plummer Elementary School back in 2009, he was already an artist.

"I like to draw and paint," the now deep-voiced thirteen-year-old says in an interview with YPT, leaning forward in his chair. "I've won a few contests for my drawing, and I've been in art shows at my school."

Back in 2009, however, Antawan wasn't a lover of writing. He found it boring, and would much rather spend his time sketching pictures of wolves and spiders than writing essays about them. But when his YPT teaching artist, Nicole, began working on writing activities with Antawan's class, he surprised himself.

"When I did it, I kind of had fun at it!" he says with a laugh. "I thought, 'I'd like to do this more often.'"

Antawan got another surprise when he discovered that he not only liked writing, but had a gift for it. His play, *Tornado Boy*, was selected for production in the **New Play Festival** from the hundreds of plays written by YPT students in 2009. *Tornado Boy* follows the story of Plummer Elementary School student Jeremy in his quest to defeat Scorch, an evil villain who is bombing houses in the city. But Jeremy has a secret advantage: his alter-ego, Tornado Boy, has the power to control wind and can travel as a tornado.

"Before YPT came [to my school], I saw the movie *Twister*," Antawan explains. "I got really into tornadoes. I started drawing them. When Nicole said we had to make up a play, I didn't have any ideas in the moment, but when I went home I ended up watching the movie again, and writing about a tornado superhero."

After *Tornado Boy* was produced, Antawan continued to focus on visual art, but found himself also looking for ways to be involved in theater. When he entered Sousa Middle School the following year, he was cast as the prince in the school's production of *Cinderella*.

"YPT pushed me more," he says. "I was already into drawing, but it pushed me to take more arts classes, and push myself more to get into it."

Antawan is now preparing to start ninth grade at Eastern High School, and while years have passed since his YPT experience, he still feels its effects.

"My imagination changed," he says, furrowing his brow thoughtfully. "Instead of writing something and doing it for a regular grade, I try and do it the best as I can."

Tornado Boy

by Antawan Taylor (2009)

ABOUT ANTAWAN

What grade were you in when you wrote your play? 5th

What school did you attend? Plummer Elementary School

Where do you go to school now? Eastern High School

What do you like to do for fun? I like to draw, write occasionally. I like doing artistic stuff.

Is there anything you'd like to say to the readers of this book?
If YPT comes to you, it's a good opportunity to try to change your life, because it changed my whole perspective on my life. I wasn't really interested in the arts before, but now I am. So just try it.

Characters:

PRINCIPAL GRAY

JEREMY/TORNADO BOY

KID

SCORCH

TWISTER

DR. STRANGE

SCENE 1: A classroom at Plummer Elementary School.

PRINCIPAL GRAY: Ring Ring Ring Ring. Teachers and students report to the basement shelter.

JEREMY: You, kid, what's happening?

KID: Scorch put bombs in the city and he is setting houses on fire.

JEREMY: I got to stop him before he hurts someone.

PRINCIPAL GRAY: Jeremy where are you going?

JEREMY: I got to check and see if my parents are okay.

PRINCIPAL GRAY: If you keep going that way you'll get suspended...or expelled.

JEREMY: Please don't suspend me Principal Gray! I am an A student and this is my first time getting in trouble. I had to go to a family emergency and my phone is off. I got to go and I wanted to tell the teacher but I was really scared.

PRINCIPAL GRAY: OK, OK, I know that you're in a rush, how about I drive

65

you home Jeremy?

JEREMY: Nooooo because my dogs don't like strangers, they might bite you.

PRINCIPAL GRAY: I can handle dogs.

JEREMY: There's four of them – are you sure you can handle them?

PRINCIPAL GRAY: What are you hiding from me?

JEREMY: I just gotta go.

(He runs away.)

SCENE 2:

(JEREMY becomes TORNADO BOY.)

TORNADO BOY: Good morning citizens! My name is Tornado Boy. I am a super hero – I have the power to control wind, travel as a tornado and control electricity. I have an enemy named Scorch. He is bad and dangerous. Watch out for him!

(SCORCH comes out with a blaze of fire.)

SCORCH: Tornado Boy, come out and fight me!

TORNADO BOY: Scorch this ends now. Whoossh!

(TORNADO BOY shoots a bolt of lightning. It starts to rain.)

TORNADO BOY: It's raining. Now I got the advantage. Whoosh!

(A big gust of wind turns into a tornado and it backfires on TORNADO BOY.)

SCORCH: That tornado will not hurt me!

(Whoosh! The tornado sucks up SCORCH, and some cars.)

TORNADO BOY: Scorch where are you? My powers are going out of control.

SCENE 3:

TORNADO BOY: Twister Twister I need your help, my powers is out of control!

TWISTER: What do you mean out of control?

TORNADO BOY: They are getting dangerous and I might harm the citizens.

TWISTER: Show an example or tell me something.

TORNADO BOY: I could have killed someone because I lost control of the wind. If somebody was in the cars that the tornado sucked up I would have stopped being a super hero.

TWISTER: We will take you to the mountain where Dr. Strange is.

TORNADO BOY: If this man called Dr. Strange can help then let's go.

SCENE 4:

DR. STRANGE: What's wrong boy?

TORNADO BOY: My powers are out of control.

DR. STRANGE: Have you been eating healthy?

TORNADO BOY: What do you mean healthy?

DR. STRANGE: Have you?

TORNADO BOY: Yes I guess so.

DR. STRANGE: Have you been eating vegetables and fruit?

TORNADO BOY: Yes one time.

DR. STRANGE: You have to always eat good with that kind of power.

TORNADO BOY: Do you got something I can use?

(DR. STRANGE digs around in a box looking for something. Then he remembers…)

DR. STRANGE: I got a Green Chamber that can help you.

TORNADO BOY: Let's try it.

(TORNADO BOY steps into a green glass chamber. He spins around, slowly at first and then quickly. White smoke comes out. He steps out feeling differently.)

SCENE 5:

TORNADO BOY: Now I got to stop Scorch. Whooshhhhh.

(TORNADO BOY flies back to Plummer. He doesn't see SCORCH. He shoots a bolt of lightning. A small fire starts. The fire comes behind his back and he jumps out of the way. The fire is SCORCH.)

SCORCH: You <u>almost</u> killed me!

TORNADO BOY: I didn't try to.

SCORCH: Yes you did!

TORNADO BOY: I am a super hero that does not kill.

SCORCH: You's a liar! You just wanted me to stop destroying houses and make me leave the city!

TORNADO BOY: If I <u>did</u>, you wouldn't be here right now.

(SCORCH gets mad. SCORCH shoots a hot wind with sparks of fire at TORNADO BOY. TORNADO BOY blows back his own gust of wind. SCORCH is exhausted. He breathes heavily.)

TORNADO BOY: It's the right time to use the vortex.

(TORNADO BOY turns into a tornado and circles really fast around SCORCH. He makes a vortex. SCORCH falls down.)

SCORCH: This vortex is not hurting me.

TORNADO BOY: It's not supposed to hurt you, it's draining your powers. I learned much from Dr. Strange.

SCORCH: Noooooooooooooooooooo my powers are gone!

TORNADO BOY: Ahh. All in a day's work for Tornado Boy. I will still watch this town in the skies!

End of Play

Playwright Profile: Julia Winkler

"The idea for my play was kind of an accident," Julia Winkler explains in an interview with YPT, pushing back a strand of blond hair. "Our YPT teaching artist told us to make up characters, and I thought it was just for fun, so I just kept coming up with these silly situations. But then I found out we had to write a play about them!"

The play Julia ended up writing, *The Enemy Attacks*, is silly indeed. It features a piece of broccoli named Broccoliti and his celery friend, Celetunia, as they work to defeat the hungry human, Timmy Jim Jim, before he can eat them off a veggie plate. They are assisted in their quest by their imaginary friends, Stickathina and Harry Green, as well as an orange named Orangellio.

When Julia finished writing her play, she was surprised to hear it had been selected for production in the 2006 *New Play Festival*. She was only in the third grade when YPT came to her class at Fillmore Arts Center, so she didn't have extensive creative writing experience.

"It impacted me in a big way," Julia says. "Just having the chance to write. And to be called upon again about this play after eight years – it's really increased my confidence."

Now heading into her junior year at Georgetown Day School, Julia has a significant amount of playwriting experience on her resume. In middle school, she wrote and composed the music for several of her school's Christmas pageants.

"Working with YPT was really helpful in teaching me how to write dialogue," Julia explains. "Even when I'm doing non-creative writing, I know now how to write emotion into words."

While Julia still writes when she has the chance, she is currently more focused on developing her skills as a guitarist and composer, and, of course, enjoying the rest of her time in high school.

"I have no idea what I want to major in in college," she says with a laugh. "I'm always performing, so maybe something in the arts. We'll see!"

The Enemy Attacks!

by Julia Winkler (2004)

ABOUT JULIA

What grade were you in when you wrote your play? 3rd

What school did you attend? Francis Scott Key Elementary School

Where do you go to school now? Georgetown Day School

What do you like to do for fun? Play guitar and sing. And I've always liked to write. I still write occasionally.

Is there anything you'd like to say to the readers of this book? If you like to write, but you're nervous about it, just do it for fun and see what happens!

Characters:

BROCCOLITI, a broccoli
HARRY GREEN, his imaginary friend
TIMMY JIM JIM, a human
CELETUNIA, a celery
STICKATHINA, her imaginary friend
ORANGELLIO, an orange
MR. TOMATO PRIEST, a priest

SCENE 1: _Takes place on and around a sectioned vegetable platter at TIMMY JIM JIM'S party._
(BROCCOLITI and his imaginary friend HARRY GREEN are talking in the broccoli section of the vegetable platter.)

BROCCOLITI: Everyone hates me, but you, my imaginary friend, who obviously has to like me, and, of course Timmy Jim Jim, who only likes me 'cause he wants to eat me. And no one can eat you, 'cause you're hardly visible to anyone. I mean, you're pale green!

HARRY GREEN: I know, but I can't eat veggie dip like you can, and all the veggies say it tastes good.

BROCCOLITI: I don't like veggie dip! It's 'cause I always get dunked in it when Timmy Jim Jim tries to eat me, and I end up swallowing lots of it and — well, it's disgusting!

HARRY GREEN: Look, take it easy, pal.

(HARRY GREEN disappears. BROCCOLITI jumps out of the vegetable platter and onto the tablecloth. He then sits at the edge of the table with feet hanging.)

BROCCOLITI: Hhmph! I can't believe it — he ditched me right in a real tight — AHHHHH!

TIMMY JIM JIM: *(Spies BROCCOLITI and approaches)* Mmmm, broccoli sounds good after a hard day like mine!

(TIMMY JIM JIM picks up BROCCOLITI and tries to eat him. BROCCOLITI runs as fast as he can, but trips on a fork and looks back.)

TIMMY JIM JIM: Arggh! Guess not!

(BROCCOLITI stands up and starts running until he nears the celery section of the vegetable platter. He does not know it's the celery section. BROCCOLITI sees a celery.)

BROCCOLITI and CELETUNIA: Eeeek!

BROCCOLITI: *(Surprised, and enunciating each word separately)* Who the heck are you?

CELETUNIA: I'm Celetunia, you, you *(Hesitates and thinks)* broccoli freak! Do you have any manners?!

(CELETUNIA turns her back.)

BROCCOLITI: *(To audience)* See, no one gives me any respect, I mean, NO ONE. No one cares about me; they don't even pay attention to me. Even if they looked at me like I was at least a green speck, I would be happy!

(BROCCOLITI starts to sob. CELETUNIA turns around.)

CELETUNIA: What's the matter?

BROCCOLITI: *(Still sobbing)* Everyone hates me!

CELETUNIA: I don't. Maybe we have a few things in common.

(Pats BROCCOLITI on back soothingly. BROCCOLITI begins to stop crying.)

BROCCOLITI: *(Sarcastically, right into CELETUNIA'S face)* Right. Everyone loves veggie dip except for me.

CELETUNIA: Veggie dip? Did you say veggie dip? YUCK!!! I hate veggie dip!!!!

BROCCOLITI: Okay, that's one thing in common, but my worst enemy is Timmy Jim Jim.

CELETUNIA: *(Gasping excitedly)* Mine is too!

BROCCOLITI: Maybe we do have some things in common.

CELETUNIA: *(Mischievously)* All right, let's get on with this. We have to defeat Timmy Jim Jim!

BROCCOLITI: Awesome, let's go!

(BROCCOLITI starts to run, but CELETUNIA pulls him back.)

CELETUNIA: Oh great, I forgot something. How are we going to get that slimy, disgusting, foul…

(CELETUNIA gets carried away with her description.)

BROCCOLITI: Hold on, I get the point, and you need to meet my special assistant, Harry Green! I said "Harry Green." Come on!

(BROCCOLITI gets irritable; folds arms. HARRY GREEN appears.)

HARRY GREEN: What? What do ya want? I was sleeping, you know! How many times do I have to tell you — don't wake me up. Seriously. *(HARRY notices CELETUNIA)* Whoa, who's that?

CELETUNIA: *(Looking at HARRY GREEN)* My name's Celetunia. *(Turns to BROCCOLITI)* Isn't this your imaginary friend? I have an imaginary friend, too! I want you to meet her. Hey, Stickathina, it's time for you to come out!

(STICKATHINA appears.)

STICKATHINA: *(Shyly and scared)* Is it okay to come out? Who are those guys?

BROCCOLITI: No — who are you?

CELETUNIA: Those guys' names are Broccoliti, and um, who's that again Broccoliti?

BROCCOLITI: Who? My imaginary friend? Oh, his name is Harry Green.

CELETUNIA: Oh, then the other one is Harry Green.

BROCCOLITI: Whoa, wait a minute, no one notices Harry! He's pale green!

CELETUNIA: Well, you can see Stickathina, and she's even paler!

CELETUNIA and BROCCOLITI: *(Amazed)* WOW! You can see my imaginary friend! We must be close!

STICKATHINA: *(Anxious)* Anyway, let's get this show on the road, and maybe Harry Green and I can be friends, just like you and Broccoliti.

(They huddle.)

CELETUNIA: *(To STICKATHINA)* Good idea. *(To everyone)* Now let's go and sneak some veggie dip to throw in Timmy Jim Jim's eye.

BROCCOLITI: And maybe some orange juice from an orange in the fruit platter, because that stings when it gets shot in someone's eye, just like veggie dip.

HARRY GREEN: Wait a minute! How are we going to get across the table to the fruit platter without anyone at Timmy Jim Jim's party noticing us?

CELETUNIA: I don't know, just give me two seconds to figure that out.

(CELETUNIA thinks, with finger pressed on her temple.)

CELETUNIA: I've got it! This is the signal. Hold two fingers up and then one finger when the coast is clear and it's safe for me to run.

STICKATHINA: Uh, I don't want to be rude, but what are we going to do?

CELETUNIA: Silly Stickathina. Come on guys, let's go!

(Everyone except STICKATHINA follows CELETUNIA off stage.)

STICKATHINA: Wait for me! *(Tumbles after everyone off stage)*

SCENE 2: *Takes place in and around fruit platter.*

CELETUNIA: I have to get into the fruit platter to get an orange!

EVERYONE except CELETUNIA: Don't you mean we?

CELETUNIA: No, I mean just me. That's where you give me the signal to come back with the orange.

EVERYONE except CELETUNIA: OH!!!

CELETUNIA: Okay. Ready, set, go!!!!!

(CELETUNIA runs to the orange section of the fruit platter and gets an orange. BROCCOLITI gives the signal and CELETUNIA runs back to them.)

EVERYONE: Phew!!!!

ORANGELLIO: *(Squirming)* Put me down!

EVERYONE except ORANGELLIO: What's your name?

ORANGELLIO: Orangellio.

BROCCOLITI: Well, sorry Orangellio. It's time to say farewell.

(HARRY GREEN picks up a toothpick that happens to be nearby and pokes a hole in ORANGELLIO.)

ORANGELLIO: OW!!

(STICKATHINA looks hurt.)

HARRY GREEN: You can squeeze him, Stickathina.

STICKATHINA: Thank you! *(Smiles)*

(STICKATHINA squeezes ORANGELLIO, and his juice goes into a glass.)

ORANGELLIO: Oh, my beautiful world! OWEE!

(ORANGELLIO falls over.)

BROCCOLITI: *(Excitedly)* All right! All we have to do is get the veggie dip!

CELETUNIA: Wait a minute. It may have looked easy getting the orange, but it wasn't. Veggie dip will be harder to get because we have to get a spoon for it.

BROCCOLITI: *(Understandingly)* Oh!

CELETUNIA, STICKATHINA, HARRY GREEN: Okay!

SCENE 3: *Takes place in and around the vegetable platter.*

STICKATHINA: *(Comes on stage with a giant spoon)* I got the spoon!

BROCCOLITI, CELETUNIA, HARRY GREEN: Hooray!

HARRY GREEN: *(Confidently)* I'll go with the spoon and get the veggie dip.

CELETUNIA: *(Uncomfortably)* You sure?

HARRY GREEN: Yup! Certainly. Don't worry. I can do it!!

STICKATHINA: *(Impatiently)* Let's go!

CELETUNIA: OK!

(HARRY GREEN runs to the veggie dip section in the middle of the vegetable platter. BROCCOLITI gives him the signal, and HARRY GREEN comes back with a spoon of veggie dip.)

CELETUNIA: Good work Harry!

HARRY GREEN: Thanks! Told you you can trust me.

BROCCOLITI: We're all set. *(Nods head)* So, bring it on. Come on! Quick! He's coming!!

TIMMY JIM JIM: YUM! Look what's here! Now I'll get to actually eat something. I'm starving!

STICKATHINA: I can do this. Yes!!

(STICKATHINA flicks the veggie dip spoon.)

BROCCOLITI, CELETUNIA, HARRY GREEN: Yay! Good shot Stickathina!

HARRY GREEN: My turn!

(Takes sip of orange juice and spits it out into TIMMY JIM JIM's eyes.)

HARRY GREEN: I did it!

TIMMY JIM JIM: Aaaah! My eyes! This party is OVER!

(He staggers off stage.)

SCENE 4: *Three weeks later. Wedding scene.*

(ORANGELLIO is also a wedding guest.)

MR. TOMATO PRIEST: Do you take this celery to be your lawfully wedded wife?

HARRY GREEN and BROCCOLITI: I do.

MR. TOMATO PRIEST: Do you take this broccoli to be your lawfully wedded husband?

STICKATHINA and CELETUNIA: I do.

EVERYONE except ORANGELLIO: YAY!!!

VOICEOVER: Now that Timmy Jim Jim no longer terrorizes the veggies and fruits, everyone lives happily ever after.

ORANGELLIO: What about me? My side still hurts!

VOICEOVER: Okay. Almost everyone lives happily ever after.

End of Play

Plays for 13 & Up

Rita

By Breena Bradford (2001)

ABOUT BREENA

What grade were you in when you wrote your play? 12th

What school did you attend? Benjamin Banneker Senior High School

What do you do now? Costumer and Wardrobe Supervisor in the film and television industry.

What do you like to do for fun? Sew and thrift shop.

Is there anything you'd like to say to the readers of this book? I am so excited and honored to be a featured playwright in this awesome project by Young Playwrights' Theater! To all of the readers of this book, I hope you enjoy the play I wrote as well as all of the other plays that are featured.

Characters:

RITA

KEVIN

VICKI

MOTHER

SCENE 1:

(RITA enters her room, takes off her hat, coat and book bag, she flops on her bed after a long day of school.)

RITA: I am so tired. *(She suddenly remembers something and sits up on her bed smiling excitedly and says very fast and anxiously.)* Okay! Okay! It is now 4 o'clock. *(Looking at her alarm clock)* When did he say he was going to call me? *(She pauses, thinking, smiling and biting her lip.)* Oh yeah! *(She hops off her bed, positioning herself to play the role of KEVIN. She says acting like she is KEVIN)* Oh! What's up Rita? *(Then she switches to the other side to play herself. Then she says, smiling and surprised to see him)* Oh! What's up Kevin? *(Then switches sides to do her part. Goes out of character back to herself and says hurryingly)* Bla Bla Bla about math class… *(Then goes back into character as KEVIN. She plays KEVIN as a guy who really likes her.)* So…I was wondering if you could, you know? Help me study for this test we're gonna have tomorrow. *(She switches places and acts like the question was no big deal.)* Oh! Okay! Sure. *(Switches places, and KEVIN says looking RITA up and down)* So...I'll call you around 7? *(RITA says smiling and flirting)* Yeah that's cool. *(RITA goes out of her character and KEVIN'S character and, as a show lady says and steps in the middle of her performance and talks to the audience saying)* And drum roll please... *(She steps to the side where she was playing KEVIN and says)* Alright, cool, what's your number? *(She falls on the bed, excited and in her own dream world and says in a playful sexy tone)* He wants me, I know it. *(Her phone begins to ring and she hops off her bed surprised and embarrassed like someone had been watching her. She picks up the phone.)* Hello?

VICKI: Hey girl!

RITA: Oh what's up Vicki?

VICKI: Nothing...

RITA: Girl where are you? I can hear the static in your cheap cell phone. *(RITA begins to laugh and then there is a knock at her room door and VICKI enters.)*

VICKI: I am in your house and don't talk about my cell phone. *(Both laughing)* Here's your math book you left in class since you were so into Kevin. *(She flops it in RITA'S hands and RITA looks at it in surprise because she did not know she had left her math book. VICKI looks at RITA inquisitively and begins to talk very fast moving closer to RITA and getting louder and excited.)*

VICKI: Speaking of Kevin...what were you all talking about? *(Pauses)* Did you get his number? Did he ask you out? He likes you, doesn't he? I knew it, I knew it. Girl why did you run out the building so fast!

RITA: *(Jumps off the bed to calm VICKI down who is very excited)* No, no!... *(Confiding)* I mean I don't know. Wait. Okay. What question do you want me to answer?

VICKI: *(Anxious for the scoop, she shouts)* Girl, just tell me everything that happened!

RITA: *(Smiling and walking towards her mirror like she has a juicy secret, says)* He just asked me for my number.

VICKI: That's it? He just said, "Can I get your number?"

RITA: *(Shrugging her arms of non-importance and says)* Well, he said something about helping him with his math homework or somet–

VICKI: *(She says laughing slightly)* Wait a minute, is Kevin trying to get with you or is he finally trying to get with the honor roll and needs your help?

(VICKI begins to laugh, which makes RITA feel a little stupid, but she smiles and

hides it.)

RITA: Whateva! I'll let you know around 8 tonight when I invite him over to study the geometric shapes we can both make with our tongues together.

(RITA and VICKI both laugh and give each other a high five. Then VICKI'S cell phone rings and she looks at her caller ID.)

VICKI: Shoot! It's my mom.

RITA: You not gonna answer it?

VICKI: Heck no! I know exactly what she is gonna say and I don't what to hear it. *(She begins to mimic her mother.)* Where are you? What are you doing? Why aren't you at home? Where is your brother?

RITA: *(She says laughing)* Oh! So that's where you get your question-asking-characteristic from?

VICKI: *(She says sarcastically)* Ha! Ha! You just make sure you are gonna be ready to answer my questions around 8:15 when I call up here to see what you are really "studying."

(VICKI begins walking out the room backwards still talking to RITA.)

VICKI: *(Smiling)* But what you really need to do is clean this filthy rooms since you "plan on" having company.

RITA: *(Smiling)* Oh you don't think I am gonna have company?

VICKI: *(As she goes down the stairs)* We'll see. 8:15.

(RITA laughs at VICKI'S bet-like comment, goes in her room and lays confused on her bed.)

SCENE 2:

(RITA has fallen asleep on her bed accidentally. She wakes up, looks at her clock and jumps off the bed.)

RITA: Oh no! It is 6:30. How did I fall asleep? *(She paces around her room and then looks at her clock again and then tries to calm herself down.)* Okay! Okay! Okay! I have about 30 minutes to get myself together. *(She then looks around the room and feels hopeless and then becomes frustrated and whines.)* Oh no! Look at my room. Okay! Okay! Okay! First, I'll clean my filthy room, then paint my nails. *(Looks at her nails)* Oh my goodness they look horrible and I know he saw them when I was writing down my number... *(She begins to pick her clothes off the floor and then suddenly she stops and stands straight up.)* Oh no! What am I gonna say when he calls? *(She continues to clean up while she practices her lines.)* Okay! Okay I can say, *(She changes into her talking-to-KEVIN voice and attitude.)* "So...you wanna come over and we can study quadratic functions?" Oh no! *(Disgusted)* I sound like a nerdy freak. Okay! Okay! Okay! What about "you wanna come over and we can just run over the things we went over in class this week?" Yeah! Okay! That sounds cool. *(RITA continues to clean up her room.)*

SCENE 3:

(RITA is walking into her room as her MOTHER yells from down stairs.)

MOTHER: Rita, I will be right back in an hour. I have to go back to the office to find some paperwork. When is the guy friend of yours coming over?

RITA: Mom, I said I might have to help him so I don't know when or if he is coming over.

MOTHER: Okay, well I can trust you, just don't do anything I would not approve of...

RITA: Mom!

MOTHER: Okay, okay I can trust you, I'll be back in less than an hour.

RITA: Ha! Ha! Funny.

MOTHER: Bye baby.

RITA: Bye Mom.

(The MOTHER is gone.)

RITA: Finally, okay what time is it? *(Looks at her watch)* Okay it is 7 o'clock on the dot so he should be calling any minute now. Or maybe he won't call? No, he'll call probably around 7:15 so he won't look pressed. *(She paces around the room looking at the phone. Then she walks over to her bed to get her textbook.)* Maybe I should look over this stuff so I won't look stupid. *(As she reaches for the book she looks at her hands and realizes they are not polished.)* Oh no, let me polish my nails now. *(She runs over to her dresser and starts to polish her nails.)* What if he doesn't want to come over? Oh no, Vicki will never let me live that down. What if he doesn't call? *(She begins to polish her fingernails faster in frustration.)* See, that's why I shouldn't even try to get involved with these athletic guys. They are all the same—dumb and self-centered. He's gonna call me when he is ready to not at the time he is supposed to which was five minutes ago and only when he needs something. Vicki is probably right, Kevin is probably trying to get a good grade on this test because he wants to stay on the football team. Okay, granted, he does look fine in his uniform and I could just see myself wearing his football jacket around school for the rest of senior year and I know all of the other girls would be so jealous—oh goodness we would have to be chosen for "best couple," him being the captain of the football team and me... well just being me but anyway...okay wait...what was I saying? *(The phone begins to ring and RITA looks at her wet nails and then the phone.)* Oh, I hope that's him. *(She runs over to the phone and struggles to answer it with her wet nail-polished-hands. She answers the phone in her boy-talk voice.)* Hello?

KEVIN: May I speak to Rita please?

(RITA begins to smile but keeps a cool voice on the phone and maintains her sweet voice.)

RITA: This is she.

KEVIN: Oh hey Rita, this is Kevin.

RITA: Oh hey Kevin, I thought you were someone else, what's going on?

KEVIN: Nothing...dang you sound different on the phone.

(RITA laughs cutely. She's glad he notices and is flattered by the comment.)

RITA: I don't sound that different...so...how do you want to do this? Do you want to start with the work we reviewed today in class?

KEVIN: Well I was calling to say that I'm too tired to study for this test tonight. I had a game today and Lester, you know Lester in our class, he made us lose that game. I was so mad. I told Lester in the huddle "Lester if you get the ball, pass it to me. I will be on the touch down to make the score." Did Lester do that? No! He tries to run the ball, gets tackled and fumbles the ball. I was so mad I could hit him. The whole team was mad at Lester.

RITA: But...Kevin I really think you should study for this test though...I mean I know you're mad and all but this is the last test of the second advisory and it counts for 50% of our grade...

KEVIN: Yo, I'm tired. I'll just fail the test and work harder third advisory. Really, I don't need school. I know I'm gonna get a football scholarship 'cause coach already told me that two schools have asked about me already...

RITA: But, Kevin anything can happen to you. You've heard it before, what if you break your leg or get hurt another way? You need to at least have good grades. I mean...I don't know you that well and all but I know you can pass this test if you study tonight.

KEVIN: But, see, Rita, I'm not like you. You're at the top of the class. I barely go to class. You make the honor roll so you can get into a good school. I'd rather just graduate and make a lot of money...

RITA: *(Very surprised and disappointed)* So you don't want to go to college?

KEVIN: I mean...yeah I would go to college if I can play football there because I plan to go all the way to the pros...

RITA: But what if that doesn't work out?

KEVIN: *(Laughs a little)* What do you mean, "What if it doesn't work out?" It will. Okay, fine, if it doesn't then I will just get a job with my cousin who fixes cars he makes about five hundred a week. I could move out my folk's house, have my own place where I can have parties and drink and smoke...

RITA: *(Not impressed at all but doesn't fully reveal it)* So that's your plan?

KEVIN: *(KEVIN speaks as though he has a sure plan for his future.)* Yeah, that's it, either play football or work, any old way I will be making that money for sure.

RITA: Well Kevin I don't want to hold you back from getting your rest so I am going to let you go and I will see you tom...

KEVIN: Wait Rita, see, I really wasn't going to study for the test at all.

RITA: *(Disappointed because she knows what he is about to say)* Really?

KEVIN: Yeah, I can just cheat off of Lester's paper tomorrow if I wanted to.

RITA: *(Feeling really stupid for liking KEVIN, begins to laugh in an embarrassed way and jokingly says)* Oh! You cheat too?

KEVIN: *(He laughs because he thinks RITA is joking.)* Yeah most of the time but I know you don't...

RITA: No! I don't.

KEVIN: See, Rita that's why I like you, you're innocent. You're a good girl but you need a little bad in your life. What cha say you wear my football jacket and be my girl?

RITA: *(Laughing out loud)* What? Is that why you asked me for my number? So you can be the bad in my good little life.

KEVIN: *(Smiling because he thinks RITA is impressed but he doesn't know she is being sarcastic. So he says in a sexy tone)* Yeah, Rita you are too pretty to be buried in those books all the time people barely even notice you. You need me to put a little fun in your world. You know what I mean? So I think...uh...me and you should hook up?

RITA: *(Stops laughing because she realizes that KEVIN is serious and did not get her sarcasm.)* Uh! Yeah...I know but that's just what I like to do. You like to play sports I like to read we are just different and really too different to be together. So this wouldn't work out if we tried but I wish you luck on your test tomorrow...

KEVIN: Wait! Hold up so you're saying you don't want to be with me?

RITA: We are just too different I'll see you tomorrow. Bye. *(She hangs up the phone quickly and laughs feeling a little embarrassed but relieved.)* Oh my goodness what a loser!

End of Play

The Stranger

by Sam Burris (2011)

ABOUT SAM

What grade were you in when you wrote your play? 8th
What school did you attend? Swanson Middle School
Where do you go to school now? Washington Lee High School
What do you like to do for fun? Sing, act and play football.
Is there anything you'd like to say to the readers of this book? Never be afraid to use your creativity to make a statement.

Characters:

LT. PARKER, ex-soldier, homeless, 24 years old, only possessions are his guitar and the clothes on his back

FEAR, part of Lt. Parker, ageless, very jumpy and untrusting

STRANGER, music producer, mid 30's, never learn any specifics

SCENE 1: Any given day on the street.
(LT. PARKER is hunched up against the side of the building, playing classic rock almost no one recognizes. Many people brush past him, and every time someone touches him he winces. FEAR is behind him, jumping at the mere sight of strangers.)

LT. PARKER: *(Very sullen)* I was a Lieutenant. I was a husband. My life was perfect. I had everything a man could want. But things were never the same after I came back from the war...I remember it like it was yesterday. It was all my fault...We were ambushed. Tricked by someone I thought I knew, who I was stupid enough to trust. Turns out they were just a stranger. Not one of my men survived. It appeared that night. And ever since then it's been nagging at my brain, telling me no one should be trusted. Not even my wife, or ex-wife should I say, haha. Our only communication was by argument. Eventually she kicked me out and I haven't seen her since. I can barely get through each day. I guess the only thing that keeps me going is my music...Not just the music itself, but the looks on peoples' faces when they pass me. To see that I gave someone at least one happy moment in their day, that's what it's all about. Especially since I have so few happy moments nowadays...And all because I'm stuck out here, just me and that goddamn Fear...

(LT. PARKER falls back and the main focus falls on FEAR.)

FEAR: *(Looking around, as if lost and scared)* I just want to protect him. I am the only one that is there for him. I am the only one who he can trust. Everyone is against him, the world is cruel and no one cares about anyone else. If he doesn't listen to me, his life will just get worse. Only I know the truth. You can't trust the strangers.

SCENE 2:

(People walk past giving LT. PARKER money.)

FEAR: *(Very angry at the people)* STOP GIVING HIM MONEY. We are doing fine on our own!

(No one hears FEAR except for LT. PARKER. People keep giving money to LT. PARKER. FEAR gets madder at the people.)

FEAR: STOP WITH THE MONEY. WE DON'T NEED IT.

(LT. PARKER finally gets irritated with FEAR.)

LT. PARKER: *(LT. PARKER looks like he's talking to himself, people begin to avoid him.)* No one can hear you! It's just me! And I need that money! YOU may think we're doing fine, but we aren't! You may not need this...But...But I do. I need this.

FEAR: *(Never seen LT. PARKER this mad before)* NO YOU DON'T NEED THEIR MONEY. WHO KNOWS WHAT THEY COULD'VE DONE TO IT?!

LT. PARKER: *(Looks at FEAR like he is an idiot)* You can't do anything to money you dumbass!

FEAR: What if...What if they, they put acid on it, huh? Acid that, that only reacts when it...uh...um...touches skin! What about that huh?

LT. PARKER: Well I guess, but why would anyone want to do that to me? There's no reason...but...I mean...I guess you're right...

(LT. PARKER stops playing, runs off stage. FEAR doesn't notice at first, but then looks up and notices LT. PARKER is gone, runs off stage after him.)

SCENE 3:

(LT. PARKER and FEAR are sitting on a different street than before. LT. PARKER is strumming a tune on his guitar, except this time no one is out. STRANGER is running, seems to be in a rush, but slows down and walks back to LT. PARKER after passing.)

STRANGER: *(Suddenly interested)* You're really good, anybody ever tell you that?

LT. PARKER: Well thanks I guess…

STRANGER: *(Flustered)* I'm guessing you have plenty of time…I work at the studio down the street, I'm the big producer around here, here's my card, maybe you'll think about stopping by sometime.

LT. PARKER: Well…thanks, I guess…

(STRANGER runs off stage.)

FEAR: You aren't seriously considering going are you?!

LT. PARKER: Hell yeah I am! This could be my one chance to get out of this hell-hole!

FEAR: But how do you know you can trust him?! Huh?! Riddle me this, Batman! He's probably just going to take advantage of you and try to hurt you!

LT. PARKER: He's not a goddamn terrorist, he's a frickin' record producer!

FEAR: How would you know?! You just met the guy! You know NOTHING. Everyone is out to get you. Just like back in the war.

LT. PARKER: Nowhere is like that place. Nowhere on Earth is that devastating. Especially not here, back in the States.

FEAR: There are bad people everywhere. EVERYWHERE.

LT. PARKER: I know that! Better than anyone.

FEAR: Then how do you not realize that he could be trying to hurt you?!

LT. PARKER: Well…you have a valid point…But that doesn't mean you can't trust anyone!

FEAR: Yeah you can definitely trust a stranger who comes up to you on the street and asks you to come to some building.

LT. PARKER: I'm a grown man! I can handle myself! But I can see where you're coming from. I have an idea that should solve this whole problem.

FEAR: I'm listening…

LT. PARKER: If I haven't gone by the end of the week, I'll never go.

FEAR: Well…fine…

SCENE 4: *Two days later.*

(LT. PARKER and FEAR are on the same street as 2 days ago. STRANGER walks by.)

STRANGER: Hey, I haven't seen you at the studio yet. What happened to stopping by?

LT. PARKER: Sorry I'm just thinking it over, it seems like a pretty big decision.

STRANGER: It's really no big deal at all. Just stop by, we can talk about recording a demo, and we'll give you some time to think about it.

LT. PARKER: OK…I guess I'll stop by…

(STRANGER leaves.)

FEAR: You can't go with him!

LT. PARKER: I have to! It may be my only ticket out of the living hell my life has become!

FEAR: But how do you know you can…

LT. PARKER: *(Cutting FEAR off)* I'm done with this! I need to get out. And this is my ONLY chance.

FEAR: Woah…But if anything happens to you, don't come crying to me.

LT. PARKER: You'll be there with me…

FEAR: Oh…yeah…

SCENE 5: In the record studio.

(STRANGER is sitting at his desk, LT. PARKER walks in, apprehensive, FEAR is close behind.)

STRANGER: You made it!

LT. PARKER: Yeah you were right, couldn't hurt to come in since we're just talking about it.

FEAR: I didn't think it was a good idea… *(Grumble grumble)*

LT. PARKER: *(Whispering to FEAR)* Shutup…

STRANGER: What was that?

LT. PARKER: Me? I…I didn't say anything!

STRANGER: OK…So from what I've heard of you, you are very, very talented. I know this seems like a lot since this is our first talk, but I was hoping you would be willing to record a demo for my boss. I feel like, with a little help, you could be a star.

LT. PARKER: Sounds simple enough…

STRANGER: It really is. All you need to do is come in, sign a few papers, we record a few songs, and you're out of here. It should only take a couple hours.

LT. PARKER: I'll think about it…but expect to see me back here haha…

SCENE 6:

LT. PARKER: I've made up my mind.

STRANGER: Well that was fast…So?

LT. PARKER: I'm gonna do it.

STRANGER: I was hoping you would, we can start tomorrow. I just need you to sign this.

(STRANGER hands LT. PARKER a paper. Just as LT. PARKER is about to sign it, FEAR appears. STRANGER freezes.)

FEAR: You aren't seriously doing this, are you?!

LT. PARKER: I have to do it...It's my only chance out of this hell-hole...

FEAR: But how do you know that you can trust him? That he won't take advantage of you? How do you know it won't end up like what happened with Martinez?

LT. PARKER: SHUTUP ABOUT MARTINEZ.

FEAR: But all your men...

LT. PARKER: THAT WASN'T MY FAULT. HOW WAS I SUPPOSED TO KNOW THAT I WAS GOING TO BE BETRAYED BY ONE OF MY OWN MEN. WE ALL THOUGHT WE COULD TRUST HIM. HOW WAS I SUPPOSED TO KNOW WHAT HE WAS GOING TO DO?

FEAR: I...I don't know...but things can always get worse! Things will always get worse!

LT. PARKER: How can things get worse from here? I have nothing! Absolutely nothing!

(LT. PARKER signs the paper and FEAR leaves the office. STRANGER unfreezes and begins talking to LT. PARKER. Lights dim on STRANGER'S office, leaving the spotlight on FEAR.)

FEAR: I never thought...I never thought he could do it...I thought everyone was against him...I just wanted to protect him...But I've learned that not everyone is out to get you, some people just want to help...

(FEAR disappears into the night, off to haunt someone else's mind.)

End of Play

Playwright Profile: Cameron Byrd

"YPT showed me that I could take my imagination and turn it into the basis for a career," Cameron Byrd says in an interview with YPT, resting his long forearms on the table. "It's something I could do professionally."

When YPT founder Karen Zacarías came to his seventh-grade classroom at Hardy Middle School in 2001, the idea of being a professional writer was already developing in Cameron's mind. That year he was a Larry Neal Writer's Award winner—an award he would go on to win four more times—and he loved writing short stories. Creating plays, however, was something unfamiliar to him.

"YPT was a pivotal point in the development of my craft," Cameron explains. "They showed me the mechanics of playwriting. They showed me I could go even further and make stories and characters come to life onstage. It's very fulfilling to see your ideas onstage. My director was able to add visuals and sounds that I didn't consider in my first draft."

Cameron's play, *Peasant Revolt*, takes place in medieval England, where the self-named protagonist Cameron Byrd is being appointed head of the king's guard. With the help of a mysterious mage, he soon begins to realize that there is something going on in the kingdom far darker than he ever expected.

"It started as a short story for a class assignment," Cameron says, his eyes lighting up at the memory. "The events of the play were moments I envisioned to set the scene and develop the characters around the central revolt."

After *Peasant Revolt* was produced in the 2002 **New Play Festival**, Cameron was inspired to continue with YPT. He participated in that year's summer intensive program as he continued to grow and refine his writing skills. Now two years out of Howard University, where he received degrees in English and African American studies, he is a professional freelance writer. When he has the time, he loves to travel to foreign places, using his experiences with other cultures as inspiration for his writing.

On a recent trip, Cameron was waiting for a flight at the airport when he ran into an old friend.

"I saw Karen Zacarías while I was getting on a plane!" he says with a grin. "She yelled, 'There's Cameron Byrd, the playwright!' Everyone turned around, thinking I was someone very important. It was a good feeling...just to be mentioned as 'Cameron Byrd, the playwright.'"

Peasant Revolt: The Play

by Cameron Byrd (2001)

ABOUT CAMERON

What grade were you in when you wrote your play? 7th

What school did you attend? Hardy Middle School

What do you do now? I graduated from Howard University in 2010 with a BA in English and a minor in African American studies. Now I'm a full-time writer. I'm in the process of writing a full-length play and I have some short stories in development.

What do you like to do for fun? Play video games, as an exercise in interactive storytelling.

Is there anything you'd like to say to the readers of this book?
I was with YPT through my whole middle school career, almost as long as I could be considered a "young playwright". I discovered that intricately charted plays are not always the best approach. Imagination and immersion are just as important. Sometimes you have to be the actor as much as the storyteller.

Characters:
CAMERON
WAGON DRIVER
1st TOWNSPERSON
2nd TOWNSPERSON
KING
1st MAN
2nd MAN
MAGE
SOLDIER
PEASANT
FATHER
MERCHANT
PRISONER

SCENE I: Dark area.

(Two soldiers fighting. One falls to his knees as the other soldier slices him with his sword.)

CAMERON: *(Wounded in the battle. A phantom soldier, holding a sword, stands* *over CAMERON.)* What am I doing here? I must make myself remember. Remember! Remember! *(He falls down from the pain. Black out, curtain down.)*

SCENE II: *Spring morning.*
(CAMERON arrives at Penter, England. The cart he is riding on passes through the massive stone walls of the town.)

WAGON DRIVER: Here we go sire, Penter, England. Remember, keep your head up. *(Whispering)* The King's guards are everywhere.

CAMERON: I will soon be captain of those guards. Show some respect!

WAGON DRIVER: No, get out! Get out, and I want my money.

CAMERON: OK, OK. Here it is!

(CAMERON gives the man some coins and jumps out of the wagon.)

WAGON DRIVER: Nice doing business with you.

CAMERON: *(Walks away from the cart. He is looking around. He smells the air.)* Hmm Lavender.

1ST TOWNSPERSON: *(Running by)* My son, my son. The King killed him. Oh no, no.

2ND TOWNSPERSON: *(Standing beside the grieving woman)* Something must be done, but what can we do.

SCENE III:
(Later CAMERON arrives at the castle and finds the KING and his soldiers nearby.)

KING: Ah, yes. You've arrived. Approach my subject and kneel before me.

(CAMERON kneels and the KING touches his sword to CAMERON'S shoulder.)

KING: Rise now, Sir Cameron from the House of Byrd. You bring honor to your house. You will now lead my forces.

(CAMERON rises and stands proudly. Everyone kneels before SIR CAMERON and says...

EVERYONE: Hail, Sir Cameron, Hail!

CAMERON: Thank you my lord. Permit me to take my leave, for I go now to join my men.

(CAMERON walks through the courtyard to the barracks. Inside the barracks, dimly lit by torches along the walls. The floor made of large blocks of stone. A few of the men are in the training field outside of the barracks, practicing with staffs and wooden swords. The men recognize CAMERON as the captain of the guard.)

CAMERON: You there, you need work on your defense...tomorrow. *(He *points to another man.)* Get control of that horse *(He says loudly)*, but good job men. Get some rest.

1ST MAN: Okay sir, I will learn.

2ND MAN: Yes, I will as well.

(CAMERON walks out to the archery section of the field. He now uses his bow and hits a bulls-eye, just as a man appears from out of nowhere. CAMERON is shocked but holds his bow firmly.)

MAGE: Well done. Of course I would only expect the best from the Captain of the Guard. I am the Great Mage, observer of all things.

CAMERON: Yes, the King told me much about you.

MAGE: Be careful of what words you believe from the King's lips.

(The MAGE disappears as quickly as he appeared. The KING walks to the training field. As he passes his subjects, they lower their heads and kneel before him. The KING approaches CAMERON.)

KING: I have a mission for you.

CAMERON: Yes, sire.

KING: I need you to retrieve a few of the local peasants for me.

CAMERON: Any of them sire? May I ask why?

KING: I am your King. Follow my orders.

CAMERON: Yes, sire.

SCENE IV: In the barracks.

(All of the men are lined up, fully armored.)

CAMERON: I am taking ten of you with me on a small mission. I want volunteers now.

(Ten men step forward.)

SOLDIER: We will be proud to fight at your side.

(Men leave the barracks and go to the stable to mount their steeds.)

CAMERON: Let's ride!

(CAMERON rides off and the men follow.)

SCENE V: The sun is high in the sky. Fall of the year.

(The leaves crunch under the horse's hooves, as they ride into the village.)

MERCHANT: Oh no, the King's men have come.

CAMERON: Hear my words: the King wants some of these peasants brought before him. *(CAMERON turns to the soldiers)* Bring them alive!

(The soldiers ride ahead, swords drawn. Peasants run in fear but some are quick to surrender.)

CAMERON: Tie them up. Our job is done.
(CAMERON and his soldiers ride their horses proudly, but the peasants are forced to walk the rocky trail back to the castle.)

SCENE VI: Outside, in the town center.
(The accused peasants are standing off to the side, guarded by pike men.)
KING: *(The KING says to everyone in the town center)* Traitors, traitors all of
    you. You deny my right to rule; well your friends and family...shall
    die!
*(One PRISONER stands proudly, unlike a man about to meet him doom. He is
brought forward and forced to stand on a barrel, with a rope around his neck,
about to be hanged. CAMERON's men hold back an otherwise all out revolt.)*
PRISONER: I die for my people. We will prevail. Your oppressive kingdom
    shall fall!
KING: *(The KING says to a SOLDIER)* Brave words from a traitor. *(He
    motions to the executioner.)* Kill the prisoner. Let us teach them a lesson.
VOICE FROM THE CROWD: No!
(A SOLDIER kicks the barrel until the peasant is raised lifeless.)
KING: Ha ha ha ha!! Cut him down.
(The KING'S men cut the PRISONER down and drag him away.)

SCENE VII: CAMERON's quarters.
(CAMERON sits on his bed thinking.)
CAMERON: Today, I witnessed the deaths of five local peasants. The King
    has continued sending me on mission after mission, retrieving
    townspeople and bringing them to die. When I first came to this town,
    I was told of rumors, of the King's evil ways...It appears these rumors
    were true. I think of treachery, but I am loyal to my lord the King.
    Something tells me I must help the people. I swore to protect them
    even if I must betray the King.
VOICE: A nobleman such as you, deciding to join sides with the rebellious
    peasants. Hmm...

SCENE VIII: Village at night. The area is lit by torches and candles.
(CAMERON walks around but soon finds himself surrounded by peasants.)
PEASANT: Why are you here? It does not matter, you will die soon. *(He says
    to the other peasants)* KILL HIM!
CAMERON: Wait, I've come to help you. Please give me a chance.

(PEASANTS still close in on CAMERON.)

MAGE: *(MAGE appears from nowhere.)* Stand down, he can be trusted.

PEASANT: But he is a knight of the King's men.

MAGE: Give him a chance. If he betrays us, do what you want with him.

(MAGE puts his hand on CAMERON's shoulder.)

SCENE IX:

(House torches light the inside, CAMERON and the PEASANTS gather around a table.)

CAMERON: I've gone over tactics and there is no way we can siege a castle with just household items. We will need more advanced weapons. If we could just capture a supply of swords, spears or even bows, we would stand a chance.

PEASANT: There are supplies in the church. Follow me.

(Everyone goes to the church.)

FATHER: Why are all of you here?

PEASANT: Father, we need the supplies. It is time.

FATHER: They are in the cellar. This way. *(In the cellar)*

CAMERON: Look at these weapons, perfectly forged swords, poison tipped arrows and spears. This will help greatly.

(The PEASANTS continued through the night, planning for their siege at dawn.)

SCENE X: *Inside the castle wall, at dawn.*

SOLDIER: Sire, sire, the barracks is on fire! The barracks is on fire!

KING: What...how?

SOLDIER: It's the peasants my lord. They are in an open rebellion.

KING: First Cameron is reported missing, now my people are revolting. What next? Just kill them all!

(Back on the battlefield)

CAMERON: Alright men, breach the gates.

(Everyone holds a truck of a tree and uses it as a battering ram.)

EVERYONE: "Heave ho...heave ho...heave ho."

(Each time, they hit the ram against the gates, while peasant archers shoot the oncoming soldiers. While the battle rages on outside, CAMERON fights his way to the KING'S throne room. When he arrives...)

CAMERON: Your reign has ended, tyrant.

KING: Only when you die.

(Both draw swords and battle each other. The KING falls and CAMERON

hesitates to make the kill.)

CAMERON: Could I really be as despicable as you?

(The KING stabs CAMERON and CAMERON falls. The KING is then impaled by a jewel-encrusted dagger. It is the MAGE. The KING falls dead.)

MAGE: We have prevailed, my brave Cameron. The tyrant is no more.

(CAMERON cough two times, takes a deep sigh, then falls dead.)

End of Play

Robbed

by Chris Chio (2011)

<u>ABOUT CHRIS</u>

What grade were you in when you wrote your play? 7th

What school did you attend? Lincoln Multicultural Middle School

Where do you go to school now? Cesar Chavez Public Charter School

What do you like to do for fun? My favorite thing to do is make movies with my friends.

Is there anything you'd like to say to the readers of this book? Thank you for checking out my play, *Robbed*. I hope to make some more funny plays!

Characters:

BOBBY, a really smart 12-year-old kid but likes to annoy people to stay away from danger

ROB, a really smart 28-year-old guy who robs rich people for the stuff he never had

MOM, a superstitious mom, she's really angry and overprotective too

LITTLE GIRL, likes to do what Bobby does, she kinda likes him

(BOBBY is in his room doing homework. ROB the robber breaks in. ROB takes out a wooden gun.)

ROB: Gimme all your money!

BOBBY: I don't have any money!

ROB: Well give me all your jewels!

BOBBY: I don't have jewels. My mom said jewels are bad.

(Flash back to BOBBY'S MOM complaining to BOBBY to not use jewels.)

MOM: Bobby, what did I tell you of playing with jewels! You know I don't like them because of what happened to my ex?

BOBBY: But mom I was just looking at them.

(Back to ROB.)

ROB: Well...give me your toys then!

BOBBY: Toys hurt you.

(Flash back to BOBBY playing with a super hero.)

BOBBY: Ooh, a toy! It's really strong. Just like in the movies. Let's see it fly!

(He stabs himself in the eyes with it. Back to BOBBY.)

BOBBY: ...My mom said I can't have them!

ROB: Well give me your gaming systems!

BOBBY: I don't have video games. My mom says they're too violent.

(Flash to when BOBBY was playing with his Xbox 360.)

BOBBY: ...Come on loser move you're too slow! No no go the other way ohh lordy. Goooooooooooo!

MOM: Bobby what did I tell you about getting mad when playing video games? And why are you playing that violent game?

BOBBY: But mom no this game is Dora the Explorer I don't know how it got to that game. Even though it is so awesome.

(Back to ROB.)

ROB: So give me your TV!

BOBBY: My mom says there are really nasty things on TV that children shouldn't watch.

(Flash back to when BOBBY was watching cartoons.)

BOBBY: Yeah yeah go Eddy! Don't give up you're almost there!

(TV changes to a violent show.)

MOM: Bobby why are you watching that violent show huh?

BOBBY: But Mommy I wasn't watching that I was watching *Ed, Edd n Eddy.*

MOM: Give me that TV.

BOBBY: OK Mommy.

(MOM throws TV out the window. Back to ROB.)

ROB: Oh my God! What does this kid have? What do you have?!

BOBBY: I have homework.

ROB: Fine. Just give me that! *(He takes it.)* Ugh, I don't even want this.

BOBBY: I want it back by tomorrow!

ROB: YEAH, yeah. Here's your home work!

BOBBY: That was fast it's not even tomorrow dude. You're fast, did you do it?

ROB: Yeah!

BOBBY: Hmm...I think that answer is wrong.

ROB: Which one?

BOBBY: Answer number two. 2+2 isn't 22!

ROB: Yeah it is. 2 and 2 equals 22.

BOBBY: It's actually 42. Come on!

ROB: You know what? Forget you I'm gonna go rob the little girl next door!

(ROB goes to the house next door.)

ROB: Gimme your TV!

LITTLE GIRL: I don't have a TV. My mom said it's nasty.

ROB: Oh come on!

End of Play

...For Which It Stands

by Kamilia Epps (2006)

ABOUT KAMILIA

What grade were you in when you wrote your play? 11th

What school did you attend? Bell Multicultural High School

What do you do now? I graduated from the University of Maryland and now work as an Equal Employment Opportunity Assistant for the Department of Labor.

What do you like to do for fun? Creative writing, spending time with family, thrifting, listening to music, playing with my two boxers Raiden and Vega.

Is there anything you'd like to say to the readers of this book? Glad to be a part of the book. Hope you enjoy my play!

Note: This play was inspired by John Gast's 1872 allegorical painting "American Progress."

Characters:
(Characters that are listed together can played by the same actors.)
BENJAMIN/JOHN O'SULLIVAN
MATTHEW
SPOOFY/SLAVE (ANTHONY BURNS)
ROXY/MANIFEST DESTINY TEMPTRESS
JODY
POLK
BODYGUARD, bodyguard for the President *(Matrix or Men in Black-like)*
MEXICAN (GIL)
NORTHERN GENERAL
PLANTER
WHITE SETTLER
NATIVE AMERICAN
MEXICAN CITIZENS
SOLDIER

ACT I, SCENE I:
(Setting: Five students are gathered at a table. Three of the students are actually sitting in the chairs [perhaps the girls] and two people are sitting on the floor.

105

They have textbooks open, notebooks, and some have pens. They are studying about Manifest Destiny and America's desire to expand to frontier lands. ROXY, the popular cheerleader girl is looking in the mirror fixing her hair and applying make-up. MATTHEW, the jock athletic guy is juggling a football. SPOOFY, the urban kid is talking on his cell phone. JODY, the quiet girl is reading along in her textbook. BENJAMIN, the nerdy preppy sort of person reads aloud.)

BENJAMIN: *(Reading)* Chapter 14: The territorial expansion of the United States. In this chapter, you will learn about two key concepts: continental expansion and the concept of Manifest Destiny and how the political effects of expansion heightened sectional tensions.

SPOOFY: BO-RING *(He says while throwing a paper airplane across the room. MATTHEW giggles with him.)*

ROXY: Come on you guys. If any of us are going to pass Mr. Fitzgerald's test tomorrow, we need to get through this.

MATTHEW: *(Says sarcastically)* Aww does little Ms. Princess have an appointment for Susan's Spa Special at seven?

ROXY: *(Says opposing him)* No...it's at six-thirty.

(Everyone sighs. ROXY looks into her mirror again and puckers her lips, then she puts it back into her purse.)

JODY: However, she does raise a good point. How about before we read the section, we tell what our standpoints are on America's Manifest Destiny. Show of hands, who thinks Manifest Destiny is a positive thing?

(JODY looks around the table. No one raises their hand except for BENJAMIN.)

BENJAMIN: How could you *not* think it's a good thing? I mean, look what it did for our economy. The more we expanded westward, we expanded slavery and slavery played a major role in our economy. Hard labor with no pay means huge profit. It's a very simple concept.

MATTHEW: *(Says questionably)* Americans expanded onto lands that were already inhabited by numerous peoples. Then they made plans of how to run that area of land. No matter who was there before them, they had to abide by their rules. Suuurrreee...simple concept. *(Pats BENJAMIN on his back)* And expanding slavery is good? Yea? For whom? You sound like a 19th century Southerner.

SPOOFY: Yo really. You know I saw your dad the other day in Walmart. I was wondering why he had a cart full of sheets. *(Puts his white hood from his jacket on and throws a fist in the air. MATTHEW laughs with SPOOFY.)*

BENJAMIN: Hardy-har-har... funny. *(Serious face)*

JODY: Let's just get through this chapter. We can argue later, you guys.

MATTHEW: *(MATTHEW continues to read. Clears his throat)* "America's rapid
   expansion had many consequences, but perhaps the most significant
   was that it reinforced Americans' sense of themselves as pioneering
   people. In the 1890's Frederick Jackson Turner, America's most famous
   historian, observed that the repeated experience of settling new
   frontiers across the continent had shaped Americans into a uniquely
   adventurous,... *(the group starts to bob their head in tiredness)* ...optimistic,
   and democratic people. Ever since the time of Daniel Boone, venturing
   into wilderness has held *(Voice goes lower in tiredness)* a special place in
   the American imagination, seen almost *(Voice lowers again)* as an
   American right. Later, John O'Sullivan, a writer for the Democratic
   Review coined the term Manifest Destiny to describe America's rapid
   expansion."

*(Everyone falls asleep. The lights turn off then back on in a matter of two seconds.
When the lights are cut back on the characters are asleep over top of their books
and others head dangling to the side. The lights are cut off again this time for five
seconds. When they are cut back on the table and chairs are gone. In walks a male
character with 19th century clothing. He is JOHN O'SULLIVAN. He has paper
in his hand and a feathery pen. He is thinking aloud. The sound effect of wind
takes place. The MANIFEST DESTINY TEMPTRESS appears on the stage. She
is dressed in all white wearing a flowy gown—angel like. She is moving
gracefully. Then she looks at the audience and puts a finger to her mouth as to say
shhh. She creeps up behind O'SULLIVAN with light steps. The sound effect of
tiptoeing takes place. O'SULLIVAN does not even notice.)*

O'SULLIVAN: *(Dangles his pen in the air and looks to the sky still walking to the
   left of the stage then he stops)* No...that's not it. *(Shakes his head. He is now
   facing the audience in deep thought.)* Maybe that would work. It's only
   reasonable. *(Still talking to himself)*

*(The TEMPTRESS is behind him. He feels like someone is behind him so he looks
left. TEMPTRESS sways left. Then he looks right. TEMPTRESS sways right. He
walks to the right of the stage. TEMPTRESS should look annoyed. She crosses her
arms and taps her feet, pouting. She huffs and puffs. Then she grins
mischievously. She dances over to where he is in a ballroom-meets-ballet sort of
way. She circles around him dancing then she runs off to the left of the stage. The
sound effect of an idea is heard as O'SULLIVAN looks enlightened and starts
writing fast. He tucks the tablet into his coat along with a pen. He begins to talk to*

the audience.)

O'SULLIVAN: *(Laughs to himself)* I've got it! Boy does it feel good to be John
   O'Sullivan right now. *(Says confidently while unbuttoning his jacket)*
   I've...got the best thing since horse and wagon. So here it is...birth rates
   are increasing. People are immigrating. We've been through a couple
   of depressions yadda yah. Basically, we just crave some elbow room.
   *(Unrolls a map tucked under his arm. The map should be the one that
   contains missing unorganized territories. He pulls out thick framed glasses
   and a pen.)* You are here. *(Points on the map with a pen to the East Coast)*
   We want to go here. *(Slides his pen across the Midwest territories)*
   Americans we should expand! Claim new territories. It doesn't matter
   if the land is already inhabited. We have the God-given right to bring
   the benefits of American democracy to...uncivilized peoples. Take
   pride and seek frontier. Come on I'm talking Manifest Destiny. We
   should take pride in our rapid development: the surge in population,
   the remarkable canals and railroads, the grand scale of the American
   enterprise. Why shouldn't it be even bigger? Manifest Destiny isn't
   complicated at all...

SCENE II:
*(Setting: During the time shortly after the Mexican-American War. President
POLK is making a speech in the town of San Suelo, Mexico. POLK should be at a
podium while swarms of people, mainly Mexicans and some Americans, are
standing and seated waiting to hear him speak. POLK takes the stand. He appears
to be costumed as a king or monarch. He has one person beside him who is his
BODYGUARD. He resembles "The Matrix" characters. POLK is arrogant and
vain.)*

POLK: Shawl.*(The BODYGUARD removes his shawl off of his shoulders.)* Cane.
   (BODYGUARD takes the cane.) Crown. *(BODYGUARD takes the crown)*
   Careful, careful. *(POLK grins wide and rests his hands on the podium.)* Boy
   do I love democracies. *(Says to BODYGUARD while leaning towards him)*
   Now uh...what's the issue today?

BODYGUARD: We've just won the Mexican-American War sir. You're here to
   tell these people why it is so good that they have the opportunity to
   become American citizens.

POLK: Ahhh yes. *(Pushes the BODYGUARD away, says proudly)* People of
   San Suelo... *(Says quickly)* thanks for Texas. *(A guy who looks like
   paparazzi should snap POLK'S photograph as POLK smiles to the audience*

with his thumbs up. Turns back to the crowd) I am pleased to be able to spread our democracy to you all. As O'Sullivan once wrote: it is our God-given right to do so. On this day, if you can all raise your right hand.

(The crowd does so.)

POLK: In order for you to become citizens you must be sworn in by the Constitution.

(A Spanish guitar plays. In walks a MEXICAN guy. He starts to clap while walking up the aisle.)

MEXICAN: Bravo, Polk, Bravo. You have managed to conquer our lands and now want our people to be as stuck up as yours. That's just dandy.

POLK: *(Laughs it off, still trying to persuade the Mexicans to become citizens)* We are American men of morals, values, and standards. We just want to share it. *(Smiles warmly)*

MEXICAN: *Los Yanquis,* so hypocritical.

POLK: *(POLK touches his head to make sure his wig is on correctly.)* Who are you? Sorry members only. *(Sticks out tongue)*

MEXICAN: I am Miguel Alvarez Fernando Lucio...the third, but you can call me Gil... Why should we be happy that you are here?

POLK: *(Tries to redirect himself to the crowd)* Well it's a good thing you asked. Our nation is one of...

GIL (MEXICAN): *(Starts to snore)* Oh sorry just taking a *napito. (Gets a little serious)* You aren't making one of your campaign speeches. Simple questions, simple answers.

POLK: *(Annoyed with him)* Fine! *(Says in a toddler spoiled tone)* You guys are backwards people and you just don't know it. You're basically crying out to be civilized like us.

(The crowd becomes shocked by the comment.)

POLK: Oh come on! You should be happy!

GIL: Beg your pardon...happy? Your military invade our lands, destroy our homes, and now you're forcing us to desert our culture to become one of you wig wearing spoons! *(Calms but in a sarcastic tone)* Oh thanks *yanquis,* how will I ever survive without you.

POLK: Oh come on, you guys need to lighten up. Where are the optimists? *(Nervous laughter)* You people always focus on the bad things. Geez. Bet you can't even think of another way our divine mission is a *(motions quotes with fingers)* "bad" idea.

(Everyone freezes and the lights darken. A light appears on the front of the stage.)

SCENE III:
(Setting: During the time of the Civil War. A black male walks onto the stage. He is the character also played by SPOOFY. He is now a runaway SLAVE. He only has one hand. He begins speaking to himself.)
SLAVE: *(Southern accent)* I hears about the white man claiming more land. Spose to make them slave states. Massah wanted to ship me off to work on one of them. I had to runaway. Miles and miles I'sa been running and I's finally... *(Drops to knees and raises both hands)* Free!
(NORTHERN REPUBLICAN GENERAL marches onto the stage from the left side. He is whistling Yankee Doodle. His whistling slows then stops as he sees the SLAVE.)
SLAVE: Uuhh uh-oh. *(Looks right. Gets up and dusts himself off)*
NORTHERN GENERAL: *(Speaks eloquently)* No need to fear now. I'm Willis Garrison Fredmont. I'm here to help. Now state your name and place of origin.
SLAVE: *(Says and looks confused)* Place of who?
NORTHERN GENERAL: Where are you from?
SLAVE: Ohh...well I'm Anthony Burns sah and I's from *(Gets interrupted)*
(White Southern PLANTER walks onto the stage from the right. Should be walking as if searching for something. He spots the SLAVE and NORTHERNER.)
PLANTER: *(Has a Southern accent as well...duh I suppose.)* Hey boy! *(Raises his finger towards the slave. He puts his nose in the air sniffing. He sneezes.)* You Northerners and your industrialization create nothing but air pollution. *(Speaks while looking into air left and right. The SLAVE hides behind the GENERAL for protection. The planter goes back to what he was saying. He walks over closer to them.)* You thought you could get away from me huh? After all the goods I done gave you boy?
SLAVE: *(Steps from behind the GENERAL)* Goods? Sah...with all due respect. I gets my finger caught in the sugar turner and you cut off my hand. *(Holds up his no hand)* I tries to do the work but I can't so's I's runaway and now you'se gonna take mah leg! *(Shakes his leg)*
NORTHERNER: No he isn't going to lay a finger on you.
SLAVE: *(Looks fast at the NORTHERNER)* What you talking about Willis?
PLANTER: Yea? What are you talking about? *(Crosses arms)*
NORTHERNER: Well...take a look at where you both stand. *(Points to the PLANTER'S side and says slowly)* Soouutthh. *(Taps foot where he stands)* Noorrtthh. *(Gestures with his feet a line)* And this is the line of

separation. *(Crosses arms and smiles. The SLAVE looks happy as well.)*

EX-SLAVE: So you mean to tell me because I'm on this side *(Points to the ground)* and Massah on that side *(Points to the other side)* that I's free and and no more his slave?

NORTHERNER: Mhmm Exactly!

(The EX-SLAVE shakes his entire body in excitement. Then he jumps back and forth over the line of separation twice. The MASTER tries to grab him.)

NORTHERNER: Tut. Tut. Tut.

(The GENERAL whistles. In walk three SOLDIERS who march in the back of him. They have blank looks on their face as they stand at attention.)

PLANTER: *(He becomes angry.)* You give me my property back!

NORTHERNER: Silly Democrat. He is no longer your property. This man here *(Pats the EX-SLAVE on his back. The EX-SLAVE should be smiling wide)* is now a contraband of war.

(The NORTHERNER takes his hat off of his head and puts it on the EX-SLAVE. The EX-SLAVE smile turns into a confused and disappointed look. The EX-SLAVE looks at the PLANTER and then at the NORTHERNER. He then runs off. They both start to chase after him.)

(Another light appears in the front center of the stage.)

SCENE IV: *In 1833, summer in Mississippi.*

(A WHITE SETTLER is planting weeds on his land. Just as he walks off the stage a NATIVE AMERICAN enters. He is carrying a sack. He starts to unpack them on the same lands where the WHITE SETTLER just planted his weeds. The WHITE SETTLER appears back on the stage, reading. He is standing directly by the NATIVE AMERICAN but neither recognizes the other's presence. Finally, he stops reading and the NATIVE AMERICAN stops unpacking. The NATIVE AMERICAN looks at the WHITE SETTLER slowly from toe to head. When they see each other they yelp, startled.)

NATIVE AMERICAN and WHITE SETTLER: *(Yelp)*

WHITE SETTLER: *(The WHITE SETTLER circles around the NATIVE AMERICAN.)* Why are "you" on my land?

NATIVE AMERICAN: Your land? This has been my land since forever. Always have the Blackfoot tribe roamed these parts.

WHITE SETTLER: *(Chuckles)* If that is so then why weren't you here when I arrived?

NATIVE AMERICAN: We're nomadic that's what we do! This is where I come for the summer because that's when lots of buffalo roam here.

WHITE SETTLER: You can't just roam here and there as you please. "We" Americans are farmers. You don't just simply migrate with wild animals. That is simply uncivilized. And besides haven't you heard? Andrew Jackson? Indian Removal Act? Has been passed now for several months. So the way I see it *you (Points to him)* gotta go. *(Crosses arms)*

NATIVE AMERICAN: Why I oughta… *(Makes strangling gesture to him)* I don't understand what do you mean Indian Removal Act?

WHITE SETTLER: Don't believe me read it for yourself? *(Hands him a rolled up newspaper from inside his jacket)*

NATIVE AMERICAN: *(Begins reading)* Yesterday evening two Bostonian men were tarred and feathered by their fellow classmates and held down by the Professor after suggesting the separation of church and state in America.

WHITE SETTLER: No not there. The story under that. *(Points)*

NATIVE AMERICAN: *(Reads)* "President Andrew Jackson has now put the Indian Removal Act which he signed three years ago in progress. The act is supposed to move all tribes east of the Mississippi River to the west where they will be given new Indian Territory. All Native Americans are to be paid fifteen cents per acre and will be given land equivalent to those owned previously. In his speech Jackson noted, 'will separate the Indians from immediate contact with settlements of whites; enable them to pursue happiness in their own way and under their own rude institutions; will retard the progress of decay, which is lessening their numbers, and perhaps cause them gradually, under the protection of the government and through the influences of good counsels, to cast off their savage habits and become an interesting, civilized, and Christian community.'"

(He stops reading and looks up angrily. He rips the newspaper.)

NATIVE AMERICAN: I for once have had enough of this. *(Looks at the ground)* Our people are ebbing away like a rapidly receding tide that will never return. *(Looks at the WHITE SETTLER)* How can your God become our God, renew our prosperity, and awaken in us dreams of returning greatness? If we have a common Heavenly Father He must be partial, for He came to His pale face children. We never saw Him. *(Stretches arms)* He gave you laws but had no word for His red children whose teeming multitudes once filled this vast continent as stars fill the firmament. No; we are two distinct races with separate origins and separate destinies. There is little in common between us.

WHITE SETTLER: Tut, tut, tut…Now don't go crying a trail of tears. I'm sure there is a way we can both live on this land together peacefully. *(Grins)* Aha! *(Digs in his pocket and pulls out his chalk drawing a line dividing them and the stage)* This is your side *(Points)* and this is my side. However, I own both sides and I will let you stay here if you give me 30% of the crops that you grow.

NATIVE AMERICAN: Are you kidding me? Sharecropping doesn't start 'til after the Civil War. This is 1833.

WHITE SETTLER: Yes, but this is also a dream which means anything goes. I didn't change anything in history just kind of fast forwarded it. *(Rocks back in forth on heels then toes)* You have two choices.

NATIVE AMERICAN: Which are?

WHITE SETTLER: Do things my way or I will alert military troops up North that you're on *my* land.

NATIVE AMERICAN: Blackmail at its best. *(Grunts)* Fine.

(WHITE SETTLER goes off again while the NATIVE AMERICAN prepares a bow and arrow for hunting. WHITE SETTLER looks over at him.)

WHITE SETTLER: *(Clears his throat)* *Ahem*

(NATIVE AMERICAN starts to pray to the gods wishing to give him good fortune with this year's hunting. As he prays he stretches his hand forward. WHITE SETTLER clears throat again.)

WHITE SETTLER: *Ahem*

(NATIVE AMERICAN starts to do a native dance. WHITE SETTLER clears his throat even louder with a little coughing.)

NATIVE AMERICAN: What is it?

WHITE SETTLER: Oh nothing.

NATIVE AMERICAN: Good. *(Goes back to dancing)*

WHITE SETTLER: It's just that you're doing it all wrong.

(Clears chalk line. Walks over to the NATIVE AMERICAN and removes his bow and arrow from him. He hands him a sign that says "Hail Andrew Jackson" and hands him a Bible.)

WHITE SETTLER: *(Sighs)* Perfect. *(Smiles and hugs the NATIVE AMERICAN)* Civilizing at its best. Carry on.

(Walks back to his side. The NATIVE AMERICAN packs his bags swiftly and walks off the stage.)

NATIVE AMERICAN: On to the West. They'll never bother me there.

(The light appears back to the POLK scene. They unfreeze.)

POLK: Well we have good news. We're making this a slave state. Good eh?
(*Chuckles*)

(*Someone says from the audience, "Good news my...[foot]" but gets interrupted by GIL's laughter and the citizens gasp.*)

GIL: That crown must be cutting off the circulation to your brain.

(*POLK touches his crown again, conscious.*)

GIL: Now you want us to endure your moral wrongs. Human bondage, torturing, racism, and discrimination on our lands and tell us it's good news?

POLK: (*Turns to the BODYGUARD. He whispers*) Wow this guy is good. You think the Northerners put him up to this? (*Says to the BODYGUARD*) Now wait'ah second. Slavery a moral wrong? Ha. Slavery is purely good says it right there in the good book and the Constitution. Look at how much it's done for our country. Where do you think we got all our wealth from? Anything that adds to the growth of the economy is welcomed by me. Besides, the slaves are much better here in a controlled environment then out in the wild. If they knew how lucky they were they would thank us.

(*Crowd gasps and is in disagreement with POLK. They start to walk out of the convention and exit the stage. GIL starts to walk out as well. Then he stops.*)

GIL: Oh by the way, you guys having a reception? Boy am I starving. (*Starts walking out again*)

POLK: (*Says to the BODYGUARD*) Quick! Last idea for persuasion? (*BODYGUARD whispers in his ear. POLK says desperately*) Uhh come to the dark side...we have cookies! (*Sighs. He appears center stage and speaks to the audience.*) Oh come on you guys are so over analytical. Manifest Destiny isn't complicated at all. Just look where we are today. Talk about progress. I can see the future now... (*On walks a small group of people holding anti-Iraq war signs*) Well who cares what they think? No one can stop me!

(*Yankee Doodle drum beat. The NORTHERN GENERAL and his two soldiers walk onto the stage. POLK looks nervous.*)

SOLDIER: What should we do with him General? (*Grabs POLK by one arm each*)

NORTHERN GENERAL: Well flogging isn't permitted here. However, good news, Polk. You're going to face Congress for treason charges. We know all about your conspiring Mexican territory. Are you familiar with the water wheel? (*Drags him off stage*)

POLK: You know the word "sorry" is thrown around a lot... *(Off stage by now)*

SCENE V:
(Back at the library MATTHEW wakes first, then JODY, ROXY, and SPOOFY. MATTHEW pops up.)

BENJAMIN: Ahh no...Not the water wheel! *(Still half sleep then realizes that it was just a dream)*

(They all speak at the same time, saying how they had the same dream. Ad-lib welcome.)

MATTHEW: Not a complicated issue eh?

BENJAMIN: *(Scratches head)* So maybe you guys had a point after all.

(They start to gather their things. Walking off stage, SPOOFY says...)

SPOOFY: I gotta stop drinking those energy drinks.

(All characters are back on stage. The MANIFEST DESTINY TEMPTRESS appears center stage and holds a shrug shoulder stance.)

End of Play

Playwright Profile: Elaine Qi Ling Li

When Elaine Qi Ling Li talks about her first day at Bell Multicultural High School in the fall of 2005, she laughs at the memory. "It was terrible," she says in an interview with YPT, shaking her head. "Everything was messed up!"

Elaine had just moved to the United States from Guangdong, China, and didn't speak a word of English. "I had one friend, a girl from China also," Elaine explains, "but she learned a lot of English in China. She went to English schools. I had to keep asking her to translate."

At the time, Bell Multicultural's Asian American population was only 7%. Nearly 80% of students spoke both English and Spanish, but very few spoke Chinese. Unfamiliar with American culture and struggling to communicate in a new language, Elaine truly felt like an outsider. At times, even some of her teachers made her feel excluded.

"This one teacher I had, he would talk to the other students in Spanish, and then say to me, 'Practice your English!' He told me I wouldn't graduate if I didn't learn English. Then he'd turn around and use Spanish to talk to other students! What's the point?"

Fortunately, Elaine soon found a mentor who was supportive and able to help her improve her English. Her math teacher was a Vietnamese man who spoke both Chinese and English. He helped her to complete scholarship essays as she applied to college, and to prepare for speeches she had to give in class. However, when her YPT teaching artist Patrick brought the *In-School Playwriting Program* to her English class in the fall of 2007, Elaine was still struggling with both her English and her confidence.

"I felt shy all the time," Elaine says, "but when I got into the program, it helped me a lot. Patrick had us work in groups on dialogues, play games, work with partners. He kept pushing me, even when I didn't want to do it. It helped me become a better writer, and learn to express my emotions."

Elaine's play, *Destiny*, tells the story of all the difficulties she faced upon coming to America. Her protagonist, Colleen, struggles with insecurities and isolation as she tries to learn English in time to make a speech that she must complete in order to graduate. Having the opportunities not only to tell her story but also to watch it performed in the 2008 *New Play Festival* was incredibly empowering for Elaine.

"I never thought my play would be that awesome!" she laughs. "It was a great experience. I learned how to inspire people."

As of last year, Elaine is officially a United States citizen. Her English is nearly flawless, and she speaks about her experiences with confidence and humor. When she completes her last semester at James Madison University this fall, she will have a degree in Computer Information Systems. Currently she is finishing an internship at the World Bank, where she hopes to get a job after graduation doing web design or data analysis.

"When I think back on that time," she says thoughtfully, "it's hard to believe how far I've come. I've enjoyed my time here more than China!"

Destiny

by Elaine Qi Ling Li (2008)

<u>ABOUT ELAINE</u>

What grade were you in when you wrote your play? 11th

What school did you attend? Bell Multicultural High School

What do you do now? I attend James Madison University for Computer Information Systems, and am interning at the World Bank.

What do you like to do for fun? I like to go hiking, watch movies and go to the theater.

Is there anything you'd like to say to the readers of this book? Control your own destiny. Don't let other people's words get to you – ignore it. If you know you can do it, then you can do it.

Characters:

COLLEEN, student
AMY, friend
JENNY, friend
MS. T., teacher
MR. G., teacher
STUDENT A
STUDENT B
STUDENT C
MS. A.
MR. B.

ACT I, SCENE 1:

(Monday morning, the school hallway is filled with loud student noise. COLLEEN is walking in the hallway to meet her friends, AMY and JENNY.)

COLLEEN: Hey, guys, 你们好吗? (How are you doing today?)

AMY: Hi, Colleen, we're okay. How are you?

JENNY: Oh, I have some news to tell you. This year we have a big presentation in the library, and it will affect your graduation.

AMY: Really bad news, Colleen.

(AMY looks at COLLEEN.)

COLLEEN: Oh, my god! 你说真的吗? (Are you serious?) I think

如果我再不努力的话，我会败在那个presentation上 (I will fail with this

119

presentation, if I don't study hard now.) I will fail!

JENNY: You won't die and you won't fail, Colleen. Just relax and do your best.

(Bell rings)

AMY: Oh, it's time to go to class. See you after school.

COLLEEN: 再见！(Bye!)

JENNY: See you later.

(JENNY and AMY exit left.)

COLLEEN: Did you see that? They not feel nervous when they hear this news. It is because they born here and they never care about their language problems. They don't need be afraid they cannot pass the presentation. But how are about me? I come here two years ago and I never speak and learn English before. Every time, when I speak out, afraid the people sneer at me and they no want be my friends. You know what? Sometimes when I talk to Jenny and Amy, I think how they feel about me and are they laugh me? 我为什么要怀疑她们呢？(Why I will doubt them?) But anyway, I should believe them. 因为在学校里面，她们是我最好的朋友 (They are my best friends in school.) But I still afraid my presentation because of this presentation I cannot get to graduate. 怎么办啊，我毕不了业啊！(What should I do, I cannot get to graduate.)

(COLLEEN moves stage right to a "classroom" set.)

MR. G: Good morning, everyone. Today we will continue to do our project. If you need the computers let me know, okay? Let's go to work.

(COLLEEN walks to MR. G.'s desk to ask him a question.)

COLLEEN: Mr. G., how you do this q...q...question? *(Trying to sound out the word)* Because I...I...I...

MR. G: Excuse me? Say it again. I don't know what you're saying?

COLLEEN: This question? *(Says slowly, sounding out the word)*

MR. G: Oh, oh, stop, I still didn't get it. What are you trying to say? Oh, my god, this is terrible!

(MR. G. starts to get mad. COLLEEN points to her paper. He tries to understand her hand gestures. But that is even worse than before. His face changes to frustration and anger.)

MR. G: Colleen, look at your paper. There are lots of grammar mistakes. Why do you turn in work like this?

COLLEEN: *(Slowly and stuttering)* I...I...I don't know and English is my second language. Hard for me…speak, write… I try my best already. *(Broken, slow, stuttering)*

MR. G: Hey, hey, listen, I still did not get it. What you are trying to say? Colleen, this is no excuse. If your English and grammar don't improve, then you will never finish high school. Never!

COLLEEN: But…

MR. G: No buts girl, oh, that reminds me. This year you have the required graduation library presentation and you have to present in front of your teachers. Your English is so bad. How do you think you can present your work to them? How can you graduate? And if you go to college, and your language or grammar has still not improved, you will definitely fail all of your classes. The teacher may kick you out of their class or never look at your papers because you cannot speak grammatically correct English! You make too many mistakes. Now go back to your desk and do your work.

COLLEEN: *(Stuttering, broken)* But I…I…I don't know how to do it? And if I not finish that, then how can I… pass your class, Mr. G?

MR. G: I still didn't get what you said or wrote. Just go back to your seat.

(COLLEEN is really sad and goes back to her seat.)

STUDENT C: *Señor* G. I don't understand this question.

MR. G: *¿Que pasa?*

(COLLEEN stares at MR. G and watches MR. G happily help the Latino students. She turns back to her paper and sighs.)

ACT I, SCENE 2:

(After school, in the hallway, COLLEEN sees her friends, AMY and JENNY. AMY is singing a song, she sees COLLEEN.)

AMY: Hey, Colleen. Are you going home now or staying after school?

COLLEEN: *(Unhappy and almost crying)* I don't know. I don't know what can I do?

JENNY: *(Sad)* Oh, Colleen, what's going on? Why are you sad? Is something wrong or has somebody hurt you? Tell me.

(JENNY hugs COLLEEN and gently touches her hair.)

COLLEEN: Jenny, tell me, 我的语法和口语是不是很差啊? (Is it my speaking and grammar are very bad?) Tell me the true thing. Is my English speaking bad?

JENNY: Why are you asking me about your speaking and grammar? Is something wrong?

COLLEEN: *(Sad)* No, nothing wrong. You just tell. That's all.

JENNY: Why are you suddenly so worried about your language?

COLLEEN: *(Mad)* Don't ask me why! You just tell me, why? Jenny, no lie.

JENNY: Okay, okay, don't get mad. Colleen, let me tell you. In my mind, your speaking is okay. But, your grammar is so-so. But that's not your fault because you've already tried your best to learn. So you don't need to feel sad because different people have different challenges in life. Not everything is going to work out smoothly. If you do your best, that's fine.

COLLEEN: En... is it true? But my teacher, Mr. G. told me, he no understand what I say and he say my grammar really bad, and say I cannot get graduate in high school.

AMY: Oh... girl. Don't feel sad because we know Chinese people face a big challenge to learn English. Stay positive, don't be so negative.

COLLEEN: But Mr. G. say if I go to presentation in library I fail and he also say whatever I present how many times I just fail, no matter. I just fail. If when I go to the college and speak to the professor and he not know what I say that mean I fail half already. Or when I write essay to give professor and he not know what I write, that mean I totally. No, I want to go to college, but I do not know how I can improve speaking and grammar. Oh, who can help me, who...GOD!! And how I graduate? Why does school have a presentation? Why other schools don't have? Not fair.

AMY: Don't complain right now. You must do something to let your teacher know you can do it. Don't let him laugh at you and don't let him say you can't graduate because of your speaking and grammar. We know you can do it.

JENNY: Yes, Amy is right. You can do it Colleen. We believe in you.

COLLEEN: Oh, you are so sweet. Yes, I know I can do it. 我不会放弃的 (I cannot give up.)

AMY: First, we have to find a teacher to help you out.

JENNY: Yea, let me see who can help you out?

AMY: Jenny, how about Ms. T.? She is a nice teacher and she likes to help the students out if they have questions.

JENNY: Yea, you're right. What do you think, Colleen?

COLLEEN: *(Worried)* 你觉得她会教我吗? (Do you think she will help me?)

Because she's not my teacher and she never teach me. She help me?
No…I don't know…

AMY: That's fine, don't worry about that. She will help you out.

COLLEEN: *(Still worried)* Okay…if you think so.

AMY: *(Smile)* Okay, let's go.

(COLLEEN stands alone center stage after AMY and JENNY exit.)

COLLEEN: Ms. T.? Who is Ms. T.? Why I never hear that teacher's name. Oh,
I'm so nervous. Is she a serious teacher? Will she hit me if I do not do
well? No, I no want to find her. 我不要去找她 (I don't want to find her).
This is my weakness. Every time when I go to see the teacher I feel
really nervous. How can I do, how can I do? But Jenny said she nice
teacher, so don't need to worry. But why I still feel so nervous? Okay,
Colleen, you calm down, calm down. You should feel happy you will
have good teacher to help you. So don't feel nervous. Everything will
be fine. Right? Yes, yes, 不会有事的 (everything will be fine). OK, let's
go.

(COLLEEN exits.)

ACT II, SCENE 1: MS. T.'s office. Same day, after school.

JENNY and AMY: Hi, Ms. T., how are you today?

MS. T: Good! Wow, you three are really working hard to stay after school
today.

JENNY and AMY: *(Smile)* Yeah!

JENNY: Go on, Colleen. Ask her.

COLLEEN: *(Nod her head)* Ms. T., I need your help.

MS. T: *(Smiles)* Yes, how can I help you, dear?

(When MS. T. looks at COLLEEN, she feels scared.)

COLLEEN: *(Nervous and looks back to JENNY and AMY)* Can you help me to
improve my English and grammar, because I want to get graduate.
And I don't want hear I cannot get graduate in high school because my
speaking and grammar.

MS. T: Yes, I can help you. English is my second language, too. My first
language is Chinese so I know how you feel. I had the same challenges
in school. So, don't worry. I will help you out. I know you can do it
because I've heard you're a hard working student.

JENNY: *(Surprised)* Are you serious? English is your second language, too? I
can't believe that. Your English is so good.

COLLEEN: *(Excited and halted speech)* What do you...do...to speak fluency English? Teach me, teach me.

MS. T: Honey, if I teach you, you'll work hard, right? If you want to speak English fluently, it's going to be a real challenge. Can you do it?

COLLEEN: *(Happy)* Yes!

MS. T: Okay, first, you have to speak more and read more to cement your vocabulary. Second, you need more practice. When you talk to your friends or family, you need to speak in English. Third, watch more movies in English. Those three things are very important. Remember.

COLLEEN: I know, I do it. I am not let you despair, Ms. T.

MS. T: Good, okay. Do you want to start today? Are you ready?

COLLEEN: I ready to accept this...chall...enge? *(As if she is not sure she's saying the correct word and saying it correctly)*

MS. T: Good. Today, I want you to do some exercises so I can determine your reading level. Tomorrow, I want you to read some articles. And, the day after tomorrow I want you to write a story about yourself so I can determine your writing level and grammar needs. Do you know why I am doing this? Because all of this information will help me determine how to help improve your English skills.

COLLEEN: Yes, I...do...my best!

(MS. T, JENNY, and AMY freeze.)

COLLEEN: *(Spotlight on COLLEEN)* Wow! She really nice teacher. I think I no need worry. I should open my mind and not be shy, not scared. 我能做得到的! (I can do this!)

ACT II, SCENE 2:

(Two days later, the school hallway. COLLEEN is walking in the hallway. She stops and overhears students talking about her.)

STUDENT A: Hey, do you know Colleen?

STUDENT B: No.

STUDENT A: That's her. *(She points to COLLEEN.)* You know what? Last week, Mr. G. was yelling at her because he didn't know what she said. She made Mr. G. get really mad. She doesn't know how to speak English. Can you believe that? She's been here for 2 years already! Wow! That's horrible. *(They laugh.)*

STUDENT B: *(Surprise)* What? Are you serious?

STUDENT A: Yes. Her English is really bad. Or you could say, stupid. You never can catch on to what she is trying to say.

STUDENT B: How come the school would accept her? That's so stupid. That could affect our reputation if people know we have a stupid student in this school.

STUDENT A: Yea, you are so right!

(The bell rings. STUDENT A and STUDENT B go to their class. But COLLEEN is really mad and sad. Stays in the corner in the hallway.)

COLLEEN: *(Crying out)* I know I'm not smarter than everyone. I know I'm not good at study, but why you say I'm stupid? No, I'm not. 我不是蠢! (I'm not stupid.) And I already try my best. Why you will say I'm stupid? It not my fault. Not my fault.

ACT II, SCENE 3: *After school, in the hallway by lockers.*

JENNY: Hi, Colleen. How is it going? How are your English lessons going?

COLLEEN: *(Unhappy)* My English still really bad. I don't know why. Jenny, I want give up, 英文对我来说真的好难学啊 (English is really hard for me.)

JENNY: *(Look at her)* What? What did you say? You say you want to give up?

COLLEEN: Yea, I give up because I'm stupid and not good at study.

JENNY: *(Angry)* What? Who told you you're stupid? Stop saying that! Do you remember what you said before? You said you want to show Mr. G. that you can learn English and you want to show other people you can do it. You are good at studying and you just need time to practice. That's all. But now, you want to give up? Oh, Colleen, I hope you're joking.

COLLEEN: No, no joke. I want to give up, Jenny. It's really hard. I can't do it. I'm not good at study.

JENNY: *(Frustrated)* Colleen, look at me.

(COLLEEN has turned her face away from JENNY.)

JENNY: I said look at me. You promised Ms. T. you can do it and that you would never give up. But now…

COLLEEN: Yes, but now I can't do it. I can't. You are not me. You no know what I feel. Your English better because you born here. So you stop talk to me, Jenny.

JENNY: *(Yelling to her)* You say you don't want to talk to me? Okay, Colleen, you've told me before, that you want to graduate from high school. You said you want to go to college, and you said you want to improve your English.

(COLLEEN puts her head down and covers her ears with her hands. She doesn't want to look at JENNY because JENNY'S words scare her and make her feel like she can't say anything.)

JENNY: *(Angry)* Let me tell you something. If Ms. T. and Amy heard what you're saying, they would be so angry and so disappointed. This is your destiny, Colleen. That's why you came here. To become a citizen and get a better life. If you give up, that means you are… *(Hesitates)* a loser and my friends aren't losers. I know, my friend, you never would…give…up. And you know what? I…I…don't want to see you anymore. We…we…are not friends anymore.

(JENNY says this reluctantly. Her plan is to motivate COLLEEN with a little tough love. Actually, in JENNY'S mind, she does not want to hurt COLLEEN'S feelings, she just knows COLLEEN needs some motivation. She knows COLLEEN is a strong person who never gives up, but lacks confidence and worries a lot.)

COLLEEN: *(Cries out)* Jenny, I…

(JENNY turns and walks out. COLLEEN stays there and cries out. But after few minutes…)

COLLEEN: *(Wipes her tears)* Jenny, I just want tell you, you said it right. I know I was wrong now. Jenny, you yell to me because you don't want me to give up. Jenny, I know you just want me to learn more. I won't let you down or myself down. I know you my best friend. Jenny, I know what I have to do now, thank you, Jenny!

(COLLEEN exits running fast to catch up to JENNY.)

ACT II, SCENE 4: Two months later, classroom.

MR. G: Good morning, everyone. Today is the last day to turn in your work to me. I've already given you one month to do this project.

(COLLEEN confidently walks to MR. G.'s desk to turn in her work and speak to him. He looks surprised.)

COLLEEN: Mr. G., is something wrong with my paper? Do you not understand what I have written? Please, don't look at me like that. It scares me.

MR. G: *(Surprised)* Oh, I'm sorry. You have done a good job on this project. You are speaking clearly better than before. I'm just surprised. How did you improve your speaking and grammar in just a few months?

COLLEEN: You know what? I got one-on-one instruction in English. Every day for hours and hours I practice speaking English.

MR. G: Wow! Good job, Colleen.

COLLEEN: *(With confidence)* So, Mr. G. please don't say I cannot graduate. I'm working hard. Mr. G. let me give you some advice. When you talk to your students about their work, please have a better attitude. It's very easy to hurt students' feelings. You should say something positive. Try to understand students who are trying to learn a new language. If you use a bad tone with students, do you think you're really a good teacher? If you don't improve, I think you'll get fired soon.

MR. G: *(Angry)* You...

COLLEEN: Also, I want to say one more thing. Whenever your Spanish speaking students ask you questions, you use Spanish to help them out. You know what? That's not fair. Sometimes, I think you are racist. Anyway Mr. G., I deserve to get a good grade in your class because I've done a good job.

(COLLEEN does not let MR. G. say anything. She turns her back to and returns to her seat. Because Mr. G. feels really angry, he could not say anything. After few minutes, the bell rings.)

ACT III, SCENE 1: After school. The school hallway.

JENNY: Hi, Colleen, how is it going today?

COLLEEN: *(Smiles)* Great! When Mr. G. looked at my papers and heard me speak English, he was surprised. He could not say a thing!

JENNY: *(Laughs)* Really?

AMY: Did he praise you at all?

COLLEEN: He just said, "Good job, Colleen." And that was it.

JENNY and AMY: Oh, not a good teacher.

(They laugh.)

COLLEEN: Oh, thank you Jenny for your help when I wanted to give up you pushed me to keep going.

JENNY: I knew you would do it you. You are definitely not a loser.

(They laugh.)

AMY: What are you guys talking about?

COLLEEN and JENNY: Oh, that's our secret.

AMY: Oh, c'mon, tell me!

COLLEEN: Oh, I almost forget. I have to thank Ms. T. for all her help.

JENNY: Yeah, you are right. Okay, let's find her!

(COLLEEN, AMY and JENNY exit happily down the hall to find MS. T.)

COLLEEN: Hi, Ms. T., how's it going?

MS. T: Oh, hi, Colleen! I'm good.

COLLEEN: Thank you for your help. If you hadn't helped me out, my English would have never improved.

MS. T: It was my pleasure to help you. You know what? You are a smart girl and you learn really fast. Faster than most people.

COLLEEN: Oh, Ms. T. don't say that. I'm going to get a big head!

(After few months, COLLEEN walks to the library to start presenting her work.)

MS. T: So, do you think you're ready for the presentation next month.

COLLEEN: Yes—I'm ready.

ACT III, SCENE 2: *The Library: day of the big presentation.*

COLLEEN: Good morning! Ms. A and Mr. B, my name is Colleen.

MS. A: Morning. Have a seat, Colleen.

MR. B: Okay, you can start your presentation now and do your best. Don't feel nervous.

COLLEEN: *(Smile)* Okay, my name is Colleen and I'm in 12th grade. Today, I want to present my graduation project on child labor. First, I will review child labor conditions in the past. Work conditions were poor, pay was low and children worked long hours.

(Lights fade and return to signify time has passed in the presentation.)

COLLEEN: So that completes my presentation. Do you have any questions?

MS. A: Yes, can you tell me why this project is important to you?

COLLEEN: This project was important to me because it helped me learn about U.S. history and one day I hope to become a U.S. citizen. And I've learned I have the courage it takes to become a citizen.

(Teacher applauds, JENNY and AMY appear at door window, COLLEEN gives a smile confidently and walks out to greet them.)

JENNY and AMY: 恭喜你啊，你做到了！(Congratulations, you did it!)

COLLEEN: 我做到了！(I did it!)

End of Play

Chicas y Gringas

by Laila Parada-Worby (2004)

ABOUT LAILA

What grade were you in when you wrote your play? 9th

What school did you attend? School Without Walls Senior High School

What do you do now? I graduated from Harvard University in May 2012. I'm currently working with the Leadership Institute of Rio (ILRIO) in São Paulo on a post-graduate fellowship through Princeton in Latin America.

What do you like to do for fun? Travel, cook and read.

Is there anything you'd like to say to the readers of this book? I am so grateful to have had the opportunity to participate in the YPT program and am amazed to see how much incredible work it has inspired and continues to inspire!

Characters:

SAM: Samantha Arguetta is a 15-year-old high school student in California. Her mother is Salvadoran and her father in Chilean and she has inherited good physical qualities from both sides. She lives with both her parents and her grandmother. Sam just wants to maintain all of her friendships harmoniously and does not understand the racial and social boundaries at her school that restrict this. Sam is a good student and often has trouble balancing her social life with her education.

LARA: Lara Ann Thomas is a 15-year-old classmate of Sam's. She used to live in Rochester with her mother, but recently moved to California to live with her father. She has never experienced intense racial segregation, and it comes as a surprise to her when she begins school in California. Lara is slightly self-absorbed and does not understand why anyone wouldn't like her. She's tall, solid, and blonde.

MARISA: Marisa Anna Caroles is a 15-year-old classmate of Sam's in California. She and all her family are from Mexico. She had been a good friend to SAM since the eighth grade and has helped her through some tough times. She has been unofficially named the leader of her, Sam, and Isabella's group. Marisa is partial to older boys with bad reputations and her stunning looks have helped her to catch many.

ISABELLA: Isabella Maria Velazquez is a 16-year-old classmate of Sam and Marisa's. She and all her family originated from Mexico and she is

small and stocky like most of her relatives. She is Marisa's childhood
friend, and became close to Sam when she began to hang out with her
and Marisa. Isabella follows Marisa's lead and pretends to enjoy boys
and partying. She secretly hopes to become a member of the clergy at
her local church, but only time will tell.

MOM: Tatiana Arguetta is a 40-year-old mother of two, Sam and her little
brother Gabriel. She is a stay at home mother, and helps to take care of
her husband's elderly mother.

ABUELA: Samantha Concepcion Arguetta is Sam's 75-year-old
grandmother. She is a deeply religious woman and always offers Sam
advice when she needs it.

SCENE I:
(LARA and SAM talk on the school field during recess.)

LARA: Sammy, hey! Where were you last night? I thought we were going to
watch *The O.C.* together!

SAM: Oh man Lara, I'm so sorry! I was a little uh...busy.

LARA: Jeez girl, you ditched me again.

SAM: Um...yeah. It's just, that me, Mari, and Isa had to practice this dance
we're doing for the assembly next week.

LARA: *(Mutters)* Whatever.

SAM: Look, I'm really sorry I skipped out on you last night, it won't happen
again.

LARA: Whatever you say, call me later, o.k.? I've got class.

SAM: Cool.

(LARA goes into the school building just as MARISA and ISABELLA walk up.)

MARISA: Hey girl, what were you doing talking to that *gringa*?

SAM: Oh, uh, *nada*, she just walked up to me and started asking me for
some homework or something.

MARISA: That little white girl should stay with her own kind, right Isa?

ISABELLA: Yeah, those white girls, always taking our guys.

SAM: *Chicas*, calm down, Lara's not after any of your boyfriends.

MARISA: What, you're defending her now?

SAM: Naw, naw, girl, I was just saying.

ISABELLA: *Oye*, I just want y'all to know that I think our dance is looking
muy fabulosa!

SAM: Yeah it really is, but could you guys tell me in advance next time
when we're going to practice?

MARISA: What did you have planned that's better than spending time with us?

SAM: *Nada*, sheesh! Isa, you're right the dance is looking really good.

(MARISA and ISABELLA look at each other incredulously.)

MARISA: Alright Sammy, we'll see you later *chica*. Hit up the cell and we'll hang out.

SCENE II:

(SAM comes home after school and finds her mother in the kitchen reading the newspaper. MOM looks up when SAM enters.)

SAM: Hey Mom!

MOM: Hi sweetie, how was your day?

SAM: Pretty good, I got a 95% on my history quiz!

MOM: That's my girl! You're grandma is in the other room, go say hello to her.

SAM: O.K., Ma. *(Goes to the other room where ABUELA is sitting in a chair)*

ABUELA: *Hola mi'ja! Ven aca* and sit beside me. How was your day at school *angelita*?

SAM: Alright Abuelita. Listen, I need to ask your advice about something. You know Marisa and the other girls, right?

ABUELA: *Si, las chicanas, no?*

SAM: Yeah, the Mexicans. Well, I have this other friend Lara, but she's white and I know Isa and Mari would make fun of me if they knew about it. I don't know what to do! I love my Latina friends, but I love my white friends too.

ABUELA: That is a problem. All I can tell you is that you should follow your heart *y Dios te ayuda*. *(Traces the cross on SAM'S forehead)*

SAM: *Gracias* Abuelita. *(Gives her a kiss just as her cell phone begins to ring)* Oh, I have to take this call, Abuelita.

SCENE III:

(SAM lies on her bed in her room stage right and talks on her cell phone to MARISA who is in her own room stage left.)

SAM: Okay Mari, what is it you wanted to talk about?

MARISA: Aight, so there's gonna be this party at Enrique's tomorrow night! And guess who's gonna be there?

SAM: Not Raul! Girl, what have I told you about my no good cousin?

MARISA: That he's no good, duh. But c'mon *chica*, he's so *guapo* and didn't he say that he thought I was cute?

SAM: Yeah girl, but he's 19, and you're only 15. Plus, my Tia Ana Maria told me that he's been in juvie twice.

MARISA: I know girl, a bad boy! Anyway, are you coming to the party with me and Isa or what?

SAM: Fine, fine. Oh, sorry girl, I've got to go, call on the other line.

MARISA: Aight girl, tomorrow night, *mi casa*, at 8:00. Peace.

(MARISA hangs up. SAM remains in her original position on her bed. LARA appears in her room talking on her cell phone stage left.)

SAM: Hello?

LARA: Hey! It's Lara.

SAM: Oh! Hey, what's up?

LARA: Not too much, I just wanted to see if you were going to the party tomorrow night that Chris and the guys are throwing.

SAM: Oh, I'm really sorry, but I'm going to this party at this kid Enrique's house tomorrow.

LARA: Oh cool, that sounds much more fun than Chris' party.

SAM: Um, I don't really think it's your kind of party Lara.

LARA: Why not? What, do I like embarrass you or something?

SAM: No! No way Lara! It's just, I mean…I don't mean to sound racist or anything, but the people at this party are going to be mostly Hispanic, and…

LARA: What, you think I don't like Hispanic people or something?

SAM: No, that's not it, it's just that I don't think you'll really fit in, they might be rude to you.

LARA: Fine, if that's the way you feel about me, then I just won't go.

SAM: God, Lara! Fine you can come, but if people are mean to you it's not my fault.

LARA: Cool! I'll see you at 8:00!

(LARA hangs up.)

SAM: Lara, wait…crud! I'm meeting Mari and Isa at 8:00! What am I going to do?

SCENE IV:

(SAM and LARA walk up to MARISA'S house, all dressed up in party clothes.)

LARA: Sam, I'm not so sure this was such a good idea.

SAM: Oh my goodness, you can't back out now! You're the one who wanted to go anyway!

(SAM rings the doorbell.)

LARA: Alright, alright.

MARISA: *(MARISA answers the door.)* Hey Sam—um, hi…

SAM: Her name's Lara.

MARISA: Hi— um come on in girls. *Chica,* can I talk to you for a second? *(MARISA pulls SAM off to the side.)*

MARISA: What do you think you're doing bringing that *gringa* with you? We are going to Enrique's party! They're gonna laugh at us, and Raul is gonna be there too! *Estupida!*

SAM: Oh c'mon, she's not going to do anything. And I'm not an *estupida.*

MARISA: Whatever you say girl, wait till Isa hears about this. She's gonna kick your butt.

SAM: What's the big deal? Lara is a really nice girl! I don't see why you guys can't accept that!

MARISA: My family crossed the border from *Mejico* 17 years ago in the back of a pick-up truck. My mother and father work in the factory, and I've got to work on the weekends to buy myself clothes. She sits all day on her pretty white behind and does *NADA!* Now ask me again why I can't accept that.

SAM: You can't blame her for your problems.

MARISA: Whatever, let's just go to this party, and *que pasa, pasa,* what happens, happens.

SCENE V:

(All of the girls are at the party, MARISA and ISABELLA are on the dance floor, while SAM and LARA talk in a corner.)

LARA: Look at them out there, Marisa is such an amazing dancer!

SAM: I know, she's been salsa dancing since she was a little kid.

LARA: See, this isn't so bad! Nobody's told me to my face that I'm a whatsitcalled? *Gringa?*

SAM: Ha ha, yeah that's what it's called.

LARA: Look, Sam, I really like your friends, and I just want them to like me too! What do I have to do?

SAM: Maybe if you apologize to Mari for years of white oppression against minorities, she'll give you a chance.

LARA: You're not serious!

SAM: Of course I'm serious! And also, if you get your butt out on that dance floor and start strutting your stuff, you might make an impression.

LARA: Alright, here goes nothing.

SCENE VI:
(LARA walks out onto the dance floor and begins to dance. ISABELLA and MARISA stop dancing and stare at her incredulously.)
MARISA: Look Isa, that *gringa's* got some ants in her pants!
ISABELLA: *(Laughing)* Yeah girl. Hey whitey, you call that dancing?
(LARA stops dancing and looks embarrassed.)
LARA: Sorry girls, I was just trying to have a good time.
MARISA: We're not your girls, and you need to take that dancing and your behind out of here before we do it for you.
LARA: Why do you have to be so mean to me? What have I ever done to you?
MARISA: Don't even get me started. You white girls have all of the advantages. You're not going to ruin my night too.
(LARA begins to cry and runs off of the dance floor. MARISA angrily walks away.)

SCENE VII:
(SAM finds LARA crying in a hallway.)
SAM: Hey girl, I've been looking for you everywhere! Are you crying? Oh man, what did she do to you?
LARA: She's so awful! How can you stand her?
SAM: I'm sorry Lara, but I did tell you that it might be like this. Marisa's a great girl, but she's just had to deal with a lot of really bad stuff in her life because she's Hispanic, and she needs somebody to blame it on. If it wasn't you, it would be some other white girl.
LARA: What can I do to make her be nice to me?
SAM: I don't know, I'll try talking to her about it, because I really can't stand to have you guys fighting.
LARA: Thanks Sam, you really are a true friend.

SCENE VIII:
(SAM finds MARISA on the dance floor again and pulls her off so that they can talk.)
SAM: Mari, can I talk to you?
MARISA: It's about that *gringa* isn't it? I told you not to bring her here!
SAM: I don't understand why you can't just give her a chance!

MARISA: Because she's a stupid, rich, little white girl!

SAM: That is the worst thing that I have ever heard you say! If you don't stop this nonsense, I don't think that I can be friends with you anymore! I don't want to have to be caught in the middle of your problems with Lara.

(SAM storms off just as ISABELLA walks up.)

ISABELLA: What was that all about?

MARISA: *Esa chica* just told me that she won't be my friend anymore if I don't give Lara a chance.

ISABELLA: What are you going to do?

MARISA: Sam has been my *chica* for a long time, and I don't want to lose her because I'm blaming my problems on one girl. I've got to apologize to Lara.

ISABELLA: Yeah, me too girl. I guess we've been acting pretty mean, huh?

MARISA: Yeah, I guess so. Poor Sam, having to deal with us.

(MARISA spots LARA.)

MARISA: Hey Lara, come over here.

(LARA cautiously makes her way towards them, her cheeks are tearstained.)

LARA: What is it? You haven't insulted me enough for one night?

MARISA: Look Lara, I really wanted to apologize for the way I've treated you. It's been really unfair to both you and to Sam.

ISABELLA: Me too girl. It was really wrong of us to make judgments without even knowing you. Giving you a chance is much better than losing Sam as a friend.

LARA: That really means a lot to me girls, and I'm sure that it means a lot to Sam also.

MARISA: I think I better go find her and apologize to her as well.

SCENE IX:

(MARISA walks over to SAM.)

SAM: Is that Lara I see out there dancing with Isa?

MARISA: Yeah it is. She dances pretty good for a white girl, *tu no crees?*

SAM: So, you going to give her a chance or what? Did you apologize to her?

MARISA: Yeah I did. I love you too much to lose you over something stupid like that *chica*. And I'm in a good mood because Raul just asked me out.

SAM: Naw girl, what have I told you about him, a thousand times?

MARISA: That he's no good, I know!

SAM: I really love you Mari, and I'm glad that you're giving Lara a chance. She's really nice, and I think you'll like her a lot. *(Reaches over to hug MARISA)*

MARISA: Eh, girl, watch yourself, there are people around! Ha ha, just kidding, c'mere *chica*.

(The girls hug.)

MARISA: *Ahora, vamos a bailar!*

(The girls go out on to the dance floor and begin to dance.)

SCENE X:

(SAM brings a tray full of food to her ABUELA who is sitting in the living room.)

SAM: Here Abuelita, I brought you your breakfast.

ABUELA: *Gracias mi'ja.* How was your party last night?

SAM: It was really fun Abuelita. And all the girls had fun together, my *amigas blancas* and my *amigas Latinas*.

ABUELA: That's good to hear *chula*, I told you that you needed to follow your heart and *Dios* would do the rest!

SAM: *Gracias* Abuelita, *te amo mucho.* *(Bends to kiss ABUELA)*

End of Play

A Playwright Visits the White House:
Mariana Pavón Sánchez

"I was a very shy student, afraid to speak out. And here I am addressing the First Lady of the United States – and it's all thanks to Young Playwrights' Theater, to the arts and humanities and the power of my own ideas."

Photo by Michael J.N. Bowles

On October 20, 2010, Young Playwrights' Theater received the National Arts and Humanities Youth Program Award, the highest honor in the nation for a youth arts program. When the President's Committee on the Arts and the Humanities announced their 2010 award recipients, they had a special request – they wanted YPT playwright Mariana Pavón Sánchez to accept the award from First Lady Michelle Obama and to speak about her experience with YPT at a private ceremony in the East Room of the White House.

YPT was one of only fifteen winners selected for this honor, from a national pool of more than 400 nominations. Mariana was the only youth participant chosen to speak at the award ceremony.

Mariana was born in Fairfax, Virginia, but her family moved to Nicaragua when she was an infant. Mariana returned to the United States in 2008. In 2009, as a tenth grader, Mariana participated in YPT's *In-School Playwriting Program*. She wrote a play titled *Mariana's Wish* about a young woman who longs to visit her mother in Nicaragua, but must first convince her father to give his permission.

Mariana's Wish was produced as part of YPT's *New Play Festival* in 2009. It's a passionate, heartfelt play. In the play, the character of Mariana talks of missing her mother so much because she was the one person with whom she could dream of her future. "She is the most important person in my life," she says. The audience was moved to tears every night, partially because of the play and partially because of Mariana herself, who spoke so

Photo by Michael J.N. Bowles

eloquently about her life's journey and her love of YPT.

It was deeply moving to watch Mariana speak about YPT's impact on her life at the National Arts and Humanities Youth Program Award ceremony. "My experience with YPT really helped me to improve my English," she told a large audience, which included the First Lady. "Now I know how to express myself better." World-renowned cellist Yo-Yo Ma, who serves on the President's Committee on the Arts and the Humanities, congratulated Mariana on her speech after the award ceremony. He told her that he could relate to her experience learning to express herself through playwriting, as a shy student who found his own voice through artistic expression.

After her speech, Mariana called her mother in Nicaragua from the White House and told her all about the experience.

Mariana's Wish

by Mariana Pavón Sanchez (2009)

ABOUT MARIANA

What grade were you in when you wrote your play? 11th

What school did you attend? Wakefield High School

What do you do now? I work at the University of the District of Columbia, and I'm starting at Northern Virginia Community College in January to get my degree in Physical Therapy.

What do you like to do for fun? I read a lot of fiction, and go on the internet.

Is there anything you'd like to say to the readers of this book? As I said in my speech at the White House, my advice to other students is: don't be afraid to express yourself in writing. Even if it's something small, it is important.

Characters:

MARIANA

PAULINO, Mariana's dad

MARIANA: I came to this country last year. First I wanted to come to learn English. Mi Mami didn't come with me because her visa expired in 2007, and she and my grandfather are both sick, so she can't travel. Now I want to go back to Nicaragua to visit, because I miss mi Mami. I miss talking to her every night. I want to taste her *vaho* that she cooks really well. We used to go outside to El Mirador de Catarina, where we spent hours walking and talking. We talked about boys. She also gave me advice about how I have to act with them. Another thing that I miss is when we talked about what I want to do for my future. I want to do those things with mi Mami again. I want to spend Christmas with mi Mami, *mi hermano, mi familia* and *mis amigos*; they are the most important people in my life. I've asked my Dad 3 times before if I can go to Nicaragua but he doesn't really take me seriously. So this morning before he leaves for work, I'll talk to him and he'll have to listen to me.

PAULINO: I moved to the United States a long time ago, I think 23 years ago, because I wanted to give my family a good life. I wanted to give my children all that my parents didn't give me when I was a child for different reasons. Last year I was talking with my daughter, and she said she wanted to come to the United States to study English. I don't talk with her mother often, so I don't know if her mother—Fanny—approves of Mariana living with me. Fanny is sick; maybe this is the reason why Mariana wants to go to see her so badly. She hasn't seen her mother this year so she wants to go to Nicaragua for winter break holiday. But I'm worried about her safety. She is too young, and maybe she would get lost in the airport. Also the ticket is too expensive. Maybe she can go next year, when she can be more responsible. I know it's important for her because she loves her mother and misses her friends, but I'm worried about her. What Mariana doesn't know is the real reason –I'm afraid that she'll go to Nicaragua and not want to come back to me. And she has a better future if she stays in the United States.

(They are talking in the kitchen at breakfast time.)

MARIANA: Hi dad! Good morning. How are you?

PAULINO: I'm good, and you?

MARIANA: I'm fine. How was your day yesterday?

PAULINO: So-so you know I had a lot of work like every day.

MARIANA: I want to ask you something.

PAULINO: Yes, what?

MARIANA: Well…

PAULINO: *Apúrate,* hurry I have to go to work.

MARIANA: Can I go to Nicaragua and visit Mami for winter break holiday?

PAULINO: We can talk about this later.

MARIANA: Dad this is more important than work. I want to go and see mi Mami.

PAULINO: You are too young, you can't go alone. You could get lost, or miss your flight and you don't speak enough English.

MARIANA: There are a lot of people that speak Spanish, I could find someone. You know what? You can go with me. You speak Spanish!

PAULINO: If I go to Nicaragua who will make money for us— your Mami, your brother and you?

MARIANA: Well, I can go alone, I'm not too young, I'm 18 years old.

PAULINO: Yeah, but you are my baby. I don't want anything bad happen to you.

MARIANA: But dad…I have good grades…

PAULINO: Your grades can't help you, if you get lost in the airport.

MARIANA: *(Crying)* I want to go and see mi Mami…you don't understand me…

PAULINO: I'm sorry, but I'm worried about your safety. NO, you can't go alone and THAT'S IT!

MARIANA: But I've done this before when I came to USA. Do you remember?

PAULINO: Yes, but you came with the flight attendant, she took care of you.

MARIANA: I know I can do it, trust me, please.

PAULINO: *Hasta aquí no mas*, enough this is as far as I go. I don't want to talk about this subject anymore.

(PAULINO starts to leave the kitchen.)

MARIANA: Mi Mami is sicker than before, and you don't know because you never talk to her. It's been three years since you have called her. Her medicine doesn't work. Mi Mami has bone cancer and it's getting worse. Please think about this. I love her. If something bad happens to her I will never forgive you, and I will never forgive myself.

PAULINO: *Lo siento*, I'm sorry Mari, I didn't know how sick she is.

MARIANA: Well you didn't know before, but you know now.

PAULINO: I love you and I want to make you happy. I hope you can forgive me! I don't want to see you sad anymore. You can go!

MARIANA: Are you serious? I can go to Nicaragua?

PAULINO: Yes my darling…

MARIANA: Thank you, dad, for trusting me, and yes I forgive you, and I love you so much! *(Screaming happily)* THANK YOU, THANK YOU, THANK YOU!!!!

MARIANA: Well, I'm so happy! My father told me that I can go to my country for winter break holiday, so I will see mi Mami, *mi hermano* and *mis amigos*. I think my father trusts me, and I know nothing bad will happen to me. Mi Mami will be so happy when she sees me in my home. I can't believe it, but I know it is the truth. The first thing that I'm going to do is give her a big hug; I think I will cry too. And I'll taste her *vaho*! *¡Que rico!*

End of Play

The Elevator

by Nora Spellane (2008)

<table><thead><tr><th colspan="2">ABOUT NORA</th></tr></thead><tbody><tr><td colspan="2">**What grade were you in when you wrote your play?** 9th</td></tr><tr><td colspan="2">**What school did you attend?** Woodrow Wilson Senior High School</td></tr><tr><td colspan="2">**Where do you go to school now?** Macalester College</td></tr><tr><td colspan="2">**What do you like to do for fun?** Horseback ride, dance, listen to music, watch black and white movies.</td></tr><tr><td colspan="2">**Is there anything you'd like to say to the readers of this book?** Art is powerful. You are powerful. Create. Produce. Get yourself out there and speak.</td></tr></tbody></table>

Characters:
GEORGE
AHMED
ELEVATOR TECHNICIAN

(Lights up)

GEORGE: *(On cell phone)* Yes, dear, I'm leaving the office to get Danny now. Yes, I have the health insurance cards. Yes I know the way to the hospital. Okay, I'll see you there.

(GEORGE enters an elevator, then AHMED runs in as the door is about to close. GEORGE is a stern looking man wearing a suit. AHMED is on his way to the mosque and he wears a long simple white robe and sandals and a white Kufi on his head, with a prayer rug in a bag over his shoulder. The two glance at each other, but don't look at each other after that. They stand apart. Suddenly the elevator stops and the lights go out. Both men startle and the lights come back on, but dimmer.)

GEORGE: *(Panicking)* What did you do? You filthy Muslim terrorist! I have a wife and children! Of all the things you could attack, why this building, hmm? What's so special about it? I thought you people only attacked important places, like the Twin Towers, but now I see you guys have no limits! Am I to spend my last minutes with you? My Destroyer? *(Checks cell phone)* Great, no service! Lord, you people are stronger than I thought! So what are you gonna do? Tell me that your god is better than mine? Tell me I'm the glorious victim of Jihad? *(Folds*

143

arms expectantly) Well?

AHMED: *(Standing quietly throughout rant, finally stirs himself to speak)* I do not know what your name is, but listen to me for a moment. I am not a terrorist. Now I know nothing about you, but I must get to the mosque within the hour. We weren't attacked by a terrorist, as you scream about, but the elevator is stuck. I would appreciate it if you would help me think of a solution to getting out of this elevator.

GEORGE: I can't trust *you* to do anything to help me! Everything you say is a lie! You have to go to your *mosque*. *(Word seems awkward and clunky when he says it)* Why don't you go back to your own country and go to your mosque there!

(Moment of silence as both men are wrapped up in their own thoughts. Suddenly, AHMED drops to one knee with both palms on the ground.)

GEORGE: *(Angry)* What the hell are you doing?

(AHMED ignores him, his brow creased in thought. He looks up at the doors questioningly.)

GEORGE: I said, what th-

AHMED: *(Cutting him off)* Do you know what floors we are stuck between?

GEORGE: How should I know? Anyway, why should I tell you? What are you doing?

AHMED: *(Sharply)* Do you want to get out of this elevator?

GEORGE: *(Suspiciously)* Yes...

AHMED: Then help me. We might be able to shift this elevator, but I need to know where we are.

GEORGE: *(Silent a moment, considering his options, then grudgingly)* I believe we are between floors 2 and 3.

AHMED: Good. I think I have a solution to get out of this elevator.

GEORGE: Why should I help you? I don't care about you getting to your mosque on time. How do I know that if we get out of this elevator, you won't do something terrible?

AHMED: *(Getting more and more agitated, then explodes)* Stop accusing me! Listen, can you do that? I am *not* a terrorist! I get grief from people like you because I worship at a mosque, because I carry a prayer rug, because I pray to *Allah* five times a day!! People like you, they ostracize me. Say behind my back that I don't belong in this country! You preach "Love thy neighbor" in your churches. But *my* neighbor called the police because I keep my blinds drawn. I do this so my wife, as blonde and fair as *any* of you, can relax without her scarf. You pride yourself on *love (spits out the word)*, but you are exempt if it is a Muslim?

GEORGE: *(Taken aback by outburst)* You...your wife...is white? You corrupted a good Christian woman?

AHMED: *(Quiet now, but still angry)* I did not "corrupt" her, as you say. She made her own decision to convert.

GEORGE: That's preposterous! Why would anyone want to do that?

AHMED: Would you believe that she educated herself in our ways and made the decision herself? We met when I was in Germany. She was working as a translator. *(Wants to say more, but stops himself, seems to shake himself out of wistful mood)* I'm sure that this will offend your religious sensibilities, but if you can suspend your inhibitions for a moment, I believe that by jumping—

GEORGE: Hold on a moment, jumping?

AHMED: Yes, jumping. I believe our combined weight might be able to shift the elevator at least a little bit, or even get it started again.

GEORGE: *(Scornfully)* That will never work.

AHMED: It won't hurt to try.

(AHMED begins to jump, GEORGE regards him disdainfully.)

GEORGE: You look like a fool.

(Elevator moves a bit.)

AHMED: There, you see?

GEORGE: *(Suspiciously)* How did you know that that was going to work?

AHMED: Well, laws of gravity aside, look at it from an engineering standpoint. The cables pull the elevator up and down, but if we use enough force; we can maybe push the cables through the pulley and move down to the next floor.

GEORGE: Are...are you an engineer?

AHMED: Hmm? Yes.

GEORGE: *(Interested)* What school did you go to? *(Catches himself, and tries to put on a casual air, but fails)*

AHMED: A university in Saudi Arabia, but when I came here I did some work in the Marines.

GEORGE: They let you—

AHMED: *(With an ironic smirk)* Yes, contrary to popular belief, they do let Muslims join the marines.

(Suddenly the elevator begins moving again. GEORGE becomes unbalanced and falls, but AHMED catches him in time. The elevator stops at the second floor.

Door opens to see an elevator technician with a worried expression.)
ELEVATOR TECHNICIAN: Are you alright?
(GEORGE gets on his feet again, his confusion and conflicting emotions showing on his face. AHMED nods to the TECHNICIAN.)
AHMED: Semper Fidelis. *(Exit)*

End of Play

Plays for 16 & Up

Playwright Profile: Kenrry Alvarado

When Kenrry Alvarado started thinking about what he wanted to study in college a few years ago, he was torn.

"I've always wanted to go into politics," he says in an interview with YPT. "The whole atmosphere is really interesting. I just like the idea that you can bring a lot of people together through politics. I watch CNN a lot. But I also love science. I want to do research on the biology of education. I want to see if there's a better way to teach, beyond the psychological. What makes us remember things and apply things that we've learned."

While struggling with this decision during his junior year at Bell Multicultural High School, Kenrry discovered he had another talent: writing. When the YPT *In-School Playwriting Program* began in his English class, writing came easily to him, and he quickly discovered that he loved it.

"I thought it was really cool that I was given the opportunity to actually write a play of my own," Kenrry says. "I'd never thought of doing that. Especially in a school setting, where there are mentors that will guide you. That in itself gave me a lot of inspiration."

Kenrry's play, *Daft Desire*, was selected for production in YPT's 2010 *New Play Festival* in the spring of 2010. The play combines elements of film noir with mafia cinema as it follows two women, Jane and Amanda, in their quest to seek revenge on Jane's ex-husband, Lucio.

Though playwriting was brand new to Kenrry, he realized that he could use it to impact society. "There aren't many powerful women [noir and mafia] films," Kenrry explains. "I felt like it was important to try to empower women through my writing."

Kenrry continues to write, using what he learned with YPT to express his

thoughts on what is happening in the world around him. He spent the
year after the performance of his play working with the *Young
Playwrights' Workshop*, YPT's after-school program, where he continued
to challenge society's views with his writing. He composed the opening
monologue for the *Workshop's* original play, *Out of the Shadow*, which
challenged the willingness of many Americans to ignore the widespread
problem of bullying.

"Many turn a blind eye on bullying without realizing dire consequences it
may have on its victims," he wrote. "We will not do that. We are going to
take a stand. We are going to emerge out of the shadow."

"YPT has really helped me to be able to express my thoughts and feelings
in words," Kenrry says in his interview. "It's helped me relate to people
more, and use the right words for different things."

Now in his sophomore year at Middlebury College in Vermont, Kenrry
has settled on a major in Neuroscience.

"It was a really tough decision," he says, smiling. "Neuroscience is pretty
strict. It's so structured. I wish I could go towards my other interests and
take other classes, but my schedule is really busy!"

Daft Desire

by Kenrry Alvarado (2010)

<u>ABOUT KENRRY</u>

What grade were you in when you wrote your play? 11th

What school did you attend? Bell Multicultural High School

Where do you go to school now? Middlebury College, Class of 2015

What do you like to do for fun? I like to go out to restaurants and try out new and exotic dishes. I like to stay up-to-date with politics in the U.S. and around the world. I also like to swim and play soccer with my friends.

Is there anything you'd like to say to the readers of this book? YPT has provided me such an amazing opportunity in producing this play I wrote for their workshop. The fact that they were able to bring my thoughts and ideas to life through this program brought me sheer joy and inspiration. I realized that I am more than just one of many, beyond a mere high school student with a negligible impact in society, and that I don't have to be Batman to distinguish myself from the crowd and have my voice heard. The boundaries were broken. The opportunities became vividly clear. I was finally capable. YPT opened my eyes to a world of endless possibilities.

Characters:

JANE

AMANDA

GOON #1

GOON #2

OLD BUTLER, Jacob

BIG BOSS, Mr. Lucio DeSanti

JOHN ACKERMAN

UNDERBOSS

CHAPTER 1, SCENE 1:

(JANE and AMANDA are in an alleyway with two GOONS standing out back of a club. They are two of LUCIO DESANTI'S personal security.)

JANE: When do you wanna attack?

AMANDA: I don't know I'm not sure about this. This whole plan may blow over.

JANE: Don't think so negatively, Amanda. Just think positive thoughts. I

151

know you're nervous, but this has to go smooth-like.

AMANDA: OK, let's go. Right now, right here.

JANE: Alright. Get ready to ambush them down and out, one guy each...
On 4.

AMANDA: Huh? Why 4?

JANE: Well "3" has been sooo overdone, don't you think? The people want
something fresh. Isn't that right people? (Stares at audience)

AMANDA: Ummm, Who are you talking to?

JANE: Uhh...no one, no one.

AMANDA: OK...start counting.

JANE: 1...

AMANDA: Prepare artillery.

(AMANDA and JANE get their hands inside their purses.)

JANE: 2...

AMANDA: Become aware of surroundings...

JANE: 3...

AMANDA: Take out cherry red lipstick and make up and apply more than
the usual.

(JANE and AMANDA take out make up and lipstick from purse at the same time,
and begin to polish up.)

AMANDA: Make up applied.

JANE: 4!

AMANDA: OK, time for sexism to take its course.

(Everything freezes, except JANE, who appears front and center, JANE begins to
inform audience about plan.)

JANE: For those who don't know, I'm Jane, and over there is my good
friend Amanda. We are trying to get into this big bonanza the Big Boss
is throwing later this week, by seducing two of his dumb-as-a-rock-
good-for-nothing lackeys. What they don't know, is that we are
planning to kill their boss in the midst of all the commotion the party
would gladly provide. ...Why do we want this guy's neck, you ask?
Let's just say he happens to be my ex-husband.

(JANE gets back in freeze frame.)

JANE: (In valley girl accent; seductive, and dumbed down) Hey there big
stallions! You think you two can...hang out with us for a little while? I
was hoping we could have some fun. Probably ride on your rough,
tough...saddles. If that's okay.

GOON #1: With you two? Certainly.

(GOON #1 kisses JANE'S right hand.)

GOON #2: But don't we gotta be looking out for…

GOON #1: SHHH! *(Whispers to GOON #2)* Shut up dude. Look what we have here, two beautiful women wandering around a dark alleyway, and their lipstick is calling our names. What are the odds? *(Speaks to JANE and AMANDA)* Uhhum, yeah, we're free.

CHAPTER 1, SCENE 2:

OLD BUTLER: Mr. DeSanti, John Ackerman would like to have a word with your excellence.

BOSS (Mr. DeSanti): May he proceed… and call me Lucio. You've known me long enough.

OLD BUTLER: I'll send him in, Lucio.

(Enter JOHN)

JOHN: Your Excellency, it's a pleasure being in your presence.

BOSS: Enough, my friend…what is it that you want?

JOHN: Well I would like to ask for a bit of…financial assistance.

BOSS: Big surprise… Go on.

JOHN: I have been struggling for quite some time. Jobs on end. Midnight and weekend shifts. Barely making it. And this coming end of the month, I don't think I have the ability for me and my buddies to pay for our sports channels and movie rentals…you see those things are… what I like to call, our meaning of existence. And without them, our souls would be devoured by sadness and despair. You understand, oh magnificent one?

BOSS: I understand.

JOHN: So please bring me the life back…I beg of you.

BOSS: You would be available any and every time I summon you?…I have your life in the palm of my hand?

(JOHN nods his head rapidly.)

BOSS: Then it is so. The check will come in the mail in about 3 days to meet your needs.

JOHN: Thank you, sir thank you!! …You don't know how much this means!

BOSS: No problem, as long as you keep with your end.

(JOHN leaves happily. BOSS no longer in "The Godfather" character.)

BOSS: Geez! In need of help? Can you believe it? I get fools like this all the freaking time…What's up with this shtick???

OLD BUTLER: Why don't you just refuse to lend him your hand, your

Excellency?

BOSS: *(Back in "The Godfather" form)* It's not the honorable way is all. I have built this empire based on me helping anyone that enters my golden gates in search of need. What kind of man would I be if I leave these men empty-handed? Not a very pleasant one I presume. I seek to become an approachable man while leading with an iron fist.

OLD BUTLER: Understood, sir.

BOSS: The more people under my control, the easier it would be to overrun this town. Soon I will be able to bite the apple that is this society. Everything in my own image. Everything!

(BOSS gets himself together.)

BOSS: Uhh, *(speaking kindly)* shall we proceed with our routines?

(UNDERBOSS arrives.)

BOSS: Oh hey there, Mr. Snipe…Are all the festivities in order?

UNDERBOSS: Everything's splendid, Boss.

BOSS: Good, good. Remember, it's a fundraiser for the mayor. He needs money pronto. With huge favors on the line, I want it to be enormous. You still think you can handle the job, lieutenant?

UNDERBOSS: Yes, Sir.

BOSS: I like your initiative. That is all.

UNDERBOSS: Anything for you.

BOSS: Old Butler, ring up the next client.

OLD BUTLER: Excuse me if I am being impolite for asking, but why do you call me "Old Butler"?

BOSS: Because *(BOSS pulls out "Daft Desire" play from his desk)* …in the play titled "Daft Desire" by one Sir Kenny Avocado…and I must say this play has an antagonist that is quite delightful. Dark, yet very charming…I digress. It clearly states here that you, sir, are called the "Old Butler." And looky here, it also says that you were gonna ask this very question. *(BOSS shows script to OLD BUTLER)* Weird huh? Does that answer your question, old friend?

OLD BUTLER: *(Looks surprised; in regular voice)* How'd you do that? Ummm… *(Back to character voice)* I mean yes. That has answered my question, sir.

UNDERBOSS: Wow, the boss is sure crafty.

BOSS: *(Not in "The Godfather" mode; almost nerdy)* Yes. I got it on Amazon. *("The Godfather" mode)* Now. I will tell you my most trusted fellows something truly remarkable. This script. The script I have in my hand is the source of all my power. With it I can write anything. Well, except for flying pigs or raining ice cream. Tried it. Didn't work. And I was still hungry. I can write <u>almost</u> anything on this and the characters in the script will follow along these lines.

UNDERBOSS: That is sheer brilliance! Very wicked, Sir.

BOSS: Lucio, Mr. Snipe…Call me Lucio.

CHAPTER 2, SCENE 1: *Walkby.*

(Walking through from end to end on stage. Two days before party.)

AMANDA: I am sooo loving this! Fooling these people into thinking we're innocent eye candy was sheer brilliance! Here we come, Lucio.

JANE: Remember, we can have our time of enjoyment, but this whole ordeal is revolved around manipulation and getting to Lucio. We are sleeping with the enemy now, Amanda.

AMANDA: I know, Jane. The saddle has been set, and now we make our way to sweet, silent revenge.

JANE: Oh yes, revenge will be saccharine. Sweet as ice tea.

CHAPTER 2, SCENE 2:

BOSS: *(After drinking ice tea)* Uhhh, eww! What is this?

JOHN: Well, it's ice tea my lord.

BOSS: Well, it tastes like dirt. Fetch me some Cola.

JOHN: All we have in the storage is a 2 liter bottle of Diet Cola, your Excellency.

BOSS: DAMN IT! Well I guess that'll do. It's closer to Cola than it is to this junk.

JOHN: Would you like a glass with that sir?

BOSS: No, I prefer drinking it from the source.

JOHN: Very well, I'll be back.

(BOSS waits for a minute while JOHN comes back with a 2 liter bottle of Diet Cola.)

JOHN: Here you go.

(Gives BOSS a 2 liter Diet Cola bottle. LUCIO freezes chugging down bottle. JANE is hiding from a distance; time freezes and JANE gets closer.)

JANE: Oh, you…you dirtclot! Wait 'til I get my hands on your neck choking you down until your head turns blue as a balloon and your eyes turn dark as night!

(JANE looks at LUCIO'S 2 liter.)

JANE: Hmmm…I guess his obsession for Cola has nothing but grown over the past few years.

CHAPTER 3, SCENE 1:
(JANE and AMANDA are arriving at LUCIO DESANTI'S big party bonanza at his mansion.)

JANE: We are in. Do you have the venom?

AMANDA: Yes, right here, in this small bottle.

JANE: Good. We've had our time of enjoyment. This is the real deal. The big boss will not see it coming. He'll be choking his words. Gasping for another breath. We were spiders swaying our mate, and now, we go in for the kill.

AMANDA: You think this is too much? I mean you said it was a long time ago.

JANE: No. This man... *(JANE shed a tear, now choked up)* This man, I used to love shattered my dreams, sucked the blood from my heart, leaving it cold and deformed. This man has to die. After countless months of searching for this snake, he will be given what he rightfully deserves.

AMANDA: Alright, Jane. As you would want it let's go forth. We will poison him and cure your broken heart with arsenic.

JANE: Yeah. You hear that Lucio!! I'ma coming for your sorry, Italian butt!! Thanks Amanda for helping me in this dilemma. Every step of the way, I can say you were there for me. Thank you. I could never ask for a better friend right now than you.

AMANDA: Awww...it's been a wild ride, Jane. Believe me. Now all we have to do is find the drink that he is wrapping his lips around tonight.

JANE: The boss has a moderate to severe Cola addiction.

AMANDA: Oh really?

JANE: Back when we were just itty-bitty immature kiddies he was always seen with a can of the soft drink in his hand. We used to call him "The Colamaster."

AMANDA: The Colamaster?

JANE: Ever since the 6th grade. He has had a huge crush on Cola.

AMANDA: You've known him for that long?

JANE: Yeah.

AMANDA: Wow... Nevertheless, all we have to do is slip the toxins into his drink. Cola, water, wine, or otherwise.

JANE: Yeah... I suppose.

CHAPTER 4: *Flashback*

(JANE and LUCIO are in the 6th grade at the playground.)

LUCIO: Hey Jane.

JANE: Hey.

(LUCIO'S drink begins to drop.)

LUCIO: I just want to say…

JANE: Ohh wait, your soda is falling!!!

LUCIO: Ohh really? …No, No, NO!!

JANE: Seeing that you're always carrying that can around, this is an utter crisis.

LUCIO: Yes. I shall now commence to cleaning up the spill with the tongue.

JANE: OK, Mr. Colamaster…*(Laughs)* What were you gonna say?

LUCIO: Oh yeah…um…you think me and you *(LUCIO begins to get nervous.)* could go to the movies tomorrow? It's Friday so…

JANE: Really? I'd love to!!

LUCIO: Really?

JANE: Yes! Let's go around 5 to the theater at 14th street.

LUCIO: Alright then.

(Both say as they look away from each other.)

JANE/LUCIO: YES!

CHAPTER 4: *Poem*

(Back at the party. JANE leaves mansion, walks on stage alone, while everyone else is at a standstill. She stands in front of the audience, and recites a poem of hers.)

JANE: "The Avian Flew" By Jane Rosenbloom-Desanti

It was a beautiful night
a cherished night that will be forever photographed in my mind
I wondered, "How was I able to be with you?"
How was I able to please you?"
the way you slowing place your warm feathers against me
sent forth electric waves of affection into my heart and core
you were my king
and the next morning
we were off to the kingdom of our dreams across the sea
As we approached the warm, ocean scented gates
Our world collapsed and faded away
It was all a dream, an illusion

The truth had revealed itself,
When I stared at the glowing sea
That I was the bird with the torn wings
And you were the bird that would keep on flying

JANE: However, something inside of me may still be able to forgive you.

CHAPTER 5, SCENE 1:
(AMANDA comes towards JANE after JANE read the poem. JANE and AMANDA are on their way outside of LUCIO'S mansion heading home while the festivities are still in progress.)
AMANDA: *(Runs to JANE)* Jane, Jane! The job has been done. I slipped the toxins in his drink when he wasn't looking. After tonight, the snake by the name of Lucio DeSanti will be no more.
(JANE begins to cry)
AMANDA: Jane, what wrong? Don't tell me you're feeling sorry for the guy in these late hours.
JANE: Well, I know it could've ended another way. Not like this. What did I do wrong? Was it the way I spoke to him? Was I letting him breathe? Or did I give him too much room?
AMANDA: You did nothing wrong. It was all his doing. He deserved every drop.
JANE: Yeah... but I really wish this did not have to end like this.
(JANE runs off.)
AMANDA: Where are you going!!!?
JANE: I am going to save him. My Lucio.
AMANDA: Don't!! He's... *(whispers to herself)* shoot...

CHAPTER 5, SCENE 2:
(JANE is running towards the mansion.)
AMANDA: Jane! Jane! *(Says to herself)* I can't believe she is doing this. Jane!
JANE: I'm sorry, Amanda, but it has to be done.
(JANE sees UNDERBOSS. JANE seems surprised and senses danger, begins to run away from UNDERBOSS and towards AMANDA. UNDERBOSS pulls out pistol and chases after AMANDA. The two are now running off-screen. He shoots off-screen. JANE believed AMANDA was killed. JANE is at a standstill, frozen, as she heard the gunshot.)
JANE: *(Everything but JANE freezes on the screen)* AMANDA! Oh dear God,

forgive me. It is my fault, my trustful friend. Why did I get you in this debacle? After all we have gone through. You had my back, from the beginning. Unfortunately, I was unable to have yours.

(Time unfreezes. UNDERBOSS approaches JANE while she is crying on the floor.)

UNDERBOSS: Are you Jane? Come with me.

(UNDERBOSS grabs JANE by the arm tight and brings other men to help take her to the boss for questioning as JANE struggles to escape.)

CHAPTER 5, SCENE 3:

(JANE is dragged into LUCIO'S quarters by henchmen. She is tied up to a chair. LUCIO appears.)

LUCIO (aka "BOSS"): Hello, stranger.

JANE: You know damn well who I am.

LUCIO: Oh do I? ...Care for a glass of wine? *(LUCIO approaches wine collection in his quarters)* Here's the unopened bottle. I'll just uncork it here.

(LUCIO begins to uncork bottle. Note LUCIO is a non-alcoholic and does not get any drink for himself.)

JANE: Why!!!

LUCIO: Why what, my lovely guest? I must say your beauty ranks high among the women that I have laid my eyes upon. All the red really envelopes your tangy body. Oh, are you talking about the drink? Serving you is mere common courtesy. You are in my presence, therefore naturally, you deserve the finest. *1945 Château Latour* sound good? Or do you prefer some tainted Cola to refresh your beak?

(LUCIO places JANE'S glass in front of her. LUCIO now looks more serious.)

JANE: *(With anger)* Why the hell did you leave me in the dirt for the animals to feast upon my emaciated soul? Tell me why! Why you left me cold and dry, and you have no sympathy? No regrets? No memory of our chapter?!

LUCIO: Oh, you are talking about that "why." It was a long time ago, Jane. Things happen, things change. The past is the past. For the best, we should just forget about it and hope for a brighter future.

JANE: I still want an answer, Lucio.

LUCIO: *(Cutting her off)* You know you ruined a perfectly good glass of Cola with that mischief.

JANE: I want an answer...

LUCIO: Trust me, Jane. Sometimes, what you want is not what you need. Now let's try to forget about our ancient history...shall we? And what a better way for you to start than with some fine wine.

JANE: Damn it, Lucio. I've gone through all of this crap to get to you. I am deserving of answers. And I want them now!

LUCIO: Very well. I will tell you...To tell you the truth, I was tired of you. You say you love me and all that...blah, blah, blah. After we married, the flame began to slowly dwindle and lose its luster...and all that was left was...a pile of soot. There was not much chemistry translating on my end. It just...didn't work well for me. So I had to leave you. I just had to leave it all. Then, later...*she* came into my life, and I was changed ever since.

(AMANDA appears in front of JANE.)

JANE: Amanda!!! How could you???!!!

AMANDA: Surprise.

JANE: What, why??

LUCIO: Yeah, she wasn't dead as you thought to believe. Quite the contrary, she is doing well alongside me. You see, I hired Amanda to spy on you, Jane.

JANE: I don't believe this. I opened up to you, Amanda. I trusted you!

LUCIO: The truth is beginning to embark its agonizing trail now, isn't it? As I was saying, I knew you were plotting to kill me, Jane. It was only a matter of time until your pain erupted and anger emerged from the depths of you. So I stayed a step ahead, tracked you down, and filed for a little insurance, which over time paid off in its own end.

(LUCIO kisses AMANDA.)

AMANDA: Sorry, Jane. We had a good run though. Now it's time for you to go "night-night."

JANE: TRAITOR! How could you, Lucio? How could you do this to me?! *(Begins to tear up)* I love!!!! ...

(JANE gets cut off by LUCIO.)

LUCIO: You were gonna say...that you loved me?

(AMANDA leaves for a second to get LUCIO some Cola.)

LUCIO: I'm sorry...but...my heart was snatched away from me by that wonderful lady over there.

(AMANDA returns.)

AMANDA: Awww...Here's your Cola, my love.

(AMANDA kisses LUCIO on cheek)

LUCIO: Thanks, my dear. I was longing for some safe, non-toxic Cola to wet my whistle. *(LUCIO drinks some of the Cola; makes "ahhh" sound after. LUCIO brings out script)* Jane, you know what this is? This is a script. And not like any old script. It's a magical script that can make my dreams reality. Everything I change in this script, will change in the real world. I led you on. I see you are the same pile of soot as I left you. An insignificant being in this world, now my world. I get to do whatever I please with this script in my hands. You see, Jane, I HAVE all the cards of the deck. And you have nothing. Nothing!

(LUCIO begins to read script.)

LUCIO: "I've got you now, you bastard."

(LUCIO begins to choke from Cola poisoning as he points at his drink. He then falls.)

LUCIO: How could have... phosphoric acid, potassium benzoate, caramel coloring and high fructose corn syrup be the source of my undoing? I loved you, Cola... I loved...

(Lucio lays motionless on the floor.)

AMANDA: *(Obtains script and writes on it)* This assembly is now under new management. Bow down before your new overlord!

(GOONS bow down.)

JANE: Oh Amanda...how did you do all this?

AMANDA: I'm sorry, Jane... *(JANE hugs AMANDA)* ...for not telling you.

EPILOGUE: *Revelation*

(AMANDA stands in front of LUCIO'S corpse.)

AMANDA: *(Looks at audience)* It is true. There I was. Holding the great brainchild of the boss, my love Lucio, the story unfolded in front of my very eyes, with me as the pilot. I befriended Jane, hoping to gain her trust, at which I was successful. There I waited for Jane to blueprint her way into killing Lucio, so that she would fall under his wrath. But during my newfound friendship with Jane, I began to bear sympathy for her. I even tried to have her believe that I killed Lucio myself and that everything was well and dandy, so that she would leave and both would part ways and live their lives feeling accomplished, but as you saw here, that did not proceed as planned. *(Looks at deceased LUCIO)* I'm sorry it had to end this way, my love. I asked myself many questions and contemplated a lot, Lucio, trust me. How was my relationship with you going to turn out? After everything I heard

about you through Jane. All of the times she cursed you. All the times I
saw her fiery eyes, wanting you dead. Were they truly justified?
Would it get to the point when you commit the same acts against me??
Would you also ditch me to the curve???
I thought deeply of this, and I had made my decision. I swiped your
script from under your nose, and created an ending that you would've
certainly not been pleased with. But it had to be done. For Jane, I, and
the good of society. Who knows what you would've ended up causing
with this much power in your hands. I'm glad I didn't find out.
Standing alongside you, the great Mafioso of the land, living the lavish
life. Being the wife of a rebel. That is my desire. Was my desire. Now I
have been enlightened…That that desire was a foolish one. That desire
was, indeed a daft desire.

(AMANDA lays a rose on LUCIO.)

AMANDA: Good bye, Lucio…Ohhhhhh, Jacob! *(OLD BUTLER arrives)* Clean
up this mess.

JACOB (OLD BUTLER): I finally have a real name!? Ummm, I mean, will do,
madam.

*(BUTLER gets mop/broom thingy and sweeps body away. JANE drinks 1945
wine.)*

End of Play

Keepin' Outta' Trouble

by Pete Hall (2007)

ABOUT PETE

What grade were you in when you wrote your play? 11th

What school did you attend? Bell Multicultural High School

What do you do now? I'm a student at California State University. I work as Northridge/Talent Crew at Pacific Theaters and am a Crew Member at Pizza Revolution.

What do you like to do for fun? Watch movies, exercise, play football, rock climb, play video games, write poetry/scripts, make funny videos, hang out with friends, eat and sleep.

Is there anything you'd like to say to the readers of this book? I am thankful for the opportunity to have been in YPT. Had I never took the chance to be in the program, I wouldn't have discovered my passion for writing. I'm on my journey trying to live my dream and be happy doing so. If the journey ever gets difficult for you and makes you want to give up – don't. When times get rough, you have to keep pushing towards your goal. Over the last few years, I've realized that myself. So I'll be jogging, running, sprinting towards my dream no matter what because I know that it's only a matter of time before I reach my goal! And if you keep pushing towards yours and never give up, I promise that you'll do the same.

Characters:

PETE

MOM

SEAN

OLD LADY

MR. URANUS

STUDENTS, at least three

MOB, at least three

MATT

SADE

GIRL

MR. DALY

OGECHI

PRINCIPAL DE OLANO

BOSS

GUARDS, at least two
NURSE

SCENE 1: _The scene opens with PETE on stage. He is the only one on stage._

PETE: Christmas. The best day of the year, besides my birthday. _(Laughs)_ I only have one more day before Winter Break comes up and then Christmas. I know this year will be good because I brought back all A's and Mom said if I brought home straight A's that I'd get that PS3. All I got to do is stay on her good side and I'm home free. I mean, how hard could that be? _(Laughs)_ If only I knew.

(PETE turns and lies in bed. In PETE'S room, it is morning now. PETE is still in bed and is late for school. His MOM yells at him off stage.)

MOM: Pete?!

(PETE snores loudly.)

MOM: _(Irritated)_ Pete?! Time to get up! _(PETE is still asleep. MOM walks on stage next to PETE, standing over him.)_ Pete!

PETE: _(Asleep)_ Oh of course I wanna' be with you Buffy... _(PETE snores loudly and turns over on his side facing the audience)_ ...you too Megan Good, just pass me the boneless Buffalo wings... _(PETE snores loudly again.)_

MOM: _(Confused)_ Buffy?! Meghan?! Boneless Buffalo wings?!?! _(Raises her voice)_ BOY, GET UP!

(MOM hits PETE on the side of the head. PETE jumps from under the covers and stands up shocked.)

PETE: _(Shocked)_ I'm up, I'm up!

(PETE rubs his eyes and walks to the left center of the stage pretending to change up. MOM follows everywhere PETE goes like a shadow.)

MOM: _(Disgusted)_ Talking 'bout some Buffalo wings in the morning. Don't make no sense. Pete, you better hurry up and get ready for school. You always late!

PETE: _(Upset)_ No I'm not!

MOM: _(In disbelief)_ That's not what the school saying. Always calling the house leaving that same old sorry message.

PETE: _(Upset)_ Mom, the school be making mistakes sometimes. I know it because I was in school yesterday and they still called.

(PETE goes to right center of stage. Mom still follows him.)

MOM: _(In disbelief)_ Yeah okay, but I know one thing, if I get a call from the school one more time, you ain't getting that Game boy for Christmas.

(PETE turns around and faces MOM.)

PETE: It's called a PS3 Mom!

MOM: *(MOM rolls her eyes.)* Whatever...*(Gets angry)* and who you raising your voice at?!

(MOM raises her hand in the air as if she is about to hit him. PETE crouches a little bit with his hands over his head.)

PETE: *(Scared)* Nobody Mom. I was just making sure you could hear me.

(MOM puts her hands on her hips and stares at him. He gets back up cautiously. She takes her hands off her hips and sighs.)

MOM: *(Sincere)* Yea okay. Hurry up and get outta' here, okay?

(MOM turns around and starts to walk away from PETE.)

PETE: *(PETE rolls his eyes.)* Okay, okay. I heard you the first time.

(PETE picks up his book bag.)

MOM: Excuse me?!

(She turns back around facing PETE looking very angry.)

PETE: *(PETE starts to panic.)* I said I...um...better get out of here before I run out of time.

(PETE walks to the down right of the stage.)

MOM: That's better. And remember, you got one more time to be messing up or no PS3. Don't make me jack you up boy!

(MOM puts her dukes up.)

PETE: *(Sighs)* I love you too Mom. Bye.

(PETE walks off stage.)

SCENE 2:

(PETE and SEAN are walking down the sidewalk. They are almost late for school. PETE and SEAN are slowly walking across the stage from stage left to stage right.)

PETE: *(Upset)* Man, we gonna' be late for school again. I can't be late for school no more! My mom said if she gets one more call from the school, I'm not gonna' get that PS3 for Christmas.

SEAN: *(SEAN puts his arm around PETE and shakes him a bit.)* Relax man. We're not going to be late for school.

PETE: *(PETE moves away from him.)* If I had a dollar for every time you said that, I'd have...um...

(PETE stops walking and starts to count his fingers. SEAN stops walking and looks at him funny. PETE puts his hands down.)

PETE: *(Angry)* Wouldn't you like to know?!

SEAN: I know you would!

(SEAN starts to laugh loudly.)

SEAN: *(SEAN stops laughing abruptly with a serious face.)* Seriously, don't
     strain your brain.

PETE: I wasn't straining.

(PETE starts to twitch a little bit.)

SEAN: *(In disbelief)* Riiight.

PETE: *(Excited)* I can't wait to get that PS3 though. I can see it now.

*(PETE looks up to the sky as if daydreaming. Then PETE looks toward the
audience and puts his hands up as if he is holding a PS3 controller. PETE presses
the buttons wildly moving left to right and putting the controller behind his back
and under his legs.)*

PETE: Yeah, I'm gonna' get you! WOOOOO, look at these graphics!

SEAN: *(Chuckles)* Yeah, that'll be fun.

(PETE still pretends to be playing a game.)

PETE: *(Excited)* Oh yeah! New high score! New high score!

SEAN: Yeah okay, you can stop now.

(PETE keeps on playing.)

SEAN: ...Well....can I have a turn?

(SEAN looks out at the audience as if he too can see the game.)

PETE: *(Smiling)* Sure buddy.

*(PETE begins to hand SEAN the controller. SEAN reaches out to grab the
controller slowly but as soon as SEAN is about to grab it, PETE pulls it away
from reach.)*

PETE: *(Looking into SEAN'S face)* SIKE!

*(Turns back to the audience playing his game and starts to laugh. SEAN starts to
pout, but gets an idea. SEAN pretends his hand is like a scissor and with one snip,
SEAN cuts the imaginary cord that connects the controller to the system.)*

PETE: Nooo!!!!!!!!!! *(Turns to SEAN looking very upset but cheers up and says to
     him)* Sike! It's a wireless controller. *(Turns back to the audience playing his
     game again laughing)*

SEAN: *(Laughs)* You got me pretty good son.

(SEAN moves in closer to PETE.)

PETE: Yup, I sure—

(SEAN smacks the imaginary controller out of PETE'S hands onto the ground.)

PETE: *(Disappointed)* Aww, you're no fun.

*(PETE takes a second to look at his watch. PETE checks the time and realizes that
he is late. He is shocked and looks at SEAN.)*

PETE: *(Worried)* Yo', we only have five minutes left to get to school before the bell rings. Let's go.

SEAN: Not yet. Gotta' go to the store and get me something to munch on during class.

PETE: *(Panicking with his hands in the air)* We don't have time!

(PETE puts his hands down.)

SEAN: *(Calmly)* Chill. I'll be quick.

(SEAN walks into the store, offstage. PETE stands there waiting, tapping his shoes. Suddenly, he can hear SEAN'S voice from offstage.)

SEAN: *(Curious)* Hmm...so what can I get in here for five cents?

(PETE'S jaw drops. PETE realizes that he won't make it to school on time waiting for SEAN so he makes a run for it. PETE runs all around stage jumping and dodging as if he's in the jungle. He keeps on running until he gets behind an OLD LADY who is blocking his way on the sidewalk. PETE jogs in place waiting for her to move faster, but she keeps on shuffling forward at a steady pace. Eventually, PETE gets impatient. So he taps her on her shoulder, the shoulder that is facing the audience. She turns in that direction facing the audience and PETE kicks her in the butt. She falls offstage yelling.)

OLD LADY: OOOOOh!

(PETE runs offstage but before he does, he turns back around with his fist in the air in an angry motion and says...)

PETE: *(Angry)* STOP HOGGING THE SIDEWALK, YA' JERK!!!

SCENE 3:

(The settings changes to PETE'S 1st period classroom. All the STUDENTS are sitting down. PETE runs into the classroom. He looks up at the clock. The bell rings. PETE yells with excitement and starts to dance in a silly manner. The STUDENTS laugh.)

MR. URANUS: *ahem*

(PETE stops dancing and turns around to MR. URANUS. He is shocked and realizes he is interrupting class.)

PETE: *(Embarrassed)* Oh...my bad.

(PETE gives a nervous chuckle but stops and takes a seat.)

MR. URANUS: Hello class. I am your substitute for today. Mr. Axelson could not make it due to an illness he caught last night.

(The class yells with joy.)

MR. URANUS: Okay, so my name is *(MR. URANUS turns around to write his name on the board)* Mr. Uranus. That's U-R-A-N--

(PETE starts to hold his laughs in. MR. URANUS turns around to see who it is but PETE looks away as if he doesn't know what's going on. MR. URANUS turns back around.)

MR. URANUS: Okay, so I, Mr. Uranus, will be picking up on the reading of
   The Crucible —

(PETE laughs again trying to hold them in. MR. URANUS turns around faster this time, now a little irritated, trying to find the person who is laughing, but PETE plays innocent again. MR. URANUS turns back around again.)

MR. URANUS: ...so like I was saying, I will be picking up on the reading of
   The Crucible, BUT —

(Once PETE heard MR. URANUS say "but," he is unable to hold in his laughs anymore and starts to laugh out loud. MR. URANUS turns around, furious.)

MR. URANUS: Would you like to tell the rest of the class the joke?! I'm sure
   we all could use a laugh.

PETE: *(Pause)* ...Okay so this cow jumped over the moon right and —

MR. URANUS: I guess you're Pete huh? Mr. Axelson told me to watch out for
   you. Do I need to give a call down to the office?

(PETE remembers his main goal, looks down and pouts.)

PETE: No sir.

(MR. URANUS smiles.)

MR. URANUS: Good. *(Looks out to the class)* Okay class, open your books to
   Act II, Scene I and start your independent reading.

(MR. URANUS and all the STUDENTS there get up and walk offstage. PETE picks up the book and starts reading it. He starts to talk to himself.)

PETE: Okay, okay. Gotta' stay focused Pete. Just gotta' read this book. Pfft! I
   mean, how hard could that be?

(He reads for a few seconds then abruptly, his head falls right into the book on the desk and falls fast to sleep snoring loud. The scenery changes around him and the stage fuses with his inner imagination. Now he is in the time of the witch craft trials and his seat is at the edge of a cliff. The weather is cold and the sun is nowhere in sight. The wind blows leaves around left and right. PETE soon wakes up to the sound of an angry MOB behind him. A man emerges from the crowd and gains the MOB'S attention with one hand motion in the air. PETE gets up out of his seat, wide awake now, and turns around to see where he is. The man turns around to PETE. Shocked, PETE'S eyes widen like saucers and he says by surprise.)

PETE: Mr. Uranus?!

MR. URANUS: Aye, it is me. Do you have anything else to say before you go?

PETE: *(Confused)* Go where? What's going on?

MR. URANUS: I'll tell you. *(MR. URANUS turns to the crowd.)* Today we are here to prove if this man is a witch or not. It is our solemn duty to purify this town of demon worshipers in the name of Our Lord and Savior. We will throw him off the cliff to test and see if he is a witch. If he flies...*(In a loud, crazy voice)* HE'S A WITCH!!! *(Goes back to normal)* If he falls to his death...*(In a loud, crazy voice)* HE'S A WITCH!!!...*(Pause)* WITCHES!!! *ahem* So, would you like to give yourself to God before it is too late?

(MR. URANUS turns back around to PETE, but PETE has fallen back to sleep snoring loudly.)

MR. URANUS: *(Angry)* Wake up boy!

(PETE wakes up in fear.)

PETE: *(Scared)* MAMA NO!!!

(PETE puts his hands up as if his MOM was going to hit him, but realizes he was asleep.)

PETE: ...Oh...my bad. Were you saying something?

MR. URANUS: *(Shocked)* He's calling out for his mama! He must be a witch!!!

(The MOB gasps and talks among each other.)

PETE: *(Confused)* Um, don't you mean warlock?

MR. URANUS: *(MR. URANUS rolls his eyes.)* Whatever, push him over.

PETE: WAIT! Isn't this America? Is it not?

(PETE looks out to the MOB.)

PETE: What happened to freedom?! Democracy?! What happened to the love for our country...and for each other? Please, stop all this nonsense. And if you can't do it for me, do it for America!

(PETE looks up into the air with his hand over his heart.)

PETE: For the red, white, and...um...

MR. URANUS: *(Confused)* Blue?

PETE: *(PETE shakes his head in disbelief.)* Naw, that's not it.

(The MOB then starts to yell out colors trying to figure out what it is.)

MOB PERSON #1: Yellow?

PETE: No.

MOB PERSON #2: Silver?

PETE: Nope.

MOB PERSON #3: Seven?

PETE: That's a number.

(There is a quick pause.)

MOB PERSON #1: Is it blue?

PETE: *(Excited)* That's it! Thanks man. Three cheers for that guy.

(He points at MOB PERSON #1.)

MR. URANUS: *(Upset)* That's what I said!

PETE: *(PETE faces MR. URANUS and talks down to him and pats him on the head as if he was a child.)* Now, now, now. Nobody likes a glory stealer.

(PETE turns back to the MOB.)

PETE: Hip hip!

MOB: Hurray!

PETE: Hip hip!

MOB: Hurray!

PETE: Hip hip!

MOB: Hurray!

(The MOB cheers MOB PERSON NUMBER #1 on. MR. URANUS grows impatient. Finally he erupts.)

MR. URANUS: Enough! Throw him over!

(It doesn't take long for the MOB to switch sides and they move closer and closer to throwing him off the cliff. PETE yells, but finds himself disappearing from the dream world — MOB walks offstage — back in his seat and wakes up to MR. URANUS calling his name over his shoulder.)

MR. URANUS: Class is over Pete.

PETE: Oh okay.

(PETE sits there for a moment and realizes that he fell asleep. He panics for a moment and tries to play it off as if he didn't.

PETE: *(Lying)* Oh...um...just to let you know, I didn't fall asleep. The story got to me so bad that it...um...put me into a deep sleep of knowledge and — and helped me to construct the true meaning of life.

(PETE smiles a cheesy one but MR. URANUS doesn't buy it. MR. URANUS stares at him for a moment before saying.)

MR. URANUS: Get out.

(PETE looks at MR. URANUS up and down.)

PETE: *(Disgusted)* Well!

(PETE walks offstage.)

<u>SCENE 4:</u>

(PETE enters from stage right. PETE is walking down the hallway when he sees his friend MATT coming from the opposite side of the stage walking down the hallway from the other direction. MATT comes up to PETE and dodges PETE'S

head as if it is taking up all the space in the hallway. PETE, along with the other STUDENTS in the hallway, laugh. PETE greets him with their handshake.)

MATT: Yo' wassup man?

PETE: Nothing. Just trying to stay out of trouble.

(MATT stares at PETE'S head amazed. PETE backs up without moving his legs.)

PETE: *(Confused)* What?

MATT: *(Loud)* Son, you head big as a mug! I bet you gotta' get your hat size custom made and erruthang!

(MATT and the rest of the STUDENTS laugh. PETE gets upset and tries to defend himself.)

PETE: *(Upset)* My head not even big though.

MATT: *(MATT tries to hold his laughs in.)* Pete, I could barely get past it in the hallway. Couldn't even see what was behind it! Thought this hallway was a dead end or something!

(The STUDENTS standing around continue to laugh.)

PETE: *(Lying)* Okay, it's kinda big, but not THAT big.

(PETE points to the sides of his head.)

PETE: See, all this is just swelling. The doctor said if I keep putting ice on it that the swelling will go down soon.

MATT: *(Grinning)* Boy, you head stuck like that for life! Your mom must of had a hard time pushing you out!

(The STUDENTS in the hallway laugh.)

PETE: *(Excited)* Hell my mom didn't push me out! She had to get a C section!

(MATT and the STUDENTS around PETE start to laugh even harder. PETE looks around and realizes that he made the situation worse.)

MATT: *(Shocked and laughing)* Dang! You head was that big!?!?!

PETE: My head is not that big!

MATT: Okay, okay, okay, but guess who I am.

(MATT takes off his book bag, unzips it, and puts his head in the book bag standing straight up.)

MATT: *(With a deep mimicking voice)* Hey look at me, I'm Pete.

(The whole hallway burst out laughing. PETE looks very upset but can't help it himself and starts to laugh with them. Soon, the STUDENTS start to walk away offstage leaving PETE and MATT in the hallway. MATT takes the book bag off his head and carries it again.)

PETE: *(PETE shakes his head.)* I swear man. You do this every day. *(Chuckles)*

MATT: *(Chuckles)* You know I'm just messing with ya'.

PETE: *(In disbelief)* Yeah, yeah, yeah. *(Chuckles)*

(PETE and MATT shake hands. While doing so, SADE walks down the hallway from stage right. She walks in front of PETE and MATT and greets them with a smile.)

SADE: Hey Pete. Hey Matt.

MATT and PETE: Hey Sade.

(SADE keeps walking down the hallway. PETE watches her go down the hallway. Somehow, time slows down with SADE still walking in slow motion. PETE eyes widen in amazement.)

PETE: *(Shocked, in a deep, slow motion voice)* WOAH MOM-MA!!!

(Time goes back to normal and SADE walks across the stage and leaves going offstage on the left side. MATT notices PETE and the way that he was looking at her. MATT taps PETE on the shoulder to get his attention again.)

MATT: You like her don't you?

PETE: *(Shocked)* How'd you know?!

MATT: *(Convinced)* I'm pretty sure that the whole "Woah Momma" was pretty obvious. *(Points to the audience)* I'm sure even the audience could see it.

(There is a slight pause.)

PETE: *(Confused)* What audience?

(MATT pauses to think about it for a second.)

MATT: Um...never mind.

(MATT smiles to the audience then turns back.)

PETE: I mean I do, but I don't know how to go up to her.

MATT: Well *(MATT grins)* lucky for you, I can teach you. I have a way with the ladies.

PETE: *(In disbelief)* Oh really?

MATT: Yeah, watch this.

(A GIRL walks across the stage from either direction.)

MATT: *(MATT looks to the GIRL and uses a seductive voice.)* 'Ey wassup baby. Dang, she got it all! Look at that phatty!

(The GIRL smiles a little bit trying to play it off that she didn't like the comment but it was quite obvious that she did.)

MATT: *(Turns to PETE)* Okay, your go.

PETE: *(Tries to deepen his voice, but it sounds silly)* HEY SWEET THANG! WOAH BABY! LOOK AT THAT GLUTEUS MAIXIMUS! IT'S HUUUGE!!!

(The GIRL looks him up and down in disgust and storms down the hallway

offstage. There is a short moment of silence. PETE turns back to MATT.)

PETE: *(Confident)* She digs me. *(PETE grins deviously.)*

MATT: Sike like!

(PETE'S face becomes sad as MATT brings him down to earth. MATT puts his hand on PETE'S shoulder.)

MATT: Look, all you got to do is do something real special that'll make her blush; something that'll make you stand out from the rest of the guys. Do that and you'll get her for sure.

PETE: *(Confused)* Okay but what?

MATT: I don't know. You gotta' figure that out on your own.

(The bell rings.)

MATT: *(Panics)* Dang, I gotta' get to class! See ya' later Pete.

PETE: Aight son.

(PETE and MATT shake one last time and dash in opposite directions offstage to class.)

SCENE 5:

(PETE walks into his math class from stage right and sits down at a desk. MR. DALY notices that he is late.)

MR. DALY: Late for my class I see?

PETE: Yeaeeaah. Sorry about that Mr. Daly.

MR. DALY: *(Smiles)* It's okay. I know how hard it is to get that big head through the doorways.

(The class laughs.)

PETE: *(Embarrassed)* Aww c'mon Mr. Daly.

MR. DALY: Okay, now I have some good news.

PETE: *(PETE rolls his eyes and sighs.)* What? More notes?

MR. DALY: Even better. A pop quiz.

(The class starts to boo.)

MR. DALY: *(Sarcastically)* Please, please. Keep the excitement level down. I told everyone the class before, while you were rushing out, there would be a pop quiz the next day. If you studied...good job. If you didn't...sucks to be you.

(A student yells out.)

STUDENT: *(Upset)* I wasn't even here yesterday.

MR. DALY: Boo hoo. A boooo hoo.

(MR. DALY uses his hands and pretends a tear is falling from his cheeks. He picks up some papers and begins to pass them around and speaks.)

MR. DALY: You have the rest of the period to finish the quiz. If you're
   talking, zoning out, or if I just don't like you, then I'll give you an F.
   Ooooookaaay...you may begin.

*(Upon hearing those words, PETE shuts out the rest of the world and is in deep
concentration. The STUDENTS and MR. DALY leave the stage.)*

PETE'S VOICE: Okay, okay. Gotta' stay focused and do my best. This is
   gonna be easy though. *(PETE grins with confidence. He reads the first
   question.)* Okay, 2 + 2? Pfft! Too easy, five—I mean four! Yeah that's it.
   (He scribbles on his paper.) Gonna 'ace this! Next question, x = y - z over
   the square root of pi is? Hmm... *(He struggles.)* ...well I'll come back to
   that one. Next one, square root of 121 is...12! Okay... *(PETE searches his
   paper for the answer but cannot find it, leaving him confused.)* Where's 12?!
   I know that's the answer! All I see is 18...5...7...and...blue?! Huh?!
   Okay maybe that's just a typo. I'll just skip that. *(PETE reads on to the
   next question.)* Train A, traveling 70 miles per hour, leaves Westford
   heading toward Eastford, 260 miles away, carrying approximately two
   hundred passengers. At the same time Train B, traveling 60 miles per
   hour, leaves Eastford heading toward Westford carrying two hundred
   and fifty passengers. If the trains continue at their current speeds...
   (PETE'S face turns in disgust.) then what color shoes will the girl wear
   boarding the train next Tuesday?! Oh stop playing?!?!

*(The bell rings and the quiz is over. MR DALY walks back on stage from either
side and comes up to PETE.)*

MR. DALY: The quiz is over.

PETE: *(In a hurry)* Okay let me just finis—

*(MR. DALY tries to take the quiz away from PETE but PETE holds on tight to
the paper.)*

PETE: *(Struggling)* Let me just finish this last part!

MR. DALY: *(Struggling)* Pete! Just give me the *(Snatches the paper from PETE'S
   hand)* quiz!

(MR. DALY looks at it for a quick second. He laughs for a second.)

MR. DALY: You failed.

PETE: *(Shocked)* What?! You barely looked at it!

MR. DALY: I know, I just don't like you.

(MR. DALY smiles. PETE smiles back too.)

PETE: *(Grins)* Haha very funny. *(PETE gets up)* I tell you, if you had your
   own show, I'd watch it every day.

MR. DALY: *(Smiles)* I know. I'll check this over the break though. Have a good day Pete.

(MR. DALY walks away offstage on stage right. SEAN enters the classroom from stage right.)

SEAN: Yo wassup Pete.

(PETE and SEAN shake hands.)

PETE: *(Curious)* Hey wassup. `Ey you got a CD I can borrow with a song on it?

SEAN: *(Unsure)* Um...*(SEAN searches through his bag)*...yeah I got one, but I don't know what song is on there. Why?

PETE: Man, I'm tired of all this bad stuff happening today. *(PETE face becomes certain.)* But it's almost Winter Break and I'm gonna' end today with a bang.

SEAN: *(Confused)* What do you mean?

PETE: *(Grins)* You'll see at lunch.

(PETE runs out of the class offstage on stage right.)

SCENE 6:

(It is lunch time. All the STUDENTS are there. PETE sees SADE hanging with her friend OGECHI. Before approaching them, PETE grabs milk off the table and drinks it with big gulps. Finished, he sets it back on the table hard as if he finished drinking a glass of beer and wiped his face looking at SADE determined. PETE walks over to SADE.)

PETE: *(Nervous)* Hey wassup Sade.

(SADE looks up and sees PETE. She greets him back with a smile.)

SADE: *(Smiling)* Hi Pete.

(PETE prepares to say more but OGECHI stands in front of SADE and interrupts the flow.)

OGECHI: *(Disgusted)* Who is you?! Don't be coming over here like You. Know. Us!

PETE: *(Sighs)* Look, can I talk to Sade for a moment please?

OGECHI: *(She makes a scene.)* BOY PLEASE! Sade don't wanna' talk to you!

(PETE gets irritated a little bit but holds back his emotions showing a calm face. He ignores her comment and keeps talking to SADE.)

PETE: Sade, I've liked you for a long time, but never knew how to say it. So instead, I'll dance it for you.

OGECHI: *(Disgusted)* Dance?! Pete you know you can't—

PETE: *(Irritated)* Shhh!

(PETE walks away to the middle of the floor with a boom box and places the CD

inside. OGECHI, still shocked that she got dissed, turns to SADE and looks at her awaiting an answer. SADE doesn't respond who is shocked as well. PETE presses the play button and gets into the middle of the floor and waits for the song to come on. When it starts playing, he hears Michael Jackson's voice and realizes what song it is. He turns to find SEAN in the cafeteria and gives him a look like "Why did you give me this song?" SEAN looks back at PETE and shrugs in shock as if he really had no clue. PETE ignored the situation and when Michael does his "Whooo" yell, PETE mimicks Michael as if he is singing. PETE turns around and starts dancing to the beat and moving his lips as if he is singing. The whole cafeteria started to laugh and cheer PETE on. SADE is embarrassed, but smiles a little bit at times. PETE keeps on dancing until PRINCIPAL DE OLANO walks in. The PRINCIPAL walks over to the boom box and turns it off, but PETE keeps on dancing with his eyes closed; too caught up in his dancing. PETE keeps on dancing backwards until he bumps into the PRINCIPAL. PETE turns around slowly and his eyes widen in fear realizing who it is.)

PRINCIPAL DE OLANO: *(Calmly but serious)* In my office Mr. Hall.

(PETE, upset and embarrassed, walks out of the cafeteria offstage on the left side down to the PRINCIPAL's office.)

SCENE 7:

(PETE sits in the PRINCIPAL'S office and waits for the PRINCIPAL to come back. Sitting there pouting, he tries to think of something to ease him a bit and calm him down. The only thing that comes to mind is his favorite game, Metal Gear Solid. Thinking of that game, PETE pretends that he is a spy like Snake from the game and stands up. PETE then calls his BOSS through his imaginary radio that he is carrying.)

PETE: *(With a serious voice)* What's the mission?

BOSS: Snake, your mission is to escape the fortress with the top secret files. Okay?

PETE: Got it.

BOSS: This radio will self-destruct.

(PETE crouches in fear trying to brace for impact.)

PETE: *(Scared)* AHH!

BOSS: *(Laughs)* Sike, I'm just playing.

(PETE sucks his teeth but gets back into the game and starts to sneak around on stage. Soon, a GUARD appears on stage. PETE sneaks up behind him and puts him in a sleeper hold. The GUARD struggles, but stops moving eventually. PETE then lays him on the ground and keeps on going. Another GUARD spots him. The

GUARD runs toward PETE attempting to punch him but PETE blocks the punch, punches him two times in the stomach, and flips him over his shoulder. PETE recovers and keeps on moving. PETE sneaks around the stage some more until he somehow gets behind the OLD LADY again. PETE jerks back in shock but keeps on moving behind her. PETE stands up and starts to wind up his foot behind him in an attempt to kick her in the butt again. As soon as he releases and starts to kick, the OLD LADY turns around, catches his foot while it is in mid-air, pulls him causing PETE to fall to the floor. PETE backs up on the ground and gets up on his feet.)

OLD LADY: *(Serious)* So you like kicking old ladies huh? Let's see what you got sonny boy!

(The OLD LADY does her karate war yells. PETE does the same. They run toward each other and start to exchange blows and blocks one after another. The fight gets pretty tough, but then the OLD LADY puts out her hand and shakes as if she's struggling to walk.)

OLD LADY: *(With a sweet OLD LADY voice)* Do you mind helping an old lady like me cross the street?

(PETE stares at her for a quick second, but smiles, letting his guard down.)

PETE: Sure thing!

(PETE puts his hand for her to grab. The OLD LADY grabs his hand in a nice manner, but then flips him onto the floor. The OLD LADY pulls out her cane and tries to stomp it on PETE. PETE sees it coming a mile away and rolls away to avoid it. The OLD LADY shuffles forward and tries it again. PETE continues to roll. After his third roll, he snatches the cane.)

OLD LADY: *(In pain)* OH MY HIP!!!

(The OLD LADY falls to the ground. PETE stands up and hypes himself up.)

PETE: *(Excited)* Oh yeah! Who da' man?! In yo' face! In yo' face! IN-YO'-FACE!!!

(The OLD LADY rolls offstage. PRINCIPAL DE OLANO walks in and calls out to PETE.)

PRINCIPAL DE OLANO: *(Angry)* PETE!

(PETE snaps back to reality.)

PETE: *(Confused)* Huh?

PRINCIPAL DE OLANO: *(Upset)* Sit down.

(PETE, realizing what had happened, sits down immediately. PRINCIPAL DE OLANO walks around him.)

PRINCIPAL DE OLANO: Pete, this has been the last straw. You've been late for class, causing trouble in class — you been into a lot of trouble and I can't ignore it. I need to have a conference with your mom.

PETE: *(Scared)* No! Please don't!

PRINCIPAL DE OLANO: *(Regretful)* I'm sorry, but you brought this upon yourself.

(PETE stands up trying to defend himself.)

PETE: *(Scared)* Please, I—

(Suddenly, PETE looks away confused and grabs his stomach. Then he loses balance. PETE staggers back and forth as if the room is spinning. He tries to keep himself up but the weight seems too much for him to bear. Finally, he falls backward and faints.)

SCENE 8:

(PETE wakes up on a bed in the NURSE'S office. He looks up at the ceiling for a moment trying to recollect his thoughts. PETE thought it may have been another dream so he pinched his arm. Ouch! Nope, it wasn't a dream. PETE then realized that the PRINCIPAL was going to call his MOM and ruin Christmas. PETE pops up on the bed, but the NURSE walks in stage left and stands beside the bed.)

NURSE: *(Worried)* Take it easy.

(PETE slows down. Sitting up now, he turns to the NURSE.)

PETE: What...happened?

NURSE: *(Smiling)* Nothing to worry about. Looks like someone had some bad milk.

(PETE looks confused for a minute but then realizes that he drank some milk at lunch today.)

NURSE: You should be okay now, but unfortunately *(The NURSE frowns,)* there's nothing I can do for your head.

PETE: *(PETE looks at her shocked)* What?!

NURSE: *(Sad)* I'm sorry.

PETE: There's nothing wrong with my head. The doctor said all I need to do is put some...you know?...ice on it, and the size should go down.

NURSE: *(Confused)* Are you sure? I put the whole school's supply of ice on it and the damage seems permanent. The milk seemed to have affected your eyebrows too.

PETE: *(PETE puts his hands over them, embarrassed)* My eyebrows?!

NURSE: *(Shocked)* Yeah I tried trimming them, but they're too thick for my razors. Too bad I left my hedge clippers at home.

(The NURSE frowns. PETE opens his mouth to defend himself more, but he gives up; too tired to care anymore.)

PETE: *(Sigh)* I'm okay now.

(PETE gets up off the bed and heads toward the door.)

NURSE: *(Smiling)* Okay. Have a good day and remember, if you turn your head sideways, you'll have an easier time walking through the doorways.

PETE: Yeah okay.

(PETE walks out of the NURSE'S office and sits out in front of the door where the chairs are set up. He sits there, thinking. While he is thinking, SADE walks up beside him, coming from offstage. PETE doesn't see her though.)

PETE: *(Upset)* Man, this has got to be the worst day ever. Got in trouble, failed a quiz, got fried too many times, and now the girl I like thinks I'm a loser.

SADE: *(Smiles)* I don't think you're a loser.

(PETE turns around and realizes that she is sitting next to him.)

PETE: *(Shocked)* Really?!

SADE: Yeah. A nerd maybe...

(PETE frowns.)

SADE: ...but a cute nerd.

(SADE smiles at him. PETE smiles back, then looks down at the floor. SADE gets up and gets the boom box.)

PETE: Thanks, but I wish I could have done a better job impressing you.

SADE: How about you start now?

(SADE presses the play button. The Michael Jackson song "Don't Stop 'til You Get Enough" plays. SADE pulls PETE up and starts to dance in front of him. PETE tries to resist, but ends up joining in with her too. Then, all the people in school join in—from offstage—and start to do their own crazy dance.)

SCENE 9:

(PETE walks through his house door happy that he improved his friendship with SADE. As soon as he closed the door, his MOM was waiting there, very angry.)

PETE: *(Shocked)* Mama?

MOM: *(Angry)* Come here!

PETE: *(Scared)* NOOOOOO!!!

(MOM runs around the stage trying to catch him and eventually does. When she gets a hold of him, MOM throws fast punches to PETE'S chest. Then she puts her arm around PETE and gives him a noogie. Finally, MOM gets behind him and pulls his underwear up. PETE looks out to the audience in pain and fear screaming.)

PETE: *(In pain)* WEEEDDDDDDGGGGGGIIIIIIIIIEEEEEEE!!!!

(MOM lets go of his underwear and PETE drops to the floor in pain. Before MOM leaves, she turns around and says)

MOM: You'll still get that PS3 okay? *(In a tough voice)* BUT I STILL HAD TO JACK YOU UP!

(MOM puts her fist up and bucks at PETE. PETE flinches. She then nods her head at him with a "Umph!" and walks offstage. PETE stands up fixing his underwear. He turns to the audience. PETE laughs and says)

PETE: *(Embarrassed)* Well...um...that's-my-Momma!

(PETE goes to his bed and falls asleep dreaming of a beautiful Christmas.)

End of Play

Unforgettable
by Zainep Mahmoud (2002)

ABOUT ZAINEP

What grade were you in when you wrote your play? 10th

What school did you attend? Benjamin Banneker Academic High School

Where do you go to school now? I'm pursuing an MBA at The Wharton School, University of Pennsylvania.

What do you like to do for fun? Read tween novels (Hunger Games!), run, spin, watch trashy reality TV with friends.

Is there anything you'd like to say to the readers of this book? Young Playwrights' Theater exposed my high school classmates and me to the incredible world of playwriting – from the idea conception phase all the way through seeing the play performed. What is most striking is seeing the creative and truly thought-provoking plots high school students compose. I hope this book provides readers with a look into the minds of our youth in a fun, creative, exciting way.

Characters:

AHMED MOHAMMED, male, in a long-term relationship with Amy

AMY MITCHELL, female, in a long-term relationship with Ahmed

YUSUF RAHMAN, (YOO-suf Rah-MAN), male

KESHIA CLARKE (Ke-SIII-ah), female, good friends with Rocio

ROCIO CIFUENTES, (Ro-CI-o Cifu-EN-tes), female, good friends with Keshia

ANNOUNCER, with a deep, dark, "God-like" voice, is never seen

MYSTERIOUS MAN

TICKET PERSON, male or female

SCENE 1: *In a coffee shop.*

(All characters are seated and there are sound effects of people conversing in the background. When characters speak, everything pauses except for the character(s) speaking. All characters are addressing the audience in the first scene unless otherwise told. AHMED MOHAMMED is fidgeting nervously. There is a ring box on the table.)

AHMED MOHAMMED: You see, there's this girl. She is the most beautiful woman I've ever met. She's smart, sweet, everything a guy could want. We've been together for 6 years now and I think I'm ready to pop the

181

question today on our anniversary…but I'm having doubts. She's aight…but her cooking can use some help. She's fine but in the morning, her breath is her…

(AHMED looks at his watch, takes a sip and motions to leave when he remembers he was talking to the audience and doesn't want to be rude. He looks at the crowd and says:)

AHMED: Sorry, got to catch my flight to LA, got to see the love of my life.

(He departs. ROCIO and KESHIA are giggling silently, watch AHMED depart rapidly, look at each other, shrug their shoulders, and look to the audience.)

ROCIO: I can't wait until I get to Harvard.

KESHIA: Me neither. I saw the campus on *Legally Blonde*, looks nice.

ROCIO: See, we've been friends for a long time and we've decided to go to the same college.

KESHIA: We're here on a college tour. First we are sightseeing here in Boston, and then we'll travel to Cambridge, Massachusetts to see Harvard.

ROCIO: Can't wait…

(Both characters look at each other and smile, and continue to chat silently while background sound effects begin again. Characters move for a short time and pause again for the introduction of the next character. YUSUF RAHMAN is wearing a head wrap—he is a Sikh. A newspaper and a red marker are lying in front of him on the table.)

YUSUF: I don't have a happy story to tell you, l don't have a sad one either. My world revolves around my family and wife, whom I love dearly. We have a baby on the way. I hope it's a girl. I have always wanted a girl to look up to me as a protector. Now I'm looking for work here in Boston. I live in Andover, Massachusetts, which isn't too far from here. I hope I have some better luck in the future.

(He takes a sip of his drink, sighs, and opens the newspaper with the red Sharpie® pen and circles two "advertisements". The background noises should have already begun. The set is dimmed and everything freezes. A dark and deep toned voice presents itself.)

ANNOUNCER: Airlines flight 11 crashed into the World Trade Centers. American Airlines flight 77 crashed into the Pentagon and United Airlines flight 175 crashed in Northern Pennsylvania. This is another day that will live in infamy.

SCENE 2:

(Scene begins with a woman with an apron on, mixing something in a bowl. She then pours the substance into a pan and puts it into an oven. She is humming and smiling while cooking.)

AMY: Today is the 6th year of my relationship with this wonderful man. I think he might ask me to marry him.

(AMY makes a gleeful shriek.)

AMY: I haven't done anything today but prepare his favorite meal squid casserole with a side of turnips and pumpkin juice. *(Another gleeful shriek)* He just adores my cooking!

(AMY prances around the kitchen, takes the food out of the oven, and places it on the stove. AMY looks at the watch, wipes her hands on her apron and takes it off. She places the apron on a chair, grabs her coat, and throws it over her arm.)

AMY: He doesn't know but I'm going to surprise him at the airport!

(AMY runs out prancing, smiling and humming.)

SCENE 3:

(Scene changes with ROCIO and KESHIA back at home. They are walking towards KESHIA'S home.)

KESHIA: I'm glad we live so close to Cambridge that we just drove home.

ROCIO: Yeah. I wish we could have stayed there longer, I wouldn't have minded a few extra hours of sleep.

(KESHIA stops dead in her tracks and notices the door to her house slightly ajar. She slowly opens the door and sees her house in ruins. KESHIA quickly looks around the house. She looks at ROCIO with tears in her eyes. She closes the door and on the back of the door it says in large letters "MUSLIM BASTARDS, GET OUT OF OUR COUNTRY". The letters are visible to the crowd and KESHIA and ROCIO both jump in shock.)

KESHIA: Why would anyone do such a thing?

(ROCIO slowly makes her way to the television and turns it on. The announcer says:)

ANNOUNCER: After this morning's terror attacks a rash of hate crimes against Muslims have occurred across the nation. Muslim women stayed inside and racial profiling is running rampant though the U.S.

(KESHIA and ROCIO look at each other with hurt, pain and worry. They slowly reach each other and hug. Lights dim. Scene changes.)

SCENE 4:

(AMY walks into the airport happily. She looks around and there are people crying all around her.)

AMY: I wonder what's wrong with those people. It's a beautiful day today.

(AMY shrugs it off and continues walking towards the terminal. She sees a ticket desk and walks up to the counter.)

AMY: Excuse me (Ma'am or sir, whichever the gender of the ticket person may be). When will Flight 93 arrive?

TICKET PERSON: Uh...ma'am—

AMY: Oh, is it delayed?

TICKET PERSON: Well, not—

AMY: Oh no, not canceled, right? I cooked his favorite dinner and everything.

(AMY'S sentence trails off. The TICKET PERSON walks over to AMY ready to console her after telling her the news.)

TICKET PERSON: Ma'am, flight 93 was one of the planes that crashed into the World Trade Center. I'm sorry for your loss—

(The TICKET PERSON is cut off by AMY'S sudden exasperation as she almost falls to the floor. The TICKET PERSON catches AMY and slowly helps her take a seat. AMY'S hands are over her face as she cries. Lights dim. Scene changes.)

SCENE 5:

(YUSUF RAHMAN is walking towards the train station with a small bag in his left hand and a cellular phone up to his right ear, talking.)

YUSUF: Yes dear...yes...but I...okay. Fine. I've got it, one quart of ice cream and a jar of pickles. No honey, after this morning all the businesses closed...No, not much luck. I know. There's always tomorrow. Okay honey, I'll be right home. Bye.

(YUSUF presses a button on his phone and slips it into his pocket. He continues walking and out of nowhere a MAN steps in front of YUSUF. YUSUF tries to walk around the man but the man is unwilling to move for him.)

YUSUF: Excuse me, sir.

MYSTERIOUS MAN: My wife was working in that tower.

YUSUF: (YUSUF, caught off guard says) My apologies sir, but I must get home to my wife.

(YUSUF motions to get around the man but the man stops him by placing his hand on YUSUF'S chest.)

MYSTERIOUS MAN: NO! You aren't going anywhere until you hear my story.

(YUSUF, having no time to answer hugs the bag of pickles and ice cream close to his chest with a bewildered look upon his face.)

MYSTERIOUS MAN: I loved that woman ever since I was in the 10th grade. She was my one and only. She was the first woman who ever loved me back.

(MAN beings to sob, his hand still on YUSUF'S chest.)

MYSTERIOUS MAN: We got married 13 years ago and next month would be our 14th anniversary. I was going to take her on the honeymoon I was never able to give her. But now because of you radical Middle Eastern Muslims, I can't experience one last kiss from my...my... *(MAN heavily sobbing now)* my only true love.

YUSUF: No, sir, you see I'm not Muslim.

(YUSUF abruptly cut off by the MYSTERIOUS MAN speaking again.)

MYSTERIOUS MAN: You did this to my wife. You did this to me and I HATE YOU FOR THIS!!

(As soon as the MAN finishes this statement, he IMMEDIATELY takes out a knife and stabs YUSUF. YUSUF falls to the ground. The man looks at the audience. He looks at YUSUF, spits at him. The MAN runs and then the lights cut off. Scene ends. 3 second pause before next scene begins.)

SCENE 6:

(Begins with the voice of the ANNOUNCER.)

ANNOUNCER: We as a nation have suffered many losses since September 11, 2001. Some losses were the product of our ignorance. We are a culturally diverse country and with cultural diversity comes the need for understanding. Understanding of one another's feelings, beliefs and customs. Be kind to one another and let us grasp the *true* concept of racial and religious harmony. Begin to take advantage of America's melting pot and let us all become united as one.

(During the reading of this paragraph, all characters should walk onto the stage in a line with their heads slightly lowered. The lights are dimmed and will rise steadily with the continuation of the paragraph. By the sentence "Be kind to one another and let us grasp the true concept of racial and religious harmony" all characters should be holding hands. With the words "united as one" all characters are still holding hands and are now raised in the air and all characters are slightly smiling.)

End of Play

Society Unjust

by Shannon Marshall (2011)

<table>
<tr><td>

<u>ABOUT SHANNON</u>

What grade were you in when you wrote your play? 11th

What school did you attend? Bell Multicultural High School

Where do you go to school now? I am a full time student at Lincoln University.

What do you like to do for fun? I like to write poetry, watch movies and hang out with family and friends.

Is there anything you'd like to say to the readers of this book? This play inspired me to think creatively to make change in my community. Overall I had tons of fun making my play.

</td></tr>
</table>

Characters:

JANE

DEVELOPER

SARAH

ALICIA

PARAMEDIC

MR. BRAXSTON

SCENE:

(JANE is a very elderly woman in her late 70's. Her home is filled with heirlooms and trinkets and they line her fireplace. There are pictures on every wall—some old, some new. In her living room sits an old couch and an older model TV with the antennas covered in aluminum foil. She is sitting down on her couch watching TV. She is all alone in the meadows of her living room speaking out to her deceased husband.)

JANE: Charles, Charles, my god I miss you. I wish you were here. Everywhere I turn there's another burden to bear. It sometimes seems as though life ain't worth living. How I wish I could lay on your chest and hear your heartbeat. My, oh my, I'm so scared, I remember in our younger years, before the children, you'd kiss me on the forehead and tell me hush my worrying everything goin' work out fine. But who's here to tell me that now? I just don't know. Just came from the doctors, they says I got cancer and my long life is short lived. They estimate a year or two time before I die out. And I can't get life insurance 'cause

I'm too old. Oh my, what am I going to do about Alicia? I raised her from knee high to a pump. All her life all she ever had was me since her mother died. And who's going take care of this big ole house when I'm gone...(*Knock at the door*) Now who the hell could this be interrupting me?

(*JANE opens the door.*)

JANE: Hello.

(*A tall medium build Caucasian man dressed in a cheap cheesy black and blue pin stripe suit and glasses approaches the door.*)

DEVELOPER: (*In a mechanical voice*) Hi I'm from Braxston Developers and Co. and I want to purchase your home.

JANE: Excuse my rudeness, but who are you?

DEVELOPER: Jim Braxston...Braxston and Co. Developers.

JANE: Purchase my home? (*Angrily*) Have you lost your mind and for what reasons?

DEVELOPER: Well, see this is an up-and-coming area and I believe this area would be a perfect spot for a coffee shop.

JANE: So mister you're telling me you want me to sell you my home full of all my memories and priceless heirlooms and fortunes so you can cook beans...Well boy I don't believe you're using the good senses God gave you. If I was your grandmother I'd beat you with an ugly stick.

DEVELOPER: I'll make you an offer you can't refuse.

JANE: Oh really? Huh. Mr. Developer Man, tell me of your offer.

DEVELOPER: I am prepared to offer you 200,000 dollars.

JANE: So you mean to tell me if I pack up all my memories and everything I have ever knew and love, all you'll give me is 200,000 dollars?

DEVELOPER: Yes indeed.

JANE: You selfish selfless son of a bitch boy if you do not get the hell off my porch I am going to stick my foot where the sun will never shine, you hear me?

(*JANE slams the door, she is very upset and mumbling. She sits back on her couch trying to calm herself down still seething anger then the phone rings.*)

JANE: Hella.

SARAH: Heyyyy girl.

JANE: Hey Sarah.

SARAH: Jane, what the matter? Take a load off your mind, gurl.

JANE: Well girl it is these developers trying to take advantage of us senior citizens like we dumb or straight trippin'. I just don't get it, what has this generation come to? Sell our souls for a sorry piece of change.

SARAH: Well girl you ain't never lied, them developers came passed my house today as well and he offered me a real pretty penny for my ole shack and I'm thinking about considering. 300,000 dollars would do my pockets just fine.

JANE: Girl I should beat the ignorance right out you…don't you remember growing up in that house and raising your kids and even still today watching your grandkids grow up?

SARAH: But hey, I've waited my whole life for something like this.

JANE: I have too, but I'd be damned if I'll sell my soul…with a greedy money hungry attitude like that you goin' die alone and your children going to rip you off for every penny…*(JANE lies)* Well girl, my granddaughter Alicia is on the other line so Ima call you back. Talk to you later.

SARAH: All right, take it easy.

JANE: Charles what am I to do? This burden is too hard to bear. I've come this far — 78 years I've been working hard tryin' to raise our family with the scrapings we were given, now my life dilemma is sell my home or die. What type of life is that to live? I'll probably end up like that woman from *Steel Magnolias*. Leave out the hospital and be watching a vacant lot questioning where is my home? Nah, not me I'm going do what I can. In addition, prepare for the worst. I sells my soul before I sell this house. Haha shoot thinking about all the time we shared here. I remember when we first got married you carried me in here — you were always big and strong. I wish you were here to take care of me.

(JANE hears a knock on the door.)

JANE: OH great, you here again. *(Sarcastically)* What you want now, a lung?

DEVELOPER: Jane, wow you are a funny woman.

JANE: Well tell that to my shoe as it's kicking your ass down these steps. Now get off my porch.

DEVELOPER: Jane I think we have really started on the wrong foot. Just think about it — you sell me your home and you'll have extra money to retire, spend on the grandkids, perhaps you have some medical bills—

JANE: *(Cuts him off)* Yeah I should have kicked your ass the first time.

DEVELOPER: Jane, I really think we have gotten off on the wrong foot. Let's be friends.

JANE: *(Angrily)* Redneck cracker please. Listen here, I do not know who misinformed you, but I ain't stupid. Do not pull that bullshit on me I've got plenty of sense and morals. One thing I know for sure is I can smell bullshit a mile away and you stink. So get your redneck cracker ass off my porch cuz this house here ain't for sale.

(JANE picks up the DEVELOPER'S brief case and throws it at him. Out falls his business card. JANE picks it up and heads back in her house startled.)

JANE: Damn Charles they just won't let me live in peace. I'm just an old lady with not too much time on my hands. My heart can stop at any point but I'm going to keep my faith, that's all I have. Growing up with no degree or no real education has it effects. I can't afford to live. But I can't give away all I have to make coffee beans. Well damn wait Charles, now I'm thinking. I'm being pretty selfish, what about the life Alicia was promised to have? I would miss our first great grandchild growing up. Damn, I won't even see it, if I don't get this cancer cured. Won't nothing work in my favor. But it is true Charles, we've always dreamed about our great grandchildren.

(There is a knock at the door. It is JANE'S granddaughter ALICIA, looking happier than usual.)

ALICIA: Hey Grandma.

JANE: *(She welcomes ALICIA inside.)* Alicia honey, I swear you look more and more grown every time I see you. How you been? I've missed you. It gets lonely in this house sometimes.

ALICIA: Wow Grandma I'm so excited I've got so much to tell you.

JANE: *(Sadly)* I've got a lot to tell you, too.

ALICIA: For real Grandma? What's wrong?

JANE: Ummm I have…I better let you tell me your news first.

ALICIA: You sure?

JANE: Yeah.

ALICIA: Well Grandma guess what? *(ALICIA takes her hand out her pocket to show a ring.)* OMG Grandma I'm getting MARRIED. I'm so excited!

JANE: I can't believe it I'm so proud. Lawd have mercy my chile is getting' married who would've believed. Wow time flies.

ALICIA: Yeah we're just trying to get finances together so we can save up for a house and a great wedding.

JANE: You just hush that whinin' and worrying. My grandbaby is getting married. You betta believe it. And afterwards you'll have this big ole place to call your own. Just promise me — whatever happens you'll *always* keep this place in the family.

ALICIA: I promise, Grandma. But Grandma I didn't come over to burden you.

JANE: Chile I ain't got no burdens.

(ALICIA'S phone rings. As she answers it, a smile comes over her face.)

JANE: It's that fiancé of yours on that telly ain't it?

ALICIA: Yeah he wants to meet me for lunch. I hate to just come and go like this.

JANE: Chile don't keep that man waiting, now go on.

(ALICIA leaves.)

JANE: Charles, Charles more and more problems. Where does this madness end? I'm tighter than a rock in a hard place right now. Maybe it is time to say goodbye to this old place. I mean I know how hard we've suffered and worked hard to make this place a home. But Alicia wants to get married and money is tighter than a fat lady in a girdle. I just don't know. If I sell this place it can give Alicia the wedding of her dreams. And if get these treatments paid for and done I can live to see it and help raise my great grandbaby. Or I can leave her the house where she can raise generation like us. Or maybe I should give her a fresh start and sell this place.

(JANE falls asleep. Two days later ALICIA knocks on JANE'S door. Left with an uneasy feeling she finds the spare key and charges open the door where she runs to JANE'S room and finds her pale and lifeless.)

ALICIA: Oh, God Jesus please do not let this be. I know I do not pray or go to church very often. But grant me this one last prayer. Lawd lawd lawd *(Tears)* my grandma is all I have, the only one I can trust, the only one who gives me support when I think I'm outta of luck. Take her and I'll be all alone.

(Begging and pleading on the floor she dials 911 hysterically crying. The PARAMEDICS enter.)

PARAMEDIC: Alicia, can I speak to you for a moment?

ALICIA: Yes.

PARAMEDIC: We have tried to revive your grandmother, but it appears she has had a heart attack.

(ALICIA drops to the ground in disbelief, screaming. The PARAMEDICS try to calm her down. They put JANE'S body on a stretcher. ALICIA walks around, looking for answers and questioning the thoughts of this bitter tragedy.)

ALICIA: *(Shaking her head with tears in her eyes)* All the dreams she instilled in

me, all the hope she gave me. Grandma, you cannot leave like this.
You are all the family I got. And all I ever had. You raised me from the
time I was a second old. Never knew my pain would be this deep.
Grandma Grandma Grandma how could you leave me all alone in this
cold, cold world? Damn Grandma, how could you?

*(ALICIA sits at her grandma JANE'S table covered in old newspapers and fixings.
ALICIA'S eyes take keen to a business card under JANE's coffee cup. It reads: Jim
Braxston Business Developer. As she moves the paper on top of the business card,
a letter written in JANE'S handwriting reads final testaments and wishes. As she
reads it, we hear JANE'S voice.)*

JANE:

Dear Alicia,

If you're reading this I'm gone to meet our maker. I've seen all I can.
Now the future and my footsteps are in your hands. Just know that
even though I've gone with the lord, I'll always be here. Just make
good of your promise and keep my home a place where my great
grandchildren can grow up. Don't shed a tear just know I'm with
Charles now — to heaven where I belong. Just grant my final wish and
keep this house a home.

Love always, Grandma.

*(She reads the will through and through while bawling tears. Then she picks up
the business card from underneath the will. She dials the phone number listed.)*

ALICIA: Hello, Mr.Braxston?

MR. BRAXSTON: Yes?

ALICIA: Well my name is Alicia Collins. I'm Ms. Jane's granddaughter. Ms.
Jane has just deceased due to natural causes and I would like to know
— did you speak with her in the last two days? I happened to find
your card next to her will.

MR. BRAXSTON: Yes, I did speak with her. I was offering to purchase her
home. Are you interested?

ALICIA: How much are you offering?

MR. BRAXSTON: $150,000 dollars.

ALICIA: Wow. I could never sell my grandma's home.

MR. BRAXSTON: Well it's been nice talking to you, but I'm late for meeting. I
must go now.

(ALICIA hangs up the phone and looks around…confused.)

ALICIA: What to do, what to do? Keep this home, or build a new one where
my family can get a fresh start? I've had my memories in here, maybe

it's time for new scenery. Too much has happened. I can't bear the
thought of being in this place without Grandma.

(ALICIA picks back up the card with an uneasy feeling and makes a call.)
ALICIA: Mr. Braxston? I reconsider.

(The effervescence of JANE'S presence left in her home is slowly heart broken. Everything JANE has ever loved is now being handed over to her worst enemy, a DEVELOPER. Her heart is cold. Her world, even smaller. Her last words echo in the heavenly skies.)

JANE:

I am all alone my childhood home where my big wheel lies.
And my inner child died
is no longer just condominiums and over priced housing.
Playgrounds are lonely, boring lots waiting to be turned into dog
parks.
Where corner stores were sacred my block feels naked for they've been
turned into coffee shops.
Where four quarters and a dollar can't even get you a cup of water.
But why the gentrification and commercialization of blocks where,
grandmothers and fathers broke backs and slaved for us to have
luxuries and see brighter days.
In which with our ignorant ways they would turn in their graves
to see we're exchanging our hard earned cash
into the government's hand because they need more land.

End of Play

Playwright Profile: Engedasew Menkir

"I want to be a filmmaker," Engedasew Menkir says in an interview with YPT, folding his hands in front of him. "Before working with YPT, that never crossed my mind."

It's no surprise that Engedasew is able to balance filmmaking ambitions, a college career and a job with the DC Restaurant Association. In the seven years since he immigrated to the United States from Ethiopia, he has excelled, graduating from Bell Multicultural High School and moving on to Colorado State University to major in biology. Now in the process of transferring to Salisbury College in Maryland, he writes when he has time between school and working. As a child in Ethiopia, he dreamed of being an artist.

"My mom was a singer," he explains with a small smile, "so I grew up with the arts, around artists. But now I'm focusing on science. Your parents want you to do science, or engineering, or be a doctor. I know they mean well. They're looking after my best interests, but at the same time, they don't consider what makes me happy, just what makes me stable for the future. Those two things are…very different."

As an eleventh grader, Engedasew was reintroduced to the arts when his YPT teaching artist, Patrick, visited his English classroom to teach the **In-School Playwriting Program**. The result of Engedasew's work in those twelve workshops is a remarkable, heartbreaking play entitled *Puzzle*. *Puzzle* explores the 9/11 terrorist attacks through the eyes of a Secret Service agent whose wife and daughter are aboard one of the planes headed for the World Trade Center.

"That was the first thing I'd written in my life," Engedasew says. "My main inspiration was my classmates coming up with their own topics because most of them wrote about teen pregnancy, immigration, love…common topics that they could really relate to. But I wanted to come

195

up with something really different."

YPT selected *Puzzle* for production in the 2008 **New Play Festival,** an experience that Engedasew still remembers well. "It's really encouraging when you write something and it's performed right there in front of you, seeing the characters come to life...it's an incredible experience."

While YPT revealed a love for script-writing that Engedasew didn't know he had, he also feels like the experience helped him in more practical ways.

"Before, when I wrote for class, I didn't read it back. I would just submit it," he says. "With YPT, there are mentors that look at your work and tell you where you should make changes. They encourage you to go back and revise, and trace back your steps to complete the puzzle. It enhanced my writing, not only with storytelling, but writing in general. Essays...even journals."

Engedasew continued working with YPT after his play was produced by joining the **Young Playwrights' Workshop,** YPT's student theater ensemble, which allowed him to further refine his writing skills. Currently, he is working on a screenplay for an action movie.

"YPT was really important because it introduced me to writing stories," he says thoughtfully. "Now I know I'm capable of creating stories. I'm independent; I don't have to rely on other's stories. I can create my own."

Puzzle
by Engedasew Menkir (2008)

ABOUT ENGEDASEW

What grade were you in when you wrote your play? 11th

What school did you attend? Bell Multicultural High School

What do you do now? I work for the DC Restaurant Association, and am in the process of transferring from Colorado State to Salisbury University in Maryland.

What do you like to do for fun? Honestly, I watch a lot of movies. But I don't watch for pure entertainment, but for how solid the plot is. The characters must be convincing, and the story must be realistic enough so that I can relate to it.

Is there anything you'd like to say to the readers of this book? This was my first attempt at writing suspense!

How far are you willing to play the game when you lost the last two pieces of the puzzle?

For what will you FIGHT?

LIVE?

DIE for?

Characters:

PATRICK

EMILY

HELEN

MARK

ALEX

ACT I, SCENE 1: *Friday, September 7, 2001. Los Angeles, CA airport.*

PATRICK: Honey, did you have everything you need in your hand bag?

EMILY: Yes, don't worry, I have everything taken care of.

PATRICK: I still can't see why you are taking Helen with you because she should stay with me until you finished your book tour.

EMILY: Didn't we discuss about this? Every time when I step outside I am constantly worried about her. Is she eating, is she alright? Is she sleeping well? Did she have her lunch?

PATRICK: You worry about this? This is what we do, we are parents. This is our job and obligation as parents to take care of this entire situation. Besides, I have her medication so what is the whole point of having her in your book tour? Wait a second, are you challenging my ability as a father?

(She smiles and puts her hand on his shoulder.)

EMILY: Well, I would say no for that trick question. *(She smiles.)* Honestly, you are incredible husband and wonderful father to our daughter. I have no doubt you are the best father any kid can ask for.

PATRICK: You know what?

EMILY: What?

PATRICK: This is the sweetest thing you ever said to me.

EMILY: What can I say, I love you.

PATRICK: The problem is I love you even more.

EMILY: The other problem I have with you is your stupid job. We need to share a quality time together, just you and me. More importantly, I want the whole family to be together like good old times. Is it too much to ask? Besides, I would do anything for us to be in that place you and I always wanted before we got married.

PATRICK: Honey I know how much you've been through because of me and I really do. But what I am going to do if I quit my job? Who's going to take care of you and our daughter? You tell me.

EMILY: Patrick, this hasn't been the issue. If you really thought through it you could have found a very decent job that pays you enough money and more importantly, a much less life threatening situation. Do you know how many times I have nightmares that one day you will not show up in our house? Do you?

PATRICK: This discussion is over. We will discuss this when you come back. But I want you to be safe and happy. I promise you, baby, I will do what ever it takes to make you happy.

(Ladies and gentlemen, Flight 284 to Boston is now boarding.)

EMILY: I guess that is us. I will call you when we land. I love you.

PATRICK: Let me talk to my beautiful little princess.

HELEN: Hi Daddy.

PATRICK: Well sweetie, I will see you after four days okay. Be behaved.

HELEN: Okay daddy.

PATRICK: Give your daddy a little sugar.

(She kisses her daddy and hugs him.)

PATRICK: That is too tight. Save me some sugar okay, baby.

HELEN: Can I give mammy some?
PATRICK: Well just a little.
HELEN: Okay.

ACT I, SCENE 2: A phone conversation between MARK (DOD) and PATRICK (airport).
PATRICK: This is Patrick.
MARK: Patrick we need you to get here immediately.
PATRICK: Talk to me, Mark.
MARK: Military chief of staff is headed to the FBI board meeting today. Sixty Secret Service members had been asked to report to the White House immediately for a debriefing.
PATRICK: Sixty Secret Services agents! What for?
MARK: I think that something horrible is going to happen.
(Department of Defense, Washington, DC. As he is passing through the working station, people are running around from one place to another. Two of his colleagues come from the conference room when they see him in the hallway.)
MARK: It is good have you back.
PATRICK: Cut to the chase, Mark. Give me an update about this situation.
ALEX: The president wants a small group of people to establish a new unit that could investigate terrorist activity in Los Angeles. The president and his advisors already sent a list of names that this team should target the most. The main point of this team is to analyze and investigate documents of all people who work for the government and retired three years ago.
PATRICK: As far as I am concerned this is priority one and top secret.
MARK: The location is here in DOD but this special unit has the most power of any other agency around the nation. Besides, all of the DOD systems run through this office and all of the other agency databases are here as well. More satellites are dedicated for this particular unit so that the investigation may proceed quickly and effectively.
PATRICK: Good job boys.
(Then, he goes to his office which is located one set of stairs above the working stations. As he reaches the top level of the stairs he turns back to make an announcement.)
PATRICK: Excuse me. Excuse me, ladies and gentlemen, may I have your attention please. As some of you may already know by now, this country received an unidentified threat. Our job is to use all of our

sources to catch these terrorists before they take the lives of millions. This special unit is officially beginning functioning, and please let us use the time wisely.

ACT I, SCENE 3: Monday, September 10, 2001 10:07 pm. Los Angeles, CA. (PATRICK is in his office doing some paper work. He glances at the clock that is attached to the wall of his office. His cell rings.)

PATRICK: Patrick speaking.

EMILY: Hi, baby, how are you holding on?

PATRICK: So far everything is alright I guess. How is it going on over there?

EMILY: It was amazing. I signed over a thousand autographs, met new people, and discovered something that I didn't know before.

PATRICK: Such as?

EMILY: I discovered how much I love you and realized how much you mean to me.

PATRICK: How much do I mean to you?

EMILY: You mean everything in the whole world to me. I would trade everything I own to be with you more than anything. How much do I mean to you?

PATRICK: I couldn't put in words how much you mean to me. To be honest, words are not good enough. Not even a melody.

EMILY: If you really mean that why don't you do one simple thing for me, quit your job?

PATRICK: Here it goes again. You are never going to drop this will you? Here in this office the situation is different. Things are changing and I can't say things precisely, but I will do something about it before you even mention it again.

EMILY: I don't know Patrick but one day my tears, my begging, and patience will hunt you down.

PATRICK: Is that a threat or a comment? I couldn't figure it out? Would you mind clarifying your statement please because I just couldn't believe what I just heard?

EMILY: You can view my statement from any perspective as you wish.

PATRICK: Thank you for the clarification, that really helps a lot. Anyhow, what flight are you taking?

EMILY: United Airlines Flight 175. I will call you from the plane.

PATRICK: Say hi to Helen and tell her daddy loves you so much. I love you.

(As soon as he finished his conversation, MARK comes in.)

MARK: Patrick you should see this.

(*PATRICK follows MARK to downstairs to see how far they are going in the investigation to find the terrorist attack.*)

PATRICK: What do we have here?

ALEX: We found something that could be the first strike. Based on accumulated sources, the attempt they have in mind is to explode the White House in Washington, D.C.

PATRICK: How reliable is the source?

ALEX: Well, the source came from the White House and they sent the voicemail here for more analysis.

PATRICK: Mark, I need two computer analysts, one field op, and two computer security programmers in the conference room in five minutes. Alex, I want you to get me Homeland Security on the phone right now. Go.

(*MARK and ALEX leave.*)

ACT I, SCENE 4: Tuesday, September 11, 2001, 6:00 AM. DOD substation, Los Angeles, CA.

(*Everybody is running around doing everything they can to protect the people of the United States 24/7.*)

PATRICK: People may I have your attention please; we have an imminent airborne security threat. Our job is to distinguish good planes from bad. As we study, the subject is targeting the Capitol. I need every plane down on the ground except Air Force One.

MARK: I need everyone to work on finding the following flight numbers: American Airlines Flight 77, United Airlines Flight 93, and United Airlines Flight 175.

PATRICK: Did you say United Airlines Flight 175?

MARK: Yes. What is going on, Patrick?

PATRICK: Where does this flight regularly depart from?

MARK: East Boston, Massachusetts. Why?

PATRICK: Oh Jesus lord, this is not happening.

(*He quickly runs to his office to confirm the ID of the real flight. He opens his office door wide open and rushes to his seat. Soon after he takes a seat, he makes a phone call to United Airlines for confirmation. After realizing his wife is on board the same plane the terrorists hijacked, he comes to his senses where he can only think of not seeing his wife for the rest of his life.*)

PATRICK: Everything shattered in front of my eyes. It hurts so bad when you are so close to losing someone you really care about. Baby, I miss you so much.

(He is on his knees and cries deeply. As he is on his knees crying, MARK runs to him to tell him an update about the planes. As soon as MARK sees him, he immediately runs toward PATRICK and asks him what is wrong with him.)

MARK: Patrick what happened? Is everything alright?

PATRICK: Oh lord, why? *(He cries more.)* Why do bad things happen to good people? I miss her so much. Now, I know. Now I know, honey, how you felt all this time.

MARK: What are you talking about?

PATRICK: Mark, Emily is on Flight 175.

(MARK takes three steps back and holds his head.)

PATRICK: I don't know what am I going to do? I am losing my mind by all of the things happening.

ACT I, SCENE 5: *Tuesday, September 11, 7:47 AM. DOD Substation, Los Angeles, CA.*

(PATRICK pulls himself together and puts on his work face as he runs to his office. As he is having a conversation with his co-workers, MARK comes over to him and tells him a new intel about where the plane is heading.)

PATRICK: I want everybody to work together because the next half an hour will be important for the investigation. There are many people's lives at risk. We should use all of our effort and time to apprehend these criminals before they make disaster. This is priority one. I need all of the information you have on screen one and every single move of Flight 175 as well because the plane just turned direction and headed to New York. Let's go people.

MARK: Patrick, you won't believe what just happened.

PATRICK: What are you talking about?

MARK: NSA was planning to eliminate the threat but failed to do so. The order came from the White House.

PATRICK: You mean to take down the Flight 175?

MARK: Yes. However, the plane is in red zone and if it continues to do what they originally planned the casualty will be hideous. *(After a few seconds)* I am sorry about this Patrick. I shouldn't have told you.

PATRICK: Don't worry, Mark, I wasn't surprised because this is the procedure you are willing to make to save millions of lives.

(PATRICK'S eyes fill with tears. MARK goes over to him and hugs him. In that

exact moment ALEX shows up in PATRICK'S office.)

ALEX: Sorry for the interruption, Patrick, but we have Flight 175 on the big screen. You should take a look at it.

(8:10 AM. Everybody is standing watching the big screen, motionless and knowing there is nothing they can do to prevent the disaster from happening. 8:13 AM. PATRICK is shaking and filled with emotion but at the same time he tries to control his feelings. All of the things are in the terrorists' hands. They can do whatever they wish to do because they have total control of the plane. Everybody is staring at the big screen that shows Flight 175, some are holding their heads in disbelief, some are crying, and some cry on others' shoulders. PATRICK moves closer to the big screen, his cellular phone rings with a tone that indicates a voicemail. He immediately opens his phone and hears his voicemail. As soon as he hears the voice of his wife, tears start to pour down from his eyes like rain.)

EMILY: *(Voice of EMILY and she is crying)* I am hoping by now you know everything what is happening in this plane. I hope one day I will see you, maybe not in this life but the next. I want you to know everything we had in our life has been wonderful. You were my friend when I had none. No matter what happens, I want you to move on in your life. The life you and I had always has a special place in my heart.

(EMILY asks her daughter to say goodbye to her dad for the last time. HELEN is crying and choking in tears as she, crumbling, says to her dad, "I love you Daddy." EMILY continues.)

EMILY: I want you to remember one thing, how much Helen and I love you. *(He consciously sits on the floor. Tears start raining relentlessly.)* For all beginnings there is an end and today mine has just ended. People should have to know what is real and what is not. Someone should guide this young species how to find joy in their life because if you are here with me witnessing all this tragedy you wouldn't believe what you see. I love you so much.

(As the voicemail ends and in a matter of seconds the big screen reveals the downfall of many innocent people in the New York twin towers.)

End of Play

Rare and Exotic

by Josh Perles (2002)

ABOUT JOSH

What grade were you in when you wrote your play? 10th
What school did you attend? Wilson High School
Where do you go to school now? New York University School of Law
What do you like to do for fun? Play ultimate frisbee. Read science fiction.
Is there anything you'd like to say to the readers of this book? If you never do anything that scares you, or makes you uncomfortable, you will never know what you are actually capable of.

Characters:
KEITH
MAN
POLICEMAN
AGENT
SECRETARY

SCENE 1:
(KEITH is walking along, pulling a MAN behind him by the hand. KEITH looks very nervous and is glancing around but the MAN has a placid, emotionless look and doesn't blink often. They walk along briefly and finally reach KEITH's car. He quickly opens the door and ushers the MAN into the back seat. He then runs around to the other side of the car, jumps in, puts his hands on the wheel and sighs in relief.)

SCENE 2:
(KEITH starts car and while they are driving along, KEITH is giving the MAN sidelong glances every once in a while. The MAN remains deadpan and emotionless except when specified and speaks in a very calm, borderline monotone voice.)
KEITH: Well, that's finally over.
MAN: It is, isn't it.
KEITH: Almost, at least. (Keeps one hand on the wheel and reaches his hand back to the MAN)
KEITH: Hi, I'm Keith, I don't think I got your name, I rarely do when...well

you know.

(MAN looks at hand, takes it after a slight delay.)

MAN: I don't believe I do know what you mean and I don't know my name.
It seems I don't know much.

KEITH: Can't blame you, living like that.

MAN: Like what?

KEITH: I'll explain later. We'll have lots of time together, getting to the
shelter for people...well people like you. We'll be friends. Friends out
of utility. Sound good to you. *(Smiles)*

(MAN smiles.)

MAN: I'd like that.

(Siren wails, KEITH looks in rear view mirror)

KEITH: It's a policeman; I'm stopping. Don't do anything out of the
ordinary. *(Looks back)* Well,...more out of the ordinary.

(POLICEMAN walks up to car)

POLICEMAN: May I see your identity card?

KEITH: Of course. *(Hands card)*

POLICEMAN: *(Looks into back seat)* Who is he?

KEITH: He's with me. I'm just taking him home for dinner.

POLICEMAN: OK, everything seems fine. *(Smiles, and relaxes posture)*
Dispatch radio'd in a theft and I'm supposed to stop every car with
two people in it. As you can see, the road isn't too busy. *(Chuckle)*
You're the first excuse to turn on my siren all day. Sorry to slow you
down, drive safely. *(Walks away from car waving)*

(KEITH restarts car and begins to drive away.)

KEITH: You hungry?

MAN: Yes, a little.

KEITH: Okay, we'll stop, I'm hungry too. We can't take too long though,
that cop is going to radio us in.

MAN: He was...

KEITH: That went a little bit too well. I can't believe he would be so stupid
as to let two people who probably fit the description he was issued go
as easy as that. Keep your eyes open.

MAN: They are.

(KEITH gives MAN sidelong glance.)

KEITH: Wait here a minute, I have to go to the bathroom. When I get back
we'll decide what we want to eat.

(KEITH is gone for a few moments and as the MAN is waiting he looks out the

windows curiously. Another man, looking furtive, approaches the car quickly. He
pulls the door open rapidly.)
AGENT: *(Yelling)* Get out! Get out now and hurry up!
(AGENT grabs MAN and pulls him quickly away. MAN looks around for
KEITH. Both characters leave as the MAN is dragged away by the AGENT.
KEITH returns to the car shortly after.)
KEITH: Damn! *(Slams fist on hood of car)*

SCENE 3:

(MAN is lying on a table. A woman is sitting behind a counter in front of the
table. A phone is on the counter. The phone rings, SECRETARY answers.)
SECRETARY: *(Begins to introduce name of store)* Bob's Rare…*(Interrupted)* Oh
    hi, Mr. McGuinness. Yeah, Jeffrey found 'im. I know! Jeff is worth
    every penny. No. Not a scratch. Just fine. Thanks, you too. Buhbye.
(The phone rings, SECRETARY answers.)
SECRETARY: Bob's Rare and Exotic Meats, how may I help you?

End of Play

In Memoriam: Edwin Ventura

Edwin Ventura dreamed of moving to a safe place with his family. His cousin had been trapped by the violence of their DC neighborhood, and he had watched his mother struggle with the impact of violence on his family. He vowed that he would not make the same mistakes. When YPT came to his eleventh-grade class, Edwin wrote a thoughtful play called *Moving Out*, which tells the tale of a family hurt by violence when the father is shot by a masked gunman during a robbery. The father survives, and by the end of the play, he and his family are planning to move to a safe new home in Florida.

On April 22, 2007, Edwin was tragically shot and killed while standing with his friends. He was only eighteen years old. Only hours before, Edwin and his family had visited the home that they hoped to buy in the Maryland suburbs.

YPT honored Edwin's passion and talent on May 21, 2007, with a public reading of *Moving Out*, as well as essays he had written and poems that inspired him. The evening brought together friends, family members, local elected officials and activists. Edwin's words served as a bridge between communities, and inspired a lively dialogue about ending neighborhood violence. As one audience member said, "What was so clear in Edwin's play is that he allowed the story to tell itself. It was his experience in the world, but that ability to take it from your head to your heart and out to others is a really wonderful thing. I'm sorry he isn't here for me to tell him this, but for him to tell this through you all is a wonderful thing."

YPT publishes this play to honor Edwin's memory.

Moving Out

by Edwin Ventura

Characters:

JOE

JENNY

CHRIS

ANA

MASKED MAN

AMBULANCE #1

AMBULANCE #2

DOCTOR

SCENE 1: *In the bedroom of a neighborhood in the Bronx, New York.*

JOE: Jenny I think we should move out of this neighborhood.

JENNY: Why do you want to move?

JOE: I don't want our two children to grow up in this bad neighborhood.

JENNY: But we don't have the money to move. I want to move as bad as you do but we just don't have the money.

JOE: Don't worry about the money. I'm going to start working extra shifts at work to make enough money so we can move.

JENNY: Don't you think you're going to be too tired to be working extra shifts?

JOE: It won't matter. I just want to move away from this neighborhood as soon as possible.

JENNY: If we do move where are we going to move?

JOE: I was thinking of a place like Florida where it's always sunny outside and people are always having fun.

JENNY: I think Florida will be a good place to live and our kids can grow up.

JOE: Tomorrow when I go to work I am going to ask my boss to give me extra shifts at work.

JENNY: I don't want you working too much because you won't have enough time for us anymore.

JOE: Don't worry about that. I will always have time for you and the kids. Family always comes first that's why I am doing this to get us out of this place.

JENNY: Well I just don't want you getting too stressed out in your work.

211

JOE: I know I will always have time for you and the kids.

JENNY: I hope so.

SCENE 2: *The next afternoon in their house.*

JOE: Jenny I asked my boss for the extra shifts at work.

JENNY: So what did he say?

JOE: He said he can give me three hours extra after quitting time.

JENNY: So when he say you can start working the extra shifts?

JOE: He says I can start working the extra shifts tomorrow and give me $400 cash every Saturday I work.

JENNY: That's good, I think I should find a job myself so we can have enough money faster.

JOE: I don't think so.

JENNY: Why not? You are going to be too tired working too much.

JOE: You need to stay home taking care of the kids and cook the food.

JENNY: Okay but if you seem too tired of working so much I am going to look for a job.

JOE: Okay. Where are the kids I haven't heard a sound out of them?

JENNY: There, in front playing.

(JENNY and JOE hear gunshots and cars going high speed outside. JOE and JENNY run outside to get their two kids CHRIS and ANA.)

JOE and JENNY: Are you kids okay? *(While JOE and JENNY hold CHRIS tightly)*

CHRIS and ANA: *(Crying)* Yes but we are scared.

JENNY: Don't worry kids you are safe now. We are going to move out of this neighborhood soon.

ANA: But I don't want to move. I have all my friends here.

JOE: But we can't stay here. This neighborhood is too dangerous for you kids to grow up in.

CHRIS: So when are we going to move? Because I can't wait to get the hell out of this neighborhood.

JENNY: Watch your mouth. We are going to be out of here when your dad makes enough money so we can move.

ANA: So where are we going to move.

JOE: Your mom and I decided we are going to move to Florida.

CHRIS and ANA: Can we go to Disney World when we get there?

JOE: Yes we are going to go as soon as I get the money.

JENNY: I think you kids should go to bed now it's getting too late.

CHRIS and ANA: Okay.

JENNY: Do you think we are going to get out of this neighborhood before something worse happens?

JOE: You should look for houses that are for sale in Florida tomorrow while I go to work.

JENNY: What part of Florida should I look into?

JOE: It doesn't matter as long as we get out of this neighborhood and we live in a good place where we can watch our children grow up and be safe.

JENNY: Okay.

JOE: I'm going to bed now I need to get up early for work tomorrow. Don't go to sleep too late.

JENNY: I won't.

SCENE 3: The next night at their home. The door slams.

JENNY: You're home.

JOE: Yeah.

JENNY: So how was work?

JOE: It was okay, there weren't a lot of people that wanted their car fixed today.

JENNY: That's good.

JOE: Yeah. So where are the kids?

JENNY: They're upstairs in their rooms. They're scared to go outside and play.

JOE: So they are probably happy that we are moving then.

JENNY: Yeah they are really happy. They really want to go to Disney World.

JOE: So did you find a house that is for sale in Florida?

JENNY: I found a big house that is for sale. It has 4 bedrooms, 3.5 bathrooms, and it has 3 floors.

JOE: Where is this house at?

JENNY: It's in Miami, Florida and it's a couple of blocks away from the beach.

JOE: Well maybe the kids will like it there.

JENNY: They can go to the beach and have fun. The newspaper says it's in a quiet neighborhood.

JOE: Okay. Let's hope we can get the house before anyone else does. I took a virtual tour in the internet and it looks nice.

JENNY: I guess this move will be good for us.

JOE: Yeah I hope so.

SCENE 4:
(The next night while JOE is getting home from work he sees a MASKED MAN following him and tries to walk faster. The MASKED MAN catches up to him.)
MASKED MAN: Give me all your money or I will shoot you.
JOE: No.
MASKED MAN: Hurry up and give it to me before I shoot you.
(JOE tries to hit the MASKED MAN before he shoots. Gun is fired, JOE gets shot in the arm. MASKED MAN runs away)
JENNY: Joe!!!!!!!!!
(JENNY runs outside and hugs JOE while crying.)
CHRIS and ANA: Daddy!!!!!!!!!!!!
JENNY: Kids go inside.
(Ambulance sirens)
AMBULANCE #1: Don't touch the wounded person.
JENNY: It's my husband.
AMBULANCE #2: We understand that but we need you to step back so we
　　can help him.
(JENNY steps back away from JOE. AMBULANCE #1 and #2 put JOE in the ambulance car and rush him to the hospital. JENNY goes in the house and gets the kids ready to go to the hospital.)
JENNY: Kids hurry up we are going to the hospital.

SCENE 5: At the hospital.
DOCTOR: Your husband has been in the emergency room for 2 hours.
JENNY: Is he going to be okay?
DOCTOR: He is going to be just fine as soon as he recovers.
JENNY: How long will it take to recover?
DOCTOR: We are not absolutely sure right now but I am thinking 3 to 5
　　days.
JENNY: Are we going to be able to see him?
DOCTOR: Yes but only for 20 minutes. We are not allowed to let anyone see
　　him but we can let you and your kids see him. Just follow me.
JENNY: Okay.
(JENNY is seeing JOE in the bed. He is sleeping.)
JENNY: Why did this have to happen? I shouldn't have let you work so
　　hard to try to get us out of this town so fast. I should have started

working to help us get out of this neighborhood.

(JENNY and the kids leave the hospital and go home.)

CHRIS: Mom is Dad going to be okay?

JENNY: Yes he is and don't worry everything is going to be okay. We are going to get out of this no matter what happens.

ANA: When is Dad going to come home?

JENNY: He is going to come home real soon. Now you kids should go to bed its getting too late.

CHRIS and ANA: Okay.

SCENE 6: 4 nights later.

(Door slams. CHRIS and ANA run to the door.)

CHRIS and ANA: Dad, you're home.

(JOE gives CHRIS & ANA a hug.)

JOE: I missed you kids a lot.

CHRIS and ANA: We missed you too dad.

JOE: Where is your mom at?

CHRIS and ANA: She's in the kitchen cooking.

JOE: Okay.

(JOE walks to the kitchen.)

JOE: Dinner smells good.

(JENNY runs to JOE and hugs him.)

JENNY: You're home.

JOE: Yeah I feel well now. The doctor says I can start working again next week.

JENNY: Are you sure you can work?

JOE: Yeah I am sure. I called my boss and he says he will count this as my vacation time so I will get paid for these days I missed.

JENNY: That is good. While you were gone I was babysitting the neighbor's kids and I made $500. Every day I babysat their kids they will give me $250 because they can't find anyone else who could babysit them. So they asked me to take care of their kids this whole week.

JOE: I hope you can handle all those kids.

JENNY: Yeah I can. All they do is sleep.

JOE: Alright.

SCENE 7: The next week.

(JOE comes home from work.)

JOE: Jenny I think we have enough money to move to Florida. I just got my check and it's a lot of money plus the money you have earned babysitting. I think we can move from here now.

JENNY: I guess we should pack all of our things then.

JOE: You should call the people from the real estate in Florida and tell them we are interested in buying the house.

JENNY: That's what I will do.

(JENNY calls the real estate.)

JENNY: The real estate people say we can go over there to check out the house to see if we like it and we can move in as soon as we want if we get approved.

JOE: Okay let's start packing our stuff so we can go.

JENNY: I'm going to go get the kids so we can pack their things up, so they will be ready to go by next week.

JOE: You know Jenny I have learned a lot from this experience I went through. I learned that no matter what obstacles you face in life if you keep trying you will always get what you want if you try hard enough.

JENNY: I think I have learned interesting things in life.

JOE: We should go upstairs and help the kids.

(The next week JOE & JENNY move to Florida with their two kids and have the best time of their lives.)

End of Play

Color Lines

by Sheila Walcott (1998)

ABOUT SHEILA

What grade were you in when you wrote your play? 12th

What school did you attend? Benjamin Banneker Academic Senior High School

What do you do now? I'm the Director of Development at HBO Films.

What do you like to do for fun? Write.

Is there anything you'd like to say to the readers of this book? Being a winner in the Young Playwrights' Theater competition is one of the main reasons I embarked on a career in entertainment, so I'm really grateful to YPT. I'm honored to be part of this book and I hope you enjoy my play.

Characters:

JALIA WASHINGTON, an 18-year-old, African American freshman at the
    University of Virginia

DYLAN McCALLAHAN, a 21-year-old, Caucasian junior at University of
    Virginia; pursuing Jalia

PATRICE SMITH, an 18-year-old, African American freshman at
    University of Virginia, Jalia's best friend

MARCUS LYLES, a 19-year-old, African American freshman at University
    of Virginia, Jalia and Patrice's friend; has a crush on Jalia

SCENE 1: _JALIA is in the U.V.A. lounge, where most students hang out_
    after/before classes. It's late in the afternoon, so it's a little crowded.
(JALIA walks into the youth lounge with her coffee and books. She spots an empty
table through a crowd of people. She walks to it and puts her coffee on the table and
book bag on the ground. She opens her bag and gets a book out. As she's opening
it, DYLAN approaches.)

DYLAN: Is anybody sitting here?

JALIA: Nope.

(DYLAN sits down.)

DYLAN: Thank God. I thought I'd never find a place to sit.

(He puts his coffee and notebook one the table. He sees JALIA'S book and
recognizes its author.)

DYLAN: What you reading?

JALIA: Devil in a Blue Dress.

DYLAN: By Walter Mosley right?

JALIA: Yep.

DYLAN: He's one of my favorite authors…So you like mystery novels.

JALIA: Yeah. They keep me in suspense. That's a switch for me because I usually know what's going to happen.

DYLAN: Well, did you know I was about to ask you your name?

JALIA: *(Smiling)* Jalia.

DYLAN: *(Extending his hand)* I'm Dylan…So, I haven't seen you around before. Are you a freshman?

JALIA: Yeah. What class are you?

DYLAN: I'm a junior…You like it here so far?

JALIA: It's okay I guess. I haven't really had time to enjoy anything but homework yet.

DYLAN: *(Smiling)* You'll get used to it. Are you far away from home?

JALIA: Yeah. I'm from Georgia.

DYLAN: *(Smiling and in a Southern accent)* Oh, so you're a Georgia peach?

JALIA: *(Smiling and in a Southern accent)* Well, I reckon you could say that. Where are you from?

DYLAN: I'm from Syracuse, New York.

JALIA: The city that never sleeps.

DYLAN: Yep, that's New York.

JALIA: Well, New York is definitely a lot different than Georgia.

DYLAN: How so?

JALIA: Okay, in Georgia, there's really not too much to do and in New York, something is always going on; in New York it's cold and in Georgia it's hot. In Georgia—

DYLAN: All right, All right. Have you ever been to New York?

JALIA: No, but—

DYLAN: Well there ya go. *(Flirtatiously)* You can't knock it 'till you try it.

(JALIA looks at him questioningly, then back at her coffee.)

DYLAN: So you say you haven't gotten a chance to look around right?

JALIA: Right.

DYLAN: Well then, allow me to rescue you from the evening rush, to show you to one of the best cafés in Richmond.

JALIA: I don't think that would be a good idea.

DYLAN: Okay. How about another time?

JALIA: *(Gathering her things)* I don't think so. It was nice talking to you. *(She gets up.)* See ya.

(JALIA exits. DYLAN sits there looking confused.)

SCENE 2: *Marcus and Patrice are sitting in the library.*
(MARCUS and PATRICE are talking.)
MARCUS: What's up with Jalia? Does she have a boyfriend?
PATRICE: For the thousandth and one time, I'm not telling you.
MARCUS: Why not?
PATRICE: Because I don't like playing cupid. If you want to know
     something about her personals then you ask her yourself. Damn, she
     don't bite.
MARCUS: So what you sayin'? You not goin' tell me?
PATRICE: Marcus, get out my face.
MARCUS: Come on Patrice, ask her for me.
PATRICE: No, Marcus. Ask her yourself—
(JALIA enters.)
JALIA: Ask who what?
MARCUS: Nothin'.
JALIA: Sounded like somethin' to me. *(Pause)* Ohhh, Marcus. You like a girl
     here don't you?! Why didn't y'all tell me? What's her name, what she
     look like?
MARCUS: *(Blushing)* No I don't like nobody.
JALIA: Oh my God. Yes you do! Marcus you're blushing. Tell me her name.
PATRICE: *(Saving MARCUS)* Girl you know how he is. He likes her, but he
     just doesn't know how to approach her.
MARCUS: *(Smiling at PATRICE then looks seriously at JALIA)* Yeah. I mean,
     she's different from most the girls I usually talk to. I just don't know
     what to say to her.
JALIA: Well does she know you like her?
MARCUS: I don't think so.
JALIA: Tell her Marcus.
PATRICE: Yeah, tell her Marcus.
MARCUS: I just don't know…
(JALIA looks at her watch.)
JALIA: Well, I'll see y'all later. I need to get some of this work done. Good
     luck on your situation.

SCENE 3: *Later on that night, Jalia and Patrice are in their dorm room sleeping.*
(The phone rings. JALIA fumbles a bit trying to find the phone in the dark and

then picks it up on the fourth ring.)
JALIA: Hello.
DYLAN: Hey Jalia. It's Dylan.
JALIA: Dylan. How'd you get my number?
DYLAN: Long story. So, what's up? What are you doing?
(JALIA looks at the time on her clock.)
JALIA: What any other normal person does at 3:19 a.m. Have you lost your
    mind?
DYLAN: No, I'm sorry. I was just sitting here reading my book, which made
    me think of Walter Mosley and that made me think of you.
JALIA: Dylan, that's very sweet, but it's late, and I'm tired, and —
DYLAN: Okay, okay. But, I can't let you get off of the phone until you
    promise to let me take you to that café I told you about.
JALIA: You are very persistent.
DYLAN: Yeah, you'd be surprised where it can get ya…So what day?
JALIA: *(Smiling)* Okay, okay, um I don't know, what day.
DYLAN: How about tomorrow at…— When's your last class over?
JALIA: About four-thirty.
DYLAN: Alright, tomorrow at five.
JALIA: Okay, cool.
DYLAN: Alright. I'll meet you in front of the lounge.
JALIA: Okay, goodnight.
DYLAN: See you tomorrow.
(They hang up. PATRICE turns on her lamp.)
PATRICE: Who was that?
JALIA: This guy I met today.
PATRICE: This guy huh? Well you don't have to tell me about him now,
    'cause I'm too tired but, you'll be grilled tomorrow. And anyways, tell
    that guy not to call here at this time of morning ever, ever, ever again
    unless they're dying. Matter fact, let me just talk to him next time.

SCENE 4: *Dylan and Jalia are in the café.*
(DYLAN and JALIA are talking.)
JALIA: So, this is the infamous café you told me so much about, huh?
DYLAN: Yep…How do you like it so far?
JALIA: It's alright, has a nice atmosphere.
DYLAN: So where do you go for a nice atmosphere in Georgia?
JALIA: Home. *(Smiling)* You go home.

(MARCUS enters, looks around and spots JALIA with DYLAN. He walks to their table.)

MARCUS: *(Distantly)* What's up Jalia?

JALIA: *(Uncomfortably)* Hey Marcus. Um, this is Dylan.

(DYLAN stands up and extends his hand.)

DYLAN: Nice to meet you.

(MARCUS looks at DYLAN'S hand then back at him. JALIA looks at MARCUS and back at DYLAN uncomfortably.)

MARCUS: *(To JALIA)* So when did you start going—like that?

JALIA: Like what?

MARCUS: *(Pointing to DYLAN)* Like that. I mean damn, I would've never guessed you'd be messing with a white boy. I never thought you'd sell out like that.

JALIA: A sell out. What?

DYLAN: I guess I oughta just go. I—

MARCUS: Naw, you don't have to go no where. I'll leave.

(MARCUS exits. JALIA looks at DYLAN, back at MARCUS walking out of the door. Then she puts her hand on her forehead and shakes her head.)

SCENE 5: *Dylan and Jalia are on the steps that lead to her dorm.*

DYLAN: You've been awful quiet.

JALIA: I'm just thinking.

(DYLAN anticipates her to continue.)

DYLAN: Okay, penny for your thoughts.

JALIA: I was right.

DYLAN: About what?

JALIA: About this. It isn't going to work. I knew it wouldn't. I don't even know why I agreed to—

DYLAN: Wait a second, hold on. What are you talking about?

JALIA: I'm talking about us. We don't work. We're just too different.

DYLAN: Huh? What do you mean, *(Imitating JALIA)* we're just too different?

JALIA: You know exactly what I mean.

DYLAN: No I don't. Please explain it to me.

JALIA: For starters, I'm black and—

DYLAN: You're what?!? I never noticed that.

(JALIA looks at him unconvinced.)

JALIA: Starting a relationship is just going to be too hard on both of us. Think about it, every time we walk down the street together, people would stare or whisper or—

DYLAN: *(Frustrated)* So what.

JALIA: So that's just too much to deal with.

DYLAN: *(Sighs)* Okay Jalia fine. If that's how you want it fine. I, I just saw a beautiful woman, who I wanted to get to know better...*(Pause)* But um, if that's too much to ask because of what people might say, then fine. I'll just go.

(DYLAN exits. JALIA watches him go.)

SCENE 6: *Patrice is in her dorm room studying.*

(JALIA enters.)

PATRICE: Hey, what's up girl?

(JALIA sits on her bed and doesn't respond. PATRICE looks at JALIA.)

PATRICE: Girl, what's wrong?

JALIA: What's right?

PATRICE: Damn, it's one of those kinda days huh? What happened?

JALIA: Where you want to start with Marcus or Dylan?

PATRICE: Who is Dylan?

JALIA: Alright, I'll start with him. I met him yesterday in the lounge. We were talking for a little while and he seems cool. But he's white.

PATRICE: And...

JALIA: What do you...

PATRICE: Okay, I'll deal with that later. Y'all haven't even gone out and you're worryin' already?

JALIA: Because, I don't want to start a relationship with him.

PATRICE: Why not?

JALIA: *(Sighing)* Patrice, if he and I started dating, it would cause too many problems.

PATRICE: Like?

JALIA: Like, like if we got serious and he wanted to meet my parents or he wanted me to meet his parents or if we all tried to kick it together, his friends and mine, that wouldn't work. Or what if we're walking down the street and the responses we get from people are negative, or what if—

PATRICE: What if? What if? All these what ifs? *(Sarcastically)* What if Grandma had balls, then she'd be Grandpa. *(Pause)* Seriously though Jalia. You taking this whole situation to another level. Y'all haven't even started dating. So what's the big deal about him and going out to get to know each other better?

JALIA: It's not as easy as you're making it seem.

PATRICE: No, it's not as difficult as you're making it seem.

(Silence for a moment.)

PATRICE: Well, Jalia, if you want my advice or perception of the situation, I'll tell you that the only person I see with the problem is you. You are the worrying too much about what "the people" are going to think. And that not what matters. What matters is what you feel.

JALIA: I just don't know what to feel about the situation.

PATRICE: Well you can't do anything until you do that.

JALIA: Alright let me tell you what happened. He called me a sell out girl, when he saw me with Dylan.

PATRICE: A sell out? Girl, just talk to Marcus. I'm sure he didn't mean what he said.

(Silence)

PATRICE: And girl, stop letting this kinda stuff get to you. Geez. That's your problem girl. You think about things too much. That's why God gave us instincts, so we wouldn't have to reason about things that have no explanation. You'll worry yourself to death.

JALIA: Well thanks, Ma.

PATRICE: *(In a southern accent)* You're welcome baby.

(Curtains close.)

SCENE 7: *Marcus is in the café that he met Jalia and Dylan in.*

(MARCUS is drinking coffee and reading a newspaper. JALIA enters, looks around and spots MARCUS. She walks to his table.)

JALIA: I been looking all over for you. What's up?

(MARCUS looks up at JALIA.)

MARCUS: *(Unenthused)* Hey.

(MARCUS goes back to reading his paper.)

JALIA: We need to talk.

MARCUS: Go ahead. Talk.

(JALIA tries to talk to him but can't see him through the newspaper.)

JALIA: *(Frustrated)* Can you put the newspaper down and look at me!

(MARCUS irritatedly puts his newspaper down, offended.)

JALIA: I mean, you don't have to approve of the people I choose to hang out with, that's fine. But you do have to respect me. An the way you came at me yesterday was completely —

MARCUS: Completely what Jalia? How you just goin' play us brothas for Opie like that?

JALIA: What?

MARCUS: You heard me. I never expected you to cross over. You just totally disrespected. I—

JALIA: I totally disrespected. What the hell did I totally disrespect! You totally disrespected me and our friendship! And this bull about me crossin' over with Opie is completely that, bull! I really resent you saying that to me. If Opie and I, I mean Dylan and I, start a relationship that's between he and I. Not you, or anybody else, brotha! I can't even believe you—

MARCUS: I'm sorry!

JALIA: What?

MARCUS: I'm sorry! ...It's just that...Man Jalia, you one of the finest black women on the campus and to see you getting down with a white boy, just, I don't know. I mean, how would you feel if I started dating Ant B?

(JALIA starts laughing.)

MARCUS: Seriously though. It really wouldn't matter if he was black or white. I probably, well I know, I wouldn't have wanted to see you with anybody else...but me.

(JALIA looks at him astonished.)

MARCUS: (Smiling) Yep. You was the girl I was talkin' about yesterday.

(JALIA punches MARCUS.)

JALIA: Why didn't you tell me?

MARCUS: I already told you why I couldn't tell you. I didn't know how.

JALIA: Well. I don't know.

MARCUS: (Smiling) It's okay. You don't have to say anything...Wow, I feel like I just sat down the ton of bricks I was carrying.

(DYLAN enters the café. As he's walking he spots JALIA and MARCUS talking. He turns around and starts heading back out the door. Before he reaches it MARCUS spots him.)

MARCUS: (Pointing to DYLAN) Hey ain't that Opie right there?

(JALIA turns to find DYLAN and sees him walk out of the door.)

JALIA: Yeah, that's him...Well, I'ma go. I need to sit down the ton of bricks I'm carrying too.

(MARCUS looks at JALIA and she looks at him.)

JALIA: (Jokingly) Now you know it would never work out between you and

I, we're too much alike to ever get along.

MARCUS: *(Smiling)* Yeah...Go unload them bricks.

JALIA: See you later?

MARCUS: Yeah.

(JALIA exits.)

SCENE 8: *Jalia and Dylan on the sidewalk in front of the café.*

(DYLAN is walking. JALIA exits the café.)

JALIA: Dylan! Dylan!

(DYLAN stops and turns around. JALIA walks to him.)

JALIA: Hey. What's up?

DYLAN: Nothing much.

JALIA: Listen, I just wanted to say that I'm sorry for what happened
   yesterday.

DYLAN: *(After a pause)* Is that all you wanted to say?

JALIA: No. I also wanted to say that, that...well, I don't really know what I
   want to say. I just want to make everything better, but the words won't
   come to me.

(Silence)

JALIA: You don't have anything to say?

DYLAN: Jalia, I already told you what I had to say. Where this goes now is
   completely up to you.

JALIA: All the what-ifs scenarios and then the thing with Marcus, it just all
   kinda got to me.

(Silence again)

JALIA: So where do you want to go from here?

DYLAN: Let's start from the beginning.

JALIA: *(Smiling)* Okay, I can do that.

DYLAN: *(Smiling)* You sure, because people will always be watching?

JALIA: *(Smiling)* Positive.

DYLAN: Good. *(He extends his hand.)* It's nice to meet you, uh...

JALIA: Jalia. Same here uh.

DYLAN: Dylan. Are you walking to campus?

JALIA: Yeah, care to join me?

DYLAN: Sure...

(They start walking. In a Southern accent:)

DYLAN: Well dear, this could be the beginning of a beautiful friendship.

(They both laugh and the curtains close.)

End of Play

Playwright Profile: Amber Faith Walton

"When I created my characters, I decided to leave the fear of judgment behind, believing that my work could change habits of hatred. I had been passive, but I now know that being an advocate for justice is the path to a better future."

Amber Faith Walton wrote this statement several months ago as part of a scholarship essay for the Federal Communications Bar Association, in which she described her experience working with YPT in 2010. She was an 11th grader at Bell Multicultural High School when her YPT teaching artist Michelle brought the *In-School Playwriting Program* to her classroom. Amber decided to use the opportunity to tackle an issue that she cared about.

"I had a gay friend, and I saw the hardship he faced in his family and his community," Amber tells YPT staff in an interview about her playwriting experience. "It just made sense to write about it."

In her scholarship essay, Amber also mentions how her own feelings of social exclusion influenced the topic she chose to address in her play: "As a biracial female I've been hurt and ostracized in both my communities. With two families, one black, one white, neither biracial, I am inevitably isolated. My protagonist also shares this frustration of not having those closest to her relate to her unique experiences."

Amber's play, *Changing Tides: Judge Me Gently*, focuses on a young lesbian woman who is riding the subway when she overhears a man on his cell phone expressing his disgust for gay people. When the train gets stuck, she tells him how offensive his words are, and, after a heated conversation, the man begins to question his biases.

"Having my play produced opened a door for me," Amber explains. "Writing hadn't taken me far at that point. Now, it's taken me further than I ever thought it would."

While Amber loved writing for years before *Changing Tides* was produced in YPT's 2011 **New Play Festival**, her experience throughout the production process, along with the audience's overwhelmingly positive reaction to her play, inspired her to realize that she could use her writing to make a difference in the world.

Amber was awarded the $10,000 prize by the Federal Communications Bar Association towards her tuition at Smith College for the essay that she submitted about her experience with YPT. At Smith, she plans to major in Biology, and hopes to one day become an epidemiologist.

"But of course I'll continue with creative writing and theater," Amber says. "I've been writing since the second grade," she adds with a smile. "It's my first love."

Changing Tides: Judge Me Gently

by Amber Faith Walton

ABOUT AMBER

What grade were you in when you wrote your play? 11th

What school did you attend? Bell Multicultural High School

Where do you go to school now? Starting Smith College in the fall

What do you like to do for fun? I like to travel. That's my number one passion. I've been to Brazil, Guatemala, and I used to live in Italy. And I like to eat!

Is there anything you'd like to say to the readers of this book? What happens in my play didn't happen to me, but it's something that happens often in our community now. I think it's important to be aware of things and care just as much as if they were happening to you.

Characters:

SUMMER GRAY

FRED

TRAIN DRIVER (voice)

SCENE 1:

SUMMER: I want to be a boy. No, wait! I don't. I want the rest of the World
to stop STARING at me...I want the absence of a...home to not
determine where I sleep at night.

The weight of my breast bends...my posture to BOW! To the harsh
petrified eyes of humanity. Yet...even though this is a challenge,
having weight in my pants would just decrease the speed at which
I...run, run from all this chaos. Why does it matter what I do in the
world, I don't hurt people, I don't judge people. I'm just a person, I
don't see myself as a problem you know. I just have a
different...ummm...sexual orientation...it's not a preference...no one
chooses to live alone in a society full of people. Ididn'tchoose it. I just
am who I am... _(Takes a deep breath)_ When I was younger and didn't
duct tape my breast to my spine you all, yes, none of you cared. Didn't
give a damn. But now! _(Gets frustrated)_ Now, that I don't wear pink!
And you can't see the development of my chest, I am wrong? I don't
want to be identified as a sex. I AM A HUMAN! Those things with
dreams and fingers! Oh well, I should probably pack my blankets and

229

get out of this basement, before anyone here wakes up. The last thing I need today is to be criticized. A day off would be nice.

SUMMER: I. Need to go. Iamjustgoingtogetonthe. Train. I'll get off. Somewhere. Who knows where. Who even—whoevencareswhere? But. I'll get off.

SUMMER: And the train just had to be packed today.
(Gets on train—sits next to FRED, a conservative businessman.)
FRED: *(Answers phone)* Hey John, How are you? *(Pause)* I heard the news; I'm sooooo…sorry to hear about your son. I had a similar story. My brother had HIV as well; in fact he actually died; and ever since I've committed myself to the church and the Bible…it really makes sense now that I am a part of the church. How about you join me this week, at my church? You learn things like…how we are designed to be with the opposite sex, right?…Society and this new generation is SO concerned with being different and standing out. Always looking for the eyes of other people; it makes them feel special…and now we are all suffering! From nonsense, false advertising, health issues, you know it's even more than AIDS! Even the government is all devoted and centralized fighting and siding with "gay marriage" and "gay rights" instead of focusing on the CRUCIAL aspects of running a country correctly, OUR COUNTRY…not theirs. *(Interrupted by SUMMER)*
SUMMER: Sir, I think you should lower your voice; you also might want to find a more appropriate place to discuss your views on such sensitive topics. *(Whispering)* More than just you around…jerk.
(FRED ignores comment—focuses back on his phone call.)
FRED: *(With attitude, and a snobbish look, stares at SUMMER)* Sorry, it's pretty loud on the train today! Everyone is being so sensitive. Ha. Anyways, I will see you at the bill preference meeting in 15 minutes. Oh by the way I think we should mention getting rid of the excessive "gay marriage bills." *(Listens)* Okay sounds good. See you soon.
FRED: *(Talks to self)* I hate it when certain people don't mind their own business; arrogant homosexuals.
SUMMER: A human can't just be a human anymore… *(Sighs)* It's so much more complicated. Not even on the train can you get away from the hate and prejudices of the world. Just problems and problems about

problems.

FRED: Little…boy, girl, whatever the hell you are, stop your croaking, please. Being on the train with you already made me upset, hearing you is just escalating that fury.

SUMMER: *(Pauses, takes a deep breath, starts directing comments at FRED)* Oh, men like you…closed-minded and simple; unable to see The JUSTICE that others want as well. Just care about them, only you. The real problem isn't that I'm a girl and you had to look twice to find out…but that you are so concerned with what I am…that is why this country doesn't get things done.

FRED: You have no right to be in my phone call. You little…indecisive eavesdropper. You people.

SUMMER: I also have a RIGHT! To be respected…who is "you people?" Sir, just be quiet, and I will too.

FRED: Excuse me! You may not have been informed but respect me, I am your elder. Besides, you should worship people like me: People who decide your fate.

SUMMER: My fate? I decide my fate.

FRED: How old are you? *(With urgency)* Where is your mother? Clearly an example of what people run away from. You are just a stupid little girl that had no guidance. Go find a church or something.

SUMMER: Oh, so now…youcanbothertodeal! I'm nineteen and I don't have a mother…*(Angry)* I am my mother now…

FRED: No wonder. You're not special. Ever think of that? None of "you" are. None. Not your tough clothing, not the flamboyant colors, none of it is special. Don't get your feelings caught in the door. You aren't doing anything. You're not helping anyone!

SUMMER: No wonder? No wonder…NO WONDER WHAT!? No wonder I turned out to be gay? Stand up for people who are disrespected by people with different views? No wonder! No wonder I'm not scared to hand it to a bastard that's been given EVERYTHING? Including respect when clearly! Clearly not deserving it! *(Get loud/angry)* You WHAT! You! Are a WASTE! A Waste! Waste of society, of your clothes, of your title, of your job, of your life, of your wife. Of my time.

FRED: I can't believe I'm even sitting here listening to this! From a baby…I have no time for you. I have more important things to be preparing for *(Whisper)* like getting rid of your nonsense.

SUMMER: How ignorant. What kind of inhumane thing are you.

FRED: I thought nineteen was an adult. Things have clearly changed. I don't have time for you. I really don't. (*Gets up, walks to the door—getting ready to exit Orange Line.*)

(*Loud crashing train noise.*)

FRED: What the HELL was that?

SUMMER: Now, that is fate. We are stuck.

FRED: No not with a freak…this can't be happening.

(*Train stops on an overpass above the Potomac River.*)

(*Intercom focusing stations.*)

TRAIN DRIVER: The train has had a stall in one of the center cars. This problem will take time to fix. Sorry for any inconveniences. Metro has already sent help. Please keep all of your valuables with you and all electronics low. No exiting cars to move to one another. Remain in current car. Metro will keep passengers informed on progress of this problem. Again, Metro sincerely apologizes. Thank you for your cooperation.

FRED: God damn, is this really happening?

SUMMER: Excuse me sir, what is your problem? Why are you so hateful? What did I ever do to you?

SCENE 2:

FRED: (*Turns from the door, walks towards the vacant side of the car. Sits down with exhaustion. Sighs.*)

SUMMER: (*Walks towards FRED. Sits directly across from him. Sits down with caution stares at FRED.*)

FRED: I can never get my fucking job completed. I went to one of the most prestigious schools in the world; not to sit at a desk and read whether or not gay marriage should be legal, yet that's what I do! I'm constantly reminded of why and how my brother died. No one gets how frustrating it is. Bygones just can't be bygones in life. I review people's complaints on how fair I am. And all I'm doing is saving people from HIV and from being hated and in return I'm hated…This unorganized society. Shouldn't we learn; this is a fatal problem. And people like you, always trying to be noticed, and show off and complicate the simplistic life. It's just too much to handle. Everything in my life has been a waste either because a gay person took it or just adds to the piles of papers I went to school not to have. I just hate the gay world. So pointless. So pointless.

SUMMER: I am a root
>An undeveloped beauty
>With an unknown fate.
>Life is a journey
>Not for the fittest
>But for the bravest.
>I bloom in the spring
>Where life itself is reborn
>With strength from the sun
>To see the light in everyone's story.
>Lay against my tree trunk
>Feel weightless from pain
>Life is a journey.
>You must forgive what hurt
>Burdens your view,
>And mend in my soils
>Where growth begins.
>Trust in your tears
>That pain is real
>Trust is in my palms,
>I will never let your story go.

FRED: Who are you? Who am I? I've never heard my voice. Oh my God, what kind of person have I become?

FRED: (*Stares into the sun shimmering off of the Potomac. He sees the first flower of spring. It's yellow.*) Hey, look at the first flower of spring…A daffodil. (*Walks back to the Metro door, look out across the Potomac and stares at the yellow flower.*)

FRED: I wish I could just start over, as that flower you know? Purify myself. Be more than what people expect me to be. Sorry for all of these years I haven't taken the time to look to see the beauty in our differences and the similarity in our hearts. Judging by the image that is handed to me by people like who I was. I refuse to be that—

TRAIN DRIVER: Thank you everyone. The train will begin operating soon. (*The train jolts forward and begins moving steadily.*)

FRED: (*Turns back to the window and stares at the flower as they move further and further away form it*) What is your name?!

(*The train gets to the end of the rail and everyone is hurrying off. FRED is awakened. He jumps to his feet and looks for SUMMER afraid she might have*

gotten off the train. He steps on something and it makes a loud noise. The
newspaper reads "The Second Chance.")

FRED: *(Picks up newspaper. Begins reading it)* Young Girl; died two days ago
   due to a hate crime. Summer Gray. That's her name! Summer.

FRED: *(Continues reading article)* Young Summer, 19 years old, without a
   home and without a family, died due to her sexual orientation.
   Saturday night making her way across town back to the home of her
   parents. Summer was found early Sunday morning by the Waste
   Management Authority, on their Sunday run. The man that found her
   Jacob Briton said, "It was nothing I had ever seen before. It was almost
   as though I was living in the time of war, her body was beaten so
   badly, her clothes were covered in blood and the passion in her eyes
   will forever live in me. I've never found a dead body and I still don't
   think I have because something in me said she wasn't done."

(FRED turns around to see a flower on the seat. He walks and picks it up, sits
down and thinks.)

FRED: Thank you, Summer. *(Calls John's voicemail)* Hey John, embrace your
   son and cherish your differences. Judge him gently.

(Falls back asleep)

End of Play

Curriculum

INTRODUCTION TO THE CURRICULUM

Young Playwrights' Theater (YPT) teaches students to express themselves clearly and creatively through the art of playwriting. We reach students with a variety of different programs; the *In-School Playwriting Program* is our oldest and largest, serving nearly 1,000 students each year. In 1995, YPT founder and accomplished playwright Karen Zacarías had just completed her graduate study in playwriting, and she wanted to put her knowledge to use serving her community. She approached several DC schools, offering to provide free instruction to students. What began as one woman operating out of her car has grown exponentially over the years, expanding to reach elementary, middle and high school students in all eight Council Wards of the District of Columbia as well as Northern Virginia and Montgomery County, Maryland.

At every partner school, the program is led by a professional YPT teaching artist. Teaching artists have expertise in the theatrical craft and in working with young people. YPT teaching artists are playwrights, actors, directors, dramaturges and designers. They bring their varied backgrounds and diverse skills to the classroom, engaging students with their real-world knowledge of professional productions. They are highly flexible and sensitive to different students' needs, using novel approaches to the playwriting process to help students succeed.

Regardless of grade level, the *In-School Program* always begins with the same question: "What is a play?" Before they begin to write, students are treated to a performance by professional actors. For many of our students, this is their first time seeing a play. For these students in particular, it is vital that they experience this theatrical performance before they can imagine creating one of their own. (Read more about this initial workshop on page 243.) The program includes instruction on characters, conflict, language, inspiration and more. These lessons provide students with the tools they need to write their own original plays. Students are also given multiple opportunities to work on writing their plays in the classroom. These writing labs serve a very important purpose: they allow the teaching artist to meet with each student individually, assisting students who are stuck and offering feedback to students as they write their plays. The program culminates in a celebration of the students' achievements. Professional actors return to the classroom, this time to perform excerpts from each student's play. This final workshop is one of the most rewarding moments for students, as they see their words come to life and delight in the work of their peers.

YPT has developed and refined the *In-School* curriculum over seventeen years. It is scaffolded for elementary, middle and high school students and addresses the Common Core State Standards for English Language Arts. Many individuals have contributed to the creation of this curriculum. It is revised each year, based on what we've learned from the previous year's program. YPT teaching artists convene for a formal "post mortem" meeting every January, offering feedback that comes directly from their experience in the classroom. Our teaching artists have made huge contributions to the program. Their training and experience in multiple arts and education methodologies enable them to provide invaluable insights as we develop our curriculum. Many exercises that we use today were originally proposed by teaching artists. We have also solicited input from teachers, administrators and principals to gain the valuable perspective of local schools and to ensure that our program supports their instructional objectives. Since 2008, we have also received support from arts education researcher Dr. Barry Oreck. In addition to working with the YPT staff to develop comprehensive assessment tools that allow us to demonstrate the impact of the *In-School Program* on student learning, Dr. Oreck has helped us ensure that our curriculum is as consistent and effective as possible. Finally, YPT students themselves have helped shape this curriculum. Through formal and anecdotal feedback, our students help us provide a rewarding, educational and fun playwriting experience.

The following workshops are a sampling from our *In-School* curriculum, organized by theme. Each lesson plan indicates a target age range (elementary, middle or high school), and lists Common Core State Standards by grade level. We hope that you will use these lessons to engage your students in learning, no matter what the content area. Playwriting can be a useful tool to teach history, social studies, science, and even math. Our curriculum has been adapted to enable students to explore the history of Jamestown, the U.S. Constitution, the life cycle of the butterfly...the possibilities are endless. When students are able to express themselves creatively, they take ownership of their education. We believe that every student has a right to participate in the arts, and we hope that this book can provide access to more students across the nation, and the world.

Understanding Plays and Playwriting

Workshop: What Is a Play?

Level: Elementary, Middle and High School

Common Core State Standards for English Language Arts addressed[1]:

Elementary School:
Writing:
- *W.5.3. Write narratives to develop real or imagined experiences or events using effective technique, descriptive details, and clear event sequences.*
- *W.5.3b. Use narrative techniques, such as dialogue, description, and pacing, to develop experiences and events or show the responses of characters to situations.*
- *W.5.5. With guidance and support from adults, develop and strengthen writing as needed by planning, revising, editing, rewriting, or trying a new approach.*

Speaking and Listening:
- *SL.5.1. Engage effectively in a range of collaborative discussions (one-on-one, in groups, and teacher-led) with diverse partners on grade 5 topics and texts, building on others' ideas and expressing their own clearly.*

Middle School:
Reading:
- *RL.8.3. Analyze how particular lines of dialogue or incidents in a story or drama propel the action, reveal aspects of a character, or provoke a decision.*

Writing:
- *W.8.3. Write narratives to develop real or imagined experiences or events using effective technique, relevant descriptive details, and well-structured event sequences.*
- *W.8.3b. Use narrative techniques, such as dialogue, pacing, description, and reflection, to develop experiences, events, and/or characters.*
- *W.8.5. With some guidance and support from peers and adults, develop and strengthen writing as needed by planning, revising, editing, rewriting, or trying a new approach, focusing on how well purpose and audience have been addressed.*

Speaking and Listening:
- *SL.8.1. Engage effectively in a range of collaborative discussions (one-on-one, in groups, and teacher-led) with diverse partners on grade 8 topics, texts, and issues, building on others' ideas and expressing their own clearly.*

---

[1] The YPT curriculum addresses the Common Core State Standards, which have been adopted by 45 U.S. states (and the District of Columbia) as of 2012. All standards included in this text are Common Core State Standards for English Language Arts. (Source: **www.corestandards.org**)

High School:
Reading:
- *RL.11-12.3. Analyze the impact of the author's choices regarding how to develop and relate elements of a story or drama (e.g., where a story is set, how the action is ordered, how the characters are introduced and developed).*

Writing:
- *W.11-12.3. Write narratives to develop real or imagined experiences or events using effective technique, well-chosen details, and well-structured event sequences.*
- *W.11-12.3b. Use narrative techniques, such as dialogue, pacing, description, reflection, and multiple plot lines, to develop experiences, events, and/or characters.*

Speaking and Listening:
- *SL.11-12.1. Initiate and participate effectively in a range of collaborative discussions (one-on-one, in groups, and teacher-led) with diverse partners on grades 11-12 topics, texts, and issues, building on others' ideas and expressing their own clearly and persuasively.*

Vocabulary[2]:
- *Play:* the stage representation of an action or a story; a dramatic composition
- *Playwright:* one who writes plays; dramatist
- *Playwriting:* the act of creating the plot, theme, characters, dialogue, spectacle and structure of a play and organizing it into a script form; the ability to imagine the entire production scene and to put it into written form so that others may interpret it for the stage
- *Actor:* a person, male or female, who performs a role in a play or entertainment
- *Audience:* the group of spectators at a public event; listeners or viewers collectively, as in attendance at a theater or concert
- *Stage:* the area where actors perform
- *Script:* the written dialogue, description, and directions provided by the playwright

Preparation:
- You will need actors to help you with this workshop. Before class begins, you should communicate with your actors to explain their role

---

[2] Throughout the YPT curriculum, we use existing definitions for theater terminology from the DC Office of the State Superintendent of Education (OSSE) Arts Education Standards, which YPT staff members helped to create in 2008.

in the workshop and ensure that they have all the materials they need.

Materials:
- A chalkboard/whiteboard, or large sheets of paper to write on
- For elementary school level: copies of the play *The Math Test* (page 247) or another play that can be stopped at the climax
- For middle and high school levels: copies of the play *My Date with Kara* (page 249) or another play that can be stopped at the climax
- Any necessary props for the play

Activities:

Introduction: Begin this initial workshop with a name game or other warm-up activity. Let the students know that you will be teaching them how to write their own original plays.

What Is a Play? Ask the students this question. Write down their responses on the board. (They will be able to revise their definition later in the workshop.)

Watching a Play: Tell the students that before they begin writing their own plays, they are going to watch a performance of a play written by YPT. Begin the performance. The actors will perform the play until it ends abruptly (at the climax).

What Happens Next? You "Write" the Ending: Ask, "How do you think this play should end?" Have the actors play out the students' suggestions. (If a student suggests an ending that requires an additional character, invite that student to play the role. You can also ask for volunteers from the group.) Discuss each suggestion after the actors perform it, encouraging the students to explore multiple possibilities. Now explain that the students have been acting as playwrights – they came up with ideas, they articulated those ideas and actors performed them for an audience. This is the essence of playwriting.

What Is a Play? Revisited: Ask if there is anything the participants would like to add to their definition of a play. Make any changes on the board, and read the students' definition aloud. Also give each student a copy of the play the students just watched, so the students can begin familiarizing themselves with written scripts.

Reflection: Why a Play? To answer this question, tell the students that there is an innate human need to tell stories. From ancient civilizations that acted out their daily life (the hunt for food) around a campfire to the modern-day phone calls we all make to tell each other about our lives, human beings have built communities through common experiences and the sharing of stories. Tell the students that you will be giving them the tools they need to tell stories through the form of playwriting. But finding the story they want to tell is up to them. It is the most important part of being a playwright, but, fortunately, it's something every human being knows how to do. Invite the students to talk about a time when something happened in their lives and they felt strongly compelled to tell someone else.

The Math Test
by YPT

SCENE 1: *An elementary school. In the hallway outside a classroom.*
(JAMIE runs in holding a piece of paper.)

JAMIE: *(Breathless)* Oh my gosh, I can't believe my terrible luck! You see, I woke up late on the day of The Most Important Math Test in the fifth grade! Even worse – I didn't study! I know, I know, how could I be so stupid? The thing is that my friend Davon just got a Nintendo Wii…oh never mind. But here's what's weird: I just found this *(Holding up piece of paper)* in the hallway. Well, I picked it up because we're *supposed* to pick up trash from the floor and throw it away, but I *had* to take a look at it first, didn't I? And do you know what it is? *(Whispers)* It's the answers to the math test! I don't know what to do. I *really* want to get a good grade on this math test. But I don't know about cheating… I…

(Suddenly JAMIE freezes. TAYLOR enters.)

TAYLOR: Look at Jamie! He looks so dumb! Oh, I'm no ordinary kid. I mean I know I look like everyone else but *I* have magic powers! I can control time with this *(Pulling a remote control out of pocket)* remote control! See?

(TAYLOR pushes the play button…)

JAMIE: …can't…

(TAYLOR pushes the pause button.)

TAYLOR: It's very useful to me. I have allllll the time in the world.

(TAYLOR sees the paper in JAMIE'S hand.)

TAYLOR: Hey! What's that?

(TAYLOR snatches the paper from JAMIE.)

TAYLOR: Oh my gosh! These are the answers to the math test!! *(While pushing the play button…)* Um, play!

JAMIE: …believe this! *(Sees TAYLOR with paper)* Uh oh.

TAYLOR: Where did you get this?!?

JAMIE: Shhhhhh! *(Whispers)* Do you want Mrs. Johnson to come out here, Taylor?

TAYLOR: So what if she does, *Jamie*? *I* won't be the one in trouble! Oh Mrs. Jo–

JAMIE: SHHHH! Please be quiet!

TAYLOR: Or what?

JAMIE: …what do you want?

TAYLOR: I know your friend Davon has a Nintendo Wii.

JAMIE: Yeah, so?

TAYLOR: I want it!

JAMIE: What? It's not mine!

TAYLOR: Well then I'm gonna tell Mrs. Johnson you're cheating!

JAMIE: No! Don't do that!

TAYLOR: So are you gonna get me the Wii or not?

This play doesn't have an ending. What do you think should happen next?

My Date with Kara
by YPT

SCENE 1: *Davon is all dressed up for homecoming. He speaks directly to the audience.*

DAVON: People told me not to date Kara. They said she was weird. Powerful. But nobody had ever liked me before. So I asked her to go to homecoming with me. She was so gorgeous. I was surprised she didn't have another date. But then she was always staring at me. It was kind of scary and kind of cool. Intense. Yeah, she was intense. When Kara came to our school was around the same time that weird things started happening. But I didn't put it together.

(DAVON steps back into the scene with his little sister, GINA. GINA is playing Witch Hunt on her Playstation 3.)

DAVON: Hey, Gina. What are you still doing here? I thought you were supposed to go shoot some hoops with your little friend, Diamond.

GINA: Why you gotta be like that?

DAVON: Like what?

GINA: Calling her my "little" friend. That's not cool.

(GINA snaps her fingers. DAVON freezes.)

GINA: My brother doesn't know I can do this. Freeze things, that is. So whenever he annoys me I like to whip this little trick out and let him hang there for a moment. It's very amusing.

(GINA snaps her fingers again.)

DAVON: Whatever, where is that little girl?

GINA: I don't know. Why are you dressed like a lawyer?

DAVON: Homecoming, son. I'm going to homecoming. Why don't you call Diamond's house?

GINA: Okay. Don't touch the PS3. I'm about to get to the next level on my game.

DAVON: That stupid Witch Hunt game?

GINA: DON'T TOUCH IT!

DAVON: Sure, whatever.

(As soon as GINA is offstage, DAVON sits down and starts messing with her game. In a few moments GINA re-enters looking shocked.)

DAVON: What's wrong? Look. I didn't mess up your game. Look!

GINA: It's not that. Diamond's mom said she ain't been home for three

249

days. The police are looking for her.

DAVON: Whoa. Okay. I'm sure she'll be okay. Don't worry. Want me to call Aunt Jo to be with you while I'm out?

GINA: No. Mom will be home in a minute.

(The doorbell rings.)

DAVON: That's my date!

GINA: She's picking YOU up?

DAVON: Well. I don't have a ride, do I? She offered.

GINA: Whatever.

(DAVON opens the door. KARA enters.)

DAVON: Wow. You look amazing. Kara, this is my sister Gina. Gina this is Kara.

(KARA puts her arm out to shake GINA'S hand. GINA snaps her fingers and everyone freezes. GINA grabs the bracelet off KARA'S wrist.)

GINA: This is Diamond's bracelet! Oh my god. What is she doing with it? *(Circling the frozen KARA cautiously)* I don't trust this girl. I don't like her at all.

(GINA steps back into place as she was before she froze everyone – except now she's holding the bracelet. She snaps to unfreeze everyone.)

GINA: This bracelet belongs to my friend Diamond!

KARA: *(Surprised that GINA has the bracelet but not skipping a beat – she leans in threateningly and snatches it.)* No, little girl, it's mine.

DAVON: *(Pulling them apart)* Sorry, Kara. Gina's a little upset. Her friend Diamond is missing. Are you ready to go?

GINA: Don't go with her.

DAVON: Gina, shut up.

GINA: She's bad.

DAVON: So sorry, Kara. Do you have a little sister?

KARA: No, but I know how disgusting little girls can be.

DAVON: You got that right. We're out of here.

(DAVON glares at GINA as they leave.)

SCENE 2: *The next morning. DAVON speaks directly to the audience.*

DAVON: I thought Gina was just acting crazy. Kara was so beautiful and intelligent. And whoever heard of a teenage girl who was out for little kids? That's just crazy. After the dance Kara asked if I wanted to go out somewhere else. I said sure and she took me to this crazy club in the basement of some building that looked abandoned. There were all kinds of people there. We danced and partied. She knew everybody. At one point a guy cut in on us dancing and I was going to start a fight, but Kara said it was okay. She told me to hold her purse and that she'd be back in a second. She and this guy were talking really intensely. I sat down. Her purse fell open. I wasn't trying to look inside. And she had crazy stuff in there. Not normal girl stuff like makeup and hair brushes. But there were vials of strange liquids, something that looked like – no joke – a magic wand and all these pieces of hair in little baggies. Each one had a name on it. There was one that said "Diamond" on it. I almost lost it when I saw that. But I played it cool 'til we got home. Then I called the police. I'm not really sure what was more stupid: going out with Kara in the first place or thinking that the police could stop this freaky girl from whatever crazy stuff she was doing.

SCENE 3: *Two days after the dance. DAVON and GINA are in the park playing basketball.*

GINA: I know you messed with my game while I was in the other room last night.

DAVON: So?

GINA: So I didn't get to the highest level in Witch Hunt. I didn't get to capture the Queen Witch.

DAVON: That must be a real letdown for you, nerd girl.

GINA: Mom was mad at you for getting home so late last night.

DAVON: Yeah. Whatever.

GINA: You're gonna get it when she gets home from work today.

DAVON: Mind your own business and stop talking or you'll never get good enough to beat me.

GINA: Why were you on the phone all night? After you got home? Who were you talking to?

DAVON: I said, mind your own business.

GINA: What are you going to do to me? Huh?

(DAVON sees KARA approaching and catches the basketball and pushes it at GINA.)

DAVON: Take this and go to Aunt Jo's house. NOW!

GINA: That ain't no threat.

DAVON: I'm serious, Gina. Get out of here.

GINA: Why? What's wrong?

DAVON: Just go. Get out of here.

KARA: *(Striding over confidently)* Hello Davon.

DAVON: Kara. I'm surprised to see you.

(DAVON pushes the ball again toward GINA – trying to get her to go away.)

KARA: Why should you be surprised? Didn't you know that I'd come looking for you after I talked to the police?

GINA: What's going on here?

KARA: Oh, and I thought you knew just about everything, little girl.

(KARA starts to reach into her purse...)

DAVON: Don't!

This play doesn't have an ending. What do you think should happen next?

Workshop: The Dramatic Form

Level: Elementary School

Common Core State Standards for English Language Arts addressed:

Reading:
- *RF.5.4. Read with sufficient accuracy and fluency to support comprehension.*
- *RF.5.4a. Read on-level text with purpose and understanding.*

Writing:
- *W.5.3b. Use narrative techniques, such as dialogue, description, and pacing, to develop experiences and events or show the responses of characters to situations.*
- *W.5.4. Produce clear and coherent writing in which the development and organization are appropriate to task, purpose, and audience.*

Speaking and Listening:
- *SL.5.1b. Follow agreed-upon rules for discussions and carry out assigned roles.*

Language:
- *L.4.3a. Choose words and phrases to convey ideas precisely.*

Vocabulary:
- *Protagonist*: the principal character who carries the main thought of the play and with whom the audience identifies most strongly
- *Antagonist:* the main opponent of the protagonist
- *Conflict:* tension between two or more characters or between action and ideas; the fundamental struggle that leads to crisis and climax of a scene or play
- *Monologue:* a long speech by a single character
- *Dialogue:* a verbal exchange between characters
- *Stage Directions:* written instructions to actors, readers and directors that are included in a play but not meant to be spoken aloud in performance
- *Drama:* a literary composition in verse or prose intended to portray a character or tell a story, usually involving conflicts and emotions exhibited through action and dialogue
- *Narrative:* a literary composition intended to tell a story to readers through the written word

Materials:
- A chalkboard/whiteboard, or large sheets of paper to write on

- Copies of a play (any play that is age-appropriate will do)

Activities:

Introduction: Begin this workshop with a warm-up activity, such as the theater game, "What are you doing?"

"What Are You Doing?" Instruct students to stand in a circle, and choose one volunteer to stand in the middle. The student in the middle must mime an action. Choose another student and instruct that student to enter the circle and ask, "What are you doing?" The student in the middle must answer with something DIFFERENT from what he or she is miming. For example, if the student is miming riding a bike, he or she could answer, "Brushing my teeth!" The student who asked the question must then mime brushing his or her teeth. Continue until all students have had a turn.

The Dramatic Form: Tell the students that they will be learning about six different playwriting terms today: protagonist, antagonist, conflict, monologue, dialogue and stage directions. Briefly define these terms for the students. Tell them that in order to understand these terms better, they're going to play a game.

The Drama Game: Before you start, have the students practice the "freeze" command with you. When you say "freeze," they should stop in their place and fall silent. Practice a couple of times as a class. To play the game, you will give the students six additional commands. While they walk around the room, they will have to respond to each one. You can explain all six commands before the game begins, or you can introduce them one at a time depending on the needs of your students. Before giving a command, have the students freeze.

The Commands:
- *Protagonist:* Students must strike the pose of a potential protagonist, or "good guy" in a story (for example, a triumphant hero standing with his or her biceps flexed).
- *Antagonist:* Students must strike the pose of a potential antagonist, or "bad guy" (for example, an evil villain clasping his or her hands together as if hatching a plot).

- *Conflict:* Students must find a partner. Without touching each other, they must strike a pose that represents a conflict (for example, a child having a tantrum and a parent trying to soothe him or her).
- *Monologue:* Students must stand in place and wait for you to give them a topic (for example, "the best vacation ever"). Call on one student at a time to deliver his or her monologue from where he or she is standing.
- *Dialogue:* Students find a partner and wait for you to give them a topic (for example, "arguing about what to eat for dinner"). Call on one pair of students at a time to deliver their dialogue from where they are standing together.
- *Stage Directions:* Students must stand in place and wait for you to give them an action (for example, "sneaking into a candy store"). They must mime the action without speaking.

Scavenger Hunt: Ask the students to return to their seats. Hand out a copy of a play that the students are familiar with (for example, YPT's *The Math Test* (page 247) from the "What Is a Play?" workshop, or any other age-appropriate play). If the students have not read a play together yet, begin this activity with an in-class reading of the play. Now tell the students to take a closer look at the script – can they find a protagonist? Antagonist? Conflict? Monologue? Dialogue? Stage directions? Ask for volunteers to give examples of each item.

Drama vs. Narrative: Ask the students to think about how the script in front of them is different from a novel or storybook. How does the writing look different? Make a list of their ideas on the board. Also ask the students why they think those differences exist. (You can guide them towards the idea that a script can be picked up by an actor and performed easily.)

Reflection: Review the six playwriting terms with the students. Ask them to tell you why they think a play needs a protagonist, an antagonist, conflict, monologue, dialogue and stage directions.

Thinking Creatively

Workshop: Inspiration and Imagination

Level: Elementary School

Common Core State Standards for English Language Arts addressed:

Writing:
- *W.5.3. Write narratives to develop real or imagined experiences or events using effective technique, descriptive details, and clear event sequences.*
- *W.5.3a. Orient the reader by establishing a situation and introducing a narrator and/or characters; organize an event sequence that unfolds naturally.*
- *W.5.3d. Use concrete words and phrases and sensory details to convey experiences and events precisely.*
- *W.5.4. Produce clear and coherent writing in which the development, organization, and style are appropriate to task, purpose, and audience.*
- *W.5.10. Write routinely over extended time frames (time for research, reflection, and revision) and shorter time frames (a single sitting or a day or two) for a range of tasks, purposes, and audiences.*

Speaking and Listening:
- *SL.5.1b. Follow agreed-upon rules for discussions and carry out assigned roles.*

Language:
- *L.5.1. Demonstrate command of the conventions of standard English grammar and usage when writing or speaking.*
- *L.5.2 Demonstrate command of the conventions of standard English capitalization, punctuation, and spelling when writing.*

Vocabulary:
- *Inspiration:* the idea, person, thing, experience, emotion, or observation that moves an artist to create; inspiration prompts action or invention
- *Tableau:* a silent and motionless depiction of a scene created by actors, often from a picture
- *Monologue:* a long speech by a single character

Materials:
- A chalkboard/whiteboard, or large sheets of paper to write on
- An ordinary object (such as a rock)

Activities:

Introduction: Begin this workshop with a warm-up activity designed to get the students to use their imaginations, such as the theater game, "Magic Clay".

"Magic Clay": Instruct the students to stand in a circle. Ask them to imagine that in your hand, you hold magic clay. This magic clay can be molded into any object in the world. Pass the clay around the circle. When the students receive the clay, they should mime molding it into an object. After they mold the clay, they must silently show the class how the object is used. (For example, after molding a toothbrush a student could brush his or her teeth.) Encourage the students to make very specific choices about what they are molding. Once they have finished using their object, they should fold the clay back into a ball and pass it to the next person. Continue until every student has had a turn.

Inspiration: Explain that all plays have to start with inspiration. Briefly define the term for the students. Tell the students that inspiration is an easy thing to learn: you just have to use your imagination.

What Is This? Tell the students that they are going to use their imaginations to change an ordinary object into something amazing. Reveal your ordinary object. First ask the students to describe it exactly as it is.

What Is This? Game: Now ask the students to imagine other things that the object could be. Instead of telling you, they have to show you. Have the students form a circle. Start the game by holding the object. Then perform an action using the object that lets the students know what it is (for example, brushing your hair with a rock tells the students that the rock is a hairbrush). Now pass the object to the next person. Continue until every student has had a turn.

What Is This? Discussion: As a class, make a list on the board of all the things the object could be. Start with the things it became during the game, and then add other ideas. The wackier the ideas, the better. If the students need help thinking of ideas you should ask questions like, "Where did it come from?" "Whose object is it?" "What can it do?"

Tableau: Tell the students that they are going to create tableaus using their ordinary object. Briefly define the term for the students, emphasizing that in a tableau actors must communicate without using movement or their voices. Explain that you will be breaking the students up into small groups of three to four and that each group should start by deciding what the ordinary object will be. They can choose an idea from the board or come up with something new. Then each group will create a tableau that will "tell" the audience about their object. The students can play characters using the object or can become the object itself. They can show the audience where the object is, who owns it, how the characters feel about the object, and how it is used. It may be helpful to demonstrate.

Rehearsal: Give the students five minutes to rehearse their tableaus. During the rehearsal period, move around the room to offer assistance and take questions.

Sharing: Ask each group to share their tableau with the class. Tell the students in the audience to imagine that they are viewing a famous work of art. They should first close their eyes while the actors set up, opening their eyes on your count of three. When they open their eyes they should say, "Ooooohh! Aaahhh!" Practice this with them before the first performance.

Writing a Monologue: Tell the students that you want them to go one step further in transforming this ordinary object: you want them to give the object a voice. To write from the object's point of view, they will create a monologue. Briefly define the term monologue for the students. Let them know that they will be learning more about monologues in a later workshop. For now, they can think of a monologue as a speech. Ask the students to imagine that they are the transformed object. What does this object want more than anything? Tell them to begin writing with the words "I want" or "I wish". Allow the students to write for the rest of the period. While they write, move around the room to offer assistance. If time allows, ask for volunteers to share their monologues.

Reflection: Ask the students to define inspiration. Why is inspiration important for a playwright?

Workshop: Character Inspiration Stations

Level: Middle School

Common Core State Standards for English Language Arts addressed:

Writing:
- *W.8.3a. Engage and orient the reader by establishing a context and point of view and introducing a narrator and/or characters; organize an event sequence that unfolds naturally and logically.*
- *W.8.4. Produce clear and coherent writing in which the development, organization, and style are appropriate to task, purpose, and audience.*
- *W.8.5. With some guidance and support from peers and adults, develop and strengthen writing as needed by planning, revising, editing, rewriting, or trying a new approach, focusing on how well purpose and audience have been addressed.*

Speaking and Listening:
- *SL.8.1. Engage effectively in a range of collaborative discussions (one-on-one, in groups, and teacher-led) with diverse partners on grade 8 topics, texts, and issues, building on others' ideas and expressing their own clearly.*

Language:
- *L.8.6. Acquire and use accurately grade-appropriate general academic and domain-specific words and phrases; gather vocabulary knowledge when considering a word or phrase important to comprehension or expression.*

Vocabulary:
- *Character:* a person, animal, or entity in a story, scene or play with specific distinguishing physical, mental and attitudinal attributes
- *Inspiration:* the idea, person, thing, experience, emotion or observation that moves an artist to create; inspiration prompts action or invention
- *Mantra:* an often repeated word, formula or phrase, often a truism

Preparation:
- Before class begins, create the six "stations" in the room.
- This is not required, but it can be helpful for the students to have a list of ideas to choose from as they move through the inspiration stations activity. You could write ten or fifteen ideas per station on slips of paper so the students can look through them, or keep a list for yourself to share with students who get stuck.

Materials:
- Idea list for each inspiration station if you choose to provide these
- If possible, some music for the students to listen to
- You may choose to prepare character questionnaires for each student to fill out or questions can be written on the board

Activities:

Introduction: Ask the students to define the word "inspiration". How do artists find inspiration for their work? Let the students know that you will guide them through an activity that will help them find inspiration for an original character during today's workshop.

Character Inspiration Stations: Divide the class into six groups. The students will be moving through different stations together, but all the writing activities they will do today are individual. Guide the student groups through the different stations, giving them five to ten minutes per station. Alternatively, students can remain at their desks while completing the activity. If you are providing idea lists these can be passed around or written on the board.

The Stations:
- Dream Jobs: At this station, students should write down five dream jobs that their character might want. They can be realistic, like "police officer" or "teacher", or fantastical, like "emperor of Mars" or "ice cream sundae tester".
- Favorite Places: At this station, students should write down five possible favorite places their character might have. They can be realistic, like "the library" or "the beach", or fantastical, like "the Xylobark galaxy" or "in the belly of a whale".
- Favorite Meals: At this station, students should write down five possible favorite meals their character might enjoy. They can be realistic, like "a burger and fries" or "empanadas", or fantastical, like "beetle smoothies" or "gold dusted kangaroo meat".
- Favorite Songs: At this station, students should write down five possible favorite songs their character might like. These can be real songs that play on the radio, a type of music (like "classical" or "heavy metal"), or the students can even invent imaginary songs (like "the

national anthem of the Dingbogians"). If possible, allow students at this station to listen to a few songs to get them started.

- Fears: At this station, students should write down five things their character might be afraid of. These could be common fears, like "spiders" or "heights", or uncommon fears like "flesh eating snails" or "people with red hair".
- Mantras ("Rules to Live By"): At this station, students should write down five possible mantras that their character might believe in. If students are unfamiliar with the term "mantra", briefly define it for them. Provide a list of common mantras for students to read through at this station. (For example, "You can't judge a book by its cover," "Just keep swimming!", or "Well behaved women rarely make history.") Students can pick their mantras from your list, they can write down mantras they already know or they can invent new ones.

Sharing: Once the groups have returned to the station at which they started, allow some time for sharing. (You should take a couple of Fears/Dream Jobs/etc. from each person who wants to share – no one student should take the time to share all six of his or her lists.)

Creating a Character: Now explain to the students that they are going to use their lists to create a character. First, ask them to pick their favorite item from each category. What ideas do they think will yield the most interesting character? Out of those six items, ask them to choose four to create a character. Give the students an example to show how these four ideas can be combined to create interesting characters, for instance, a woman who dreams of being a yoga instructor, loves the beach, listens to Miley Cyrus and is afraid of clowns. Could you write a play about such a character?

Character Questionnaire: Now ask each student to answer a series of questions about his or her character. Students should write down their answers, and you can add or subtract questions as needed.

Questions:
- What is your character's name?
- How old is your character?
- What is your character's job?

- Where does your character live?
- What does your character love?
- What does your character hate?
- What does your character want more than anything in the world? Why?
- What is stopping your character from getting what they want?
- What does your character need to tell somebody? Who does he or she need to tell?
- What is one more thing we need to know about your character?

Reflection: What did you discover about your character today? Are there any aspects of your personality that are similar to your character's? Any aspects that are different?

Workshop: Visioning

Level: High School

Common Core State Standards for English Language Arts addressed:

Reading:
- *RL.11-12.3. Analyze the impact of the author's choices regarding how to develop and relate elements of a story or drama (e.g., where a story is set, how the action is ordered, how the characters are introduced and developed)*
- *RL.11-12.5. Analyze how an author's choices concerning how to structure specific parts of a text (e.g., the choice of where to begin or end a story, the choice to provide a comedic or tragic resolution) contribute to its overall structure and meaning as well as its aesthetic impact.*

Writing:
- *W.11-12.3d. Use precise words and phrases, telling details, and sensory language to convey a vivid picture of the experiences, events, setting, and/or characters.*
- *W.11-12.5. Develop and strengthen writing as needed by planning, revising, editing, rewriting, or trying a new approach, focusing on addressing what is most significant for a specific purpose and audience.*
- *W.11-12.10. Write routinely over extended time frames (time for research, reflection, and revision) and shorter time frames (a single sitting or a day or two) for a range of tasks, purposes, and audiences.*

Vocabulary:
- *Vision:* for an artist, vision is a vivid, imaginative sense of what his/her creation will be; a specific idea about the finished product
- *Stage directions:* written instructions to actors, readers and directors that are included in a play but are not meant to be spoken aloud in performance

Materials:
- A chalkboard/whiteboard, or large sheets of paper to write on
- Opening stage directions from two very different plays (such as *Like a Raisin in the Sun* by Lorraine Hansberry and *Dead Man's Cell Phone* by Sarah Ruhl)
- Copies of the play *Mariana's Wish* (page 139)

Activities:

Introduction: Tell the students that they will be discussing the concept of artistic vision. Ask them what they think the word "vision" means for an artist. Why is vision important?

Visioning a Classroom: Now ask the students to close their eyes. Tell them to picture a bare stage. Encourage them to focus on this stage and develop a specific picture of what it looks like. Now ask them to imagine two elements (set pieces, props) that they can put on that stage to clearly suggest a classroom. Encourage them to focus on the stage once again and choose the two most essential elements they would need to show a classroom to the audience. When they know what their two elements are, they can open their eyes. Ask for volunteers to share their elements with the class. Make a list of all the different elements on the board. Using their ideas, take the exercise a step further: what different kinds of classroom could we show onstage with just two elements? (For example, what is the difference between a smart board and a stool versus a green chalkboard and one broken piece of chalk?) Encourage the students to consider specific details, as everything you put onstage will communicate something to an audience.

Visioning Your Play: Ask the students to close their eyes again. Tell them to picture that same bare stage. Now ask them to think about the play that they are writing. What two elements would they put onstage to create the world of their play? What are the first things they want the audience to see? Tell them to consider the mood they want to create at the beginning of their play. When they know what their two elements are, they can open their eyes. Ask for volunteers to share their elements with the class.

Setting the Scene: Explain that in order to communicate the ideas the students just came up with, a playwright uses stage directions. Briefly define this term for the students. Tell them that the first stage direction in a play or scene is of particular importance: often, the first stage direction communicates the playwright's vision and sets the mood for the whole play.

Example Stage Directions: Share the opening stage directions from two different plays with the students (for example, *A Raisin in the Sun* by Lorraine Hansberry and *Dead Man's Cell Phone* by Sarah Ruhl). Discuss the differences between the stage directions and why the playwrights may have chosen to begin their plays with those words. You can also invite the students to guess what the plays might be about solely based on the opening stage directions.

Writing Stage Directions: Now ask the students to write the opening stage direction for the play they're writing. They can use the two elements they came up with earlier as a starting point. While the students write, move around the room to offer assistance. You can give them five to ten minutes to complete their work.

Sharing: Ask for volunteers to share their stage directions. After each sharing, ask the class to make guesses about the plays their peers are writing based on the stage directions. What does the first stage direction tell us about the rest of the play?

Reflection – Mariana's Wish: As a class, read the play *Mariana's Wish* by YPT alumna Mariana Pavón Sánchez. (Note: Mariana's play is written in English with some Spanish words and phrases. Be sure to let the students know this before they begin to read aloud, and assist any non-Spanish speakers with words they don't know.)

Mariana's Story: Before you begin the reading, you can tell the students a little about Mariana herself. She returned to the United States from Nicaragua when she was sixteen, and when YPT first came into her classroom, she didn't think she could write a play at all. Her play inspired YPT's reading committee, and it was professionally produced by YPT in April 2010. The DVD of *Mariana's Wish* attracted the attention of the White House and First Lady Michelle Obama when YPT was honored with the National Arts and Humanities Youth Program Award. Mariana was the only student invited to speak at the award ceremony. She read a selection from her play for the audience, which included Mrs. Obama and distinguished members of the President's Committee on the Arts and the Humanities (such as cellist Yo Yo Ma, actor and director Edward Norton and actor and producer Sarah Jessica Parker).

Discussion: Ask the students: what do you think Mariana's vision was? What did she want the audience to feel when they watched her play? What did she want them to think about? If you were directing Mariana's play, how would you use the stage to achieve her vision?

Creating Characters

Workshop: Finding Inspiration for a Play

Level: Elementary School

Common Core State Standards for English Language Arts addressed:

Writing:
- *W.5.3d. Use concrete words and phrases and sensory details to convey experiences and events precisely.*
- *W.5.5. With guidance and support from peers and adults, develop and strengthen writing as needed by planning, revising, editing, rewriting, or trying a new approach.*
- *W.5.10. Write routinely over extended time frames (time for research, reflection, and revision) and shorter time frames (a single sitting or a day or two) for a range of tasks, purposes, and audiences.*

Speaking and Listening:
- *SL.5.1b. Follow agreed-upon rules for discussions and carry out assigned roles.*

Vocabulary:
- *Inspiration:* the idea, person, thing, experience, emotion or observation that moves an artist to create; inspiration prompts action or invention
- *Character:* a person, animal or entity in a story, scene or play with specific distinguishing physical, mental and attitudinal attributes

Materials:
- Unlined paper and colored pencils, crayons or markers
- If desired, printouts of the "Creating a Character" questions (these can also be written on the board)

Activities:

Introduction: Begin this workshop with a warm-up activity designed to get the students to use their imaginations, such as the game "Rock, Paper, Anything".

"Rock, Paper, Anything": This game is a variation on the classic "rock, paper, scissors." Ask the students to sit in a circle and select two volunteers to stand in the middle. The students should then turn their backs to each other while you say, "Rock, paper, anything, SHOOT!" The students should then turn to each other and strike a pose. They can pose as

a rock, paper or anything else, but they must be ready to describe what they are to the class. Encourage them to be as outrageous and creative as possible. (For example, "a unicorn flying to Mars while eating cotton candy.") All the students close their eyes, and then vote on who has the best pose. The winner goes up against another volunteer. (To keep things fair, if the same student wins again, he or she has to sit down and allow two new people to play.) Repeat until everyone has had a turn.

Character: Tell the students that today they are going to create original characters. Some characters are people, but some are animals or objects. The only limit to what their characters can be is their imagination! In the following game, students will focus on characters that are objects.

"No! You Can't Take Me!" Break the class into small groups (three to five students per group). Assign each group a room in the house (the bedroom, the living room, the kitchen – avoid assigning the bathroom!). Don't let the students know what rooms the other groups have. Within each group, have each student choose one thing that would be found in the room. (For example, if the room is the bedroom, one student might be the bed, etc.) After choosing an object, each student should practice posing as that object. Encourage the groups to work together to create a picture of the room. Also ask each student to think of at least one good reason why his or her object is important to the room. Tell the students to ask themselves what would happen if their objects were not there.

Sharing: Now ask the students to return to their seats. Before sharing, explain the rules of the game. You will call one group to the front of the room. The audience should close their eyes while the actors set up, and then open their eyes on your count of three. The performances will follow this script:

> TEACHER: Look at all this useless stuff! I've got to get rid of some of this junk!
> *(The TEACHER selects one student.)*
> TEACHER: *(To STUDENT)* I think I'll take…THIS!
> STUDENT: No! You can't take me!
> TEACHER: Why not?

The student must answer without saying the name of his or her object. For example, if the student's object is the bed, he or she might reply like this:

STUDENT: If you take me away, no one will get any sleep!

Now the audience must guess what object the student is portraying. Continue until each student in the group has had a turn. Then ask the audience to guess what room the actors were in. Repeat with the other student groups.

Important Object: To help the students find inspiration for their characters, ask each student to think of an object that is important to him or her. It could be any object he or she chooses, for example a bracelet given to him or her by a loved one or a video game system. There are no wrong answers. If you like, you can ask the students to share their ideas as a group before they commit to their choices. Now, have the students close their eyes and picture the object in their minds. What does it look like? How does it feel to touch? Why is it important to them? Give the students a few minutes to draw their objects on a blank sheet of paper. When they finish their drawing, they can share their object with a partner, explaining what it is and why they selected it.

Creating a Character: Now tell the students that they are going to use their object to create a character. They can use their imaginations to change anything they want about their real object – professional playwrights do this all the time. To create their character, students must first make a choice: do they want to make their object into a character? Or do they want their character to be a person or animal that is connected to their object? (For example, they could write about a talking bracelet, or a boy who loves video games.) After they make their choice, they should answer the following questions on a piece of paper:

- What is your character's name?
- What does your character love?
- What does your character hate?

- What does your character want more than anything in the world? Why?
- What is one more thing we need to know about your character?

Allow the students most of the class period to write down their answers. While they work, move around the room, offering assistance. If the students finish early, they can draw a picture of their characters.

Sharing: To share their characters, lead the students in a "character parade"! Ask them to stand up and form two parallel lines, facing each other. You should be the first person in one of the lines. Explain that instead of telling the class about their characters, you want the students to show them. Ask the students to close their eyes. When they open their eyes, they will become their characters. They will introduce themselves to the group by saying "Hello, my name is _____." Encourage the students to think about how their character would speak. Does their character have a high voice, or a deep voice? Does their character have an accent? Is their character happy or sad? Tell the students to open their eyes. Take your turn first, walking between the two lines until you get to the back of the line. Make bold choices with your character voice so that the students will follow suit. After you, the next person should come from the opposite line (so that it goes back and forth). Continue until every student has introduced his or her character.

Reflection: Review the terminology you used in this lesson. What is a character? What is inspiration? How does a playwright find inspiration for a character?

Workshop: Character and Monologue

Level: Middle School

Common Core State Standards for English Language Arts addressed:

Writing:
- W.8.3. *Write narratives to develop real or imagined experiences or events using effective technique, well-chosen details, and well-structured event sequences.*
- W.8.3a. *Engage and orient the reader by establishing a context and point of view and introducing a narrator and/or characters; organize an event sequence that unfolds naturally and logically.*
- W.8.3b. *Use narrative techniques, such as dialogue, pacing, description, and reflection, to develop experiences, events, and/or characters.*
- W.8.4. *Produce clear and coherent writing in which the development, organization, and style are appropriate to task, purpose, and audience.*
- W.8.10. *Write routinely over extended time frames (time for research, reflection, and revision) and shorter time frames (a single sitting or a day or two) for a range of tasks, purposes, and audiences.*

Language:
- L.8.1. *Demonstrate command of the conventions of standard English grammar and usage when writing or speaking.*
- L.8.2. *Demonstrate command of the conventions of standard English capitalization, punctuation, and spelling when writing.*

Vocabulary:
- *Character:* a person, animal or thing in a play or story with specific distinguishing traits. Characters are "the agents of action" in a play because they make things happen
- *Monologue:* a long speech by a single character

Preparation:
- Prepare a list of stock characters to assign students in the character sculptures activity.

Materials:
- Printed images of people, enough for every student to have one (these will be your "picture people")

Activities:

Introduction: Tell the students that they will be exploring the concept of character today. Ask them to define the word character. What are some of their favorite characters from books, TV and movies? What about those characters is compelling? Now lead a warm-up activity that will deepen the students' understanding of character, such as the theater game "Character Sculptures".

"Character Sculptures": Divide the students into pairs. Ask each pair to decide who will be "A" and who will be "B". Assign each student a stock character (for example, teacher, body builder, or super hero). "A" will begin the exercise by molding the body of his or her partner into a statue of the stock character. Encourage the partners to be willing to move as directed and to remember their poses. When "A" has finished sculpting, he or she should think of one line that the stock character might say. (For example, the teacher might say, "Be quiet class!") "B" must memorize this line. Now "A" and "B" switch, with "B" sculpting "A" into the character. When all the partnerships have finished, ask for volunteers to perform their sculptures. To perform, have "A" help "B" get into his or her pose. When the sculpture is set, "A" should tap "B" on the shoulder to cue "B" to speak the given line. The class must guess the character that "B" is portraying. Then the partners switch. Allow a few other partnerships to share.

Finding Inspiration for a Character: Ask the students how they created their sculptures based on their given characters. Lead a discussion about how inspiration for characters and plays comes from our experiences and observations of the world around us.

Monologue: Tell the students that they will continue to explore characters by writing monologues. Briefly define the term for the students. Explain that monologues are often used to express a character's feelings or reveal new information about the character. For this reason, they are useful tools when creating a new original character.

Picture People: Lay out your "picture people" images on a table in the classroom. Invite the students to select one image from the table. When they return to their seats, they must begin creating a monologue for the character in the image. Tell them to start by giving their character a name, and deciding who he or she is talking to. Allow the students most of the class period to write. While they work, move around the room, offering assistance.

Sharing: Ask for volunteers to read their monologues to the class.

Reflection: Ask the students what they learned today about the concept of character that they did not know before. Was it hard or easy to create a character using an image? Why?

Workshop: Creating an Original Character

Level: High School

Common Core State Standards for English Language Arts addressed:

Writing:
- *W.11-12.3. Write narratives to develop real or imagined experiences or events using effective technique, well-chosen details, and well-structured event sequences.*
- *W.11-12.3a. Engage and orient the reader by setting out a problem, situation, or observation and its significance, establishing one or multiple point(s) of view, and introducing a narrator and/or characters; create a smooth progression of experiences or events.*
- *W.11-12.3b. Use narrative techniques, such as dialogue, pacing, description, reflection, and multiple plot lines, to develop experiences, events, and/or characters.*
- *W.11-12.4. Produce clear and coherent writing in which the development, organization, and style are appropriate to task, purpose, and audience.*
- *W.11-12.5. Develop and strengthen writing as needed by planning, revising, editing, rewriting, or trying a new approach, focusing on addressing what is most significant for a specific purpose and audience.*
- *W.11-12.10. Write routinely over extended time frames (time for research, reflection, and revision) and shorter time frames (a single sitting or a day or two) for a range of tasks, purposes, and audiences.*

Vocabulary:
- *Character:* a person, animal or entity in a story, scene or play with specific distinguishing physical, mental and attitudinal attributes
- *Protagonist:* the principal character who carries the main thought of the play and with whom the audience identifies most strongly
- *Antagonist:* the main opponent of the protagonist

Activities:

Introduction: Begin today's class by telling students that they will be exploring character. Ask them to define the word character. What are some of their favorite characters from books, TV and movies? Why do they like those characters?

Three Word Characters: Now tell the students that they're going to create simple characters in only two minutes, using just three words. The first word must be a physical descriptor, like "tall", "fat" or "bald". The second word must be an emotional descriptor, like "happy", "angry" or "paranoid". The third word must be an occupation or type, like "student", "ballerina" or "father". If you like, you can write a list of words to choose from up on the board, or you can create three lists as a class before you begin. Share an example character with the students before they begin to write, for instance a "bald paranoid ballerina." Give the students two minutes to select their three words.

Characters Come to Life: Now ask the students to choose a partner. Within their partnerships they should select one person to be the actor and one person to be the director. Next, they should pick which of their two characters they will work with. Ask the actors and directors to work together to create a short solo performance that will introduce this character to the audience. The character can speak, but cannot use any of the three words the students selected. Instruct the students to think about all the ways they can show who their character is: body language, spoken words, manner of speaking, etc. You can give them an example by creating a short solo performance for the bald paranoid ballerina character.

Rehearsal: Give the students five to ten minutes to craft and rehearse their solo pieces. Make sure that the student actors are getting up on their feet to rehearse, not just sitting and imagining what they will do onstage.

Performance: Ask for volunteers to share their performances. After each performance, ask the students how they would describe the character they just saw. Compare the students' guesses to the real character that the actor was portraying.

Real Life Characters: Tell the students that they are going to create another simple character, this time using inspiration from their real lives. Ask the students to divide a piece of paper into two columns. In the first column, they should make a list of ten adjectives that describe them. In the second column, they should make a list of ten roles they play in their lives (i.e. student, son/daughter, trumpet player, etc.). Finally, ask them to circle one item from each list that they think is the most interesting. These two items make up another character (for example, a "shy student" or "energetic trumpet player").

Visualization: Have the students close their eyes and imagine the character they've just created. They should picture this character in their minds, as you ask the following questions: How old is your character? What do they look like? How do they dress? Where are they from? What is their job? What is their family like? What is important to them? What do they want more than anything? What do they fear? Ask the students to open their eyes and jot down only the most vivid and important details they imagined during the visualization.

Protagonist and Antagonist: Now ask the students to shift their focus to their own plays. How will they create interesting, active characters that audiences will identify with? Briefly go over the terms protagonist and antagonist. The relationship between protagonist and antagonist creates conflict and keeps the audience interested.

Writing Period: Explain to the students that they have created two characters today: one using only three simple words, and one based on their own lives. They may already have a different character in mind that they'd like to write about. Ask the students to choose the protagonist of their play now. Who do they need to create in order to tell the story they want to tell? What does this character struggle for? Ask the students to write a monologue for their protagonist, beginning with one of three phrases: 1) "I want..." 2) "I wish..." 3) "I feel..." (Even if they don't decide to include this monologue in their final play, it's a great way for them to start discovering their protagonist.) Give them the rest of the class to write. While they write, move around the room to offer assistance. If time allows, ask for volunteers to share their monologues.

Reflection: Ask the students what they learned about finding inspiration for an original character today. What makes a character compelling? You can also review the terms protagonist and antagonist.

Developing Conflict

Workshop: Protagonist and Antagonist

Level: Elementary School

Common Core State Standards for English Language Arts addressed:

Writing:
- *W.5.3d. Use concrete words and phrases and sensory details to convey experiences and events precisely.*
- *W.5.4. Produce clear and coherent writing in which the development and organization are appropriate to task, purpose, and audience.*
- *W.5.10. Write routinely over extended time frames (time for research, reflection, and revision) and shorter time frames (a single sitting or a day or two) for a range of tasks, purposes, and audiences.*

Speaking and Listening:
- *SL.5.1. Engage effectively in a range of collaborative discussions (one-on-one, in groups, and teacher-led) with diverse partners on grade 5 topics and texts, building on others' ideas and expressing their own clearly.*
- *SL.5.1b. Follow agreed-upon rules for discussions and carry out assigned roles.*

Language:
- *L.5.3. Use knowledge of language and its conventions when writing, speaking, reading, or listening.*

Vocabulary:
- *Protagonist:* the principal character who carries the main thought of the play and with whom the audience identifies most strongly
- *Antagonist:* the main opponent of the protagonist
- *Conflict:* tension between two or more characters or between action and ideas; the fundamental struggle that leads to crisis and climax of a scene or play

Materials:
- An ordinary object (you can use something already in the classroom if you like)

Activities:

Introduction: Begin this workshop with a warm-up activity designed to get the students to use their imaginations, such as the theater game

"Sticky Floor".

"Sticky Floor": Instruct the students to stand on one side of the room, forming multiple lines facing the other side of the room. There should be four or five students in each row. You will call out a substance, and the students in the first row must cross the room as if they are moving through that substance. (For example, lava, mousetraps, mud, ice or gum.) Repeat with the other rows of students.

Give Me Back My Phone! Reveal your ordinary object to the students. Tell them that this object is not whatever it is, but a phone (or anything else that is very important to your students). Explain that in this game you will be playing the role of a teacher who caught one of his or her students playing with a phone in class. As a result, you have taken the phone from the student. Ask for a volunteer actor to play the scene with you. Instruct the actor to enter the "classroom" and ask you for the phone. When the student actor asks, simply hand over the phone. Now ask the class what they thought of the scene. Was it interesting to watch? Why or why not? Ask for another volunteer actor. Give the actor the same instructions, but this time when he or she asks for the phone you should put up a fight. (You could say, for example, "Why should I give you back this phone? I know you're only going to play with it during my class again.") Challenge the student actor to try different tactics to get the phone back. After the performance, ask the students if they liked that scene better. Why or why not?

Conflict: Point out to the students that the difference between the first scene and the second scene was the presence of conflict. Ask the students to give you their definition of conflict. Write their ideas on the board, supplementing if necessary. Explain that conflict is essential to drama – it is what makes plays interesting to watch. To create a conflict in a play, you need a protagonist and an antagonist. Define those terms for the students.

Protagonist Interviews: Tell the students that in the next exercise, they are going to become characters that might be protagonists. The protagonist is kind of like the hero of the story or the "good guy", the one the audience roots for. Assign each student a stock character (for example, teacher, body builder or superhero) and divide the students into pairs. Explain that the students will take turns interviewing each other – one student will be in character, the other will be the interviewer. The interviewer will ask seven pre-written questions and one original question. Give the students a couple of minutes to write down their original interview question before you begin. As they write, move around the room offering assistance.

Interview Questions:
1.   What is your name?
2.   What is your job?
3.   What do you like to do for fun?
4.   Who is your best friend (or best friends)?
5.   Who is your worst enemy (or enemies)?
6.   Tell me about a time when you were really mad.
7.   Tell me about a time when you were really happy.

Becoming Your Character: Within each partnership, ask the students to decide who will be "A" and who will be "B." Then ask the "A" partners to stand up and close their eyes. Tell the students to visualize their character. What does the character look like? Tall or short? What color eyes? What color hair? What clothes are they wearing? How does the character feel right now? At the end of the visualization exercise, tell the students that when they open their eyes they will become this character. Now the "B" partners interview the "A" partners. Allow five minutes to do this. During the interview, the "B" partners' job is to remember at least one interesting answer that the actor gives. As the interviews take place, move around the room, ensuring that the student actors are speaking in the first person. At the end of five minutes, repeat the visualization exercise, this time with the "B" partners. Afterwards, allow five minutes for the "A" partners to interview the "B" partners.

Sharing: Ask the students to share what they learned about their partners' characters.

Creating an Antagonist: Now that the students have their protagonists, what they need are antagonists. The antagonist stands in the way of the protagonist, sort of like a "bad guy". But just like bad guys in the movies, all antagonists have reasons for what they do. The audience may not agree, but the writer has given the character an inner life that explains his or her actions. Ask the students to name some super villains they are familiar with and explain the reasons behind their actions. (Magneto from *X-Men* is a great example: he is distrustful of humans because of his experience in a concentration camp as a young boy.) Now tell the students that they will be creating an original antagonist to oppose their protagonist. Brainstorm a few pairings as a class. (For example, if your protagonist is a teacher, the antagonist could be a student.)

Writing Period: Have the students select their antagonists and then answer the following questions on a piece of paper:

- What is your antagonist's name?
- What does your antagonist love?
- What does your antagonist hate?
- What does your antagonist want more than anything in the world? Why?
- What is one more thing we need to know about your antagonist?

While the students write, move around the room offering assistance. If they finish early, they can draw a picture of their antagonists.

Reflection: Allow volunteers to tell the class about the antagonists they created. Ask the students what they learned about conflict today. How does a playwright create conflict onstage?

Workshop: Conflict and Dialogue

Level: Middle School

Common Core State Standards for English Language Arts addressed:

Reading:
- *RL.8.3. Analyze how particular lines of dialogue or incidents in a story or drama propel the action, reveal aspects of a character, or provoke a decision.*

Writing:
- *W.8.4. Produce clear and coherent writing in which the development, organization, and style are appropriate to task, purpose, and audience.*
- *W.8.10. Write routinely over extended time frames (time for research, reflection, and revision) and shorter time frames (a single sitting or a day or two) for a range of tasks, purposes, and audiences.*

Speaking and Listening:
- *SL.8.1. Engage effectively in a range of collaborative discussions (one-on-one, in groups, and teacher-led) with diverse partners on grade 8 topics, texts, and issues, building on others' ideas and expressing their own clearly.*
- *SL.8.1b. Follow rules for collegial discussions, track progress toward specific goals and deadlines, and define individual roles as needed.*

Vocabulary:
- *Conflict:* tension between two or more characters or between action and ideas; the fundamental struggle that leads to crisis and climax of a scene or play
- *Objective:* the desired goal of a character that motivates action
- *Obstacle:* Anyone or anything that prevents a character from reaching his or her objective
- *Dialogue:* A verbal exchange between characters

Materials:
- Printed images of people, enough for every student to have one (these will be your "picture people")

Activities:

Introduction: Begin today's class with the active theater game, "Kitty Wants a Corner".

"Kitty Wants a Corner": Ask the students to stand in a circle. Select one person to stand in the middle – this person becomes the Kitty. The Kitty should walk up to anyone in the circle and say, "Kitty wants a corner." That person must respond with, "Ask my neighbor." The Kitty then asks the next person for a corner. While this is happening, the other players try to switch places in the circle without the Kitty noticing. When the Kitty notices people trying to switch places, he or she must try to take one of the open spaces in the circle before another person does. If Kitty succeeds, the person left in the middle becomes the new Kitty. If Kitty fails, he or she continues asking for a corner. (If your students need more structure, play this game by forming a circle of chairs and having all the students except Kitty sit in their chairs.)

The Role of Conflict in Drama: Use the game you just played to unpack the concept of conflict. Ask the students what the Kitty wanted in the game. What was preventing the Kitty from getting it? What would happen if a player simply gave Kitty a space in the circle? Introduce the terms objective and obstacle. Explain that when a character has a strong objective, but is met with an obstacle, conflict is created. Conflict is essential to drama. It is what makes plays interesting because it keeps the audience guessing about what will happen next and allows them the chance to root for one character over another.

Dialogue: Tell the participants that one of the primary tools a playwright uses to reveal and develop conflict is dialogue. Briefly define the term for the students.

Picture People Duet Dialogues: Lay out your "picture people" images on a table in the classroom. Invite the students to select one image from the table. When they return to their seats, they must select a writing partner. Tell the students that they will be writing duet dialogues in their partnerships. Writing a duet dialogue is very similar to passing notes in class. Each pair of students will write their duet dialogue on one piece of paper. The first writer begins by writing one line for his character. Without speaking, he hands the paper to the second writer. The second writer must read her partner's line and write her character's response. Then she passes the paper back to her partner. Before he or she begins writing, each student should first select a name for his or her character. For this exercise, the conflict between the two characters will be that one character has something that the other character wants. The students must also decide what their two characters are arguing over. (After they make those choices, the students should write silently.) Encourage the students to consider how their character speaks when writing a dialogue with their partner and to be sure to respond to what their partner is writing. The characters should not only be arguing for their own personal objectives but also responding to their partner's points. Give the students five to ten minutes to write. Their goal should be to arrive at a resolution of the conflict. While they write, move around the room, offering assistance.

Sharing: Have groups volunteer to share their work. Ask the class to discuss the conflict in each scene.

Reflection: Ask the students why conflict is important to drama. How do playwrights create conflict?

Workshop: Java Jones

Level: High School

Common Core State Standards for English Language Arts addressed:

Writing:
- *W.11-12.3: Write narratives to develop real or imagined experiences or events using effective technique, well-chosen details, and well-structured event sequences.*
- *W.11-12.3a. Engage and orient the reader by setting out a problem, situation, or observation and its significance, establishing one or multiple point(s) of view, and introducing a narrator and/or characters; create a smooth progression of experiences or events.*
- *W.11-12.3b. Use narrative techniques, such as dialogue, pacing, description, reflection, and multiple plot lines, to develop experiences, events, and/or characters.*
- *W.11-12.4. Produce clear and coherent writing in which the development, organization, and style are appropriate to task, purpose, and audience.*
- *W.11-12.10. Write routinely over extended time frames (time for research, reflection, and revision) and shorter time frames (a single sitting or a day or two) for a range of tasks, purposes, and audiences.*

Speaking and Listening:
- *SL.11-12.1. Initiate and participate effectively in a range of collaborative discussions (one-on-one, in groups, and teacher-led) with diverse partners on grade 11-12 topics, texts, and issues, building on others' ideas and expressing their own clearly and persuasively.*

Vocabulary:
- *Character:* a person, animal or entity in a story, scene or play with specific distinguishing physical, mental and attitudinal attributes
- *Conflict:* tension between two or more characters, or between action and ideas; the fundamental struggle that leads to crisis and climax of a scene or play
- *Objective:* the desired goal of a character that motivates action
- *Obstacle:* anyone or anything that prevents a character from reaching his or her objective
- *Monologue:* a long speech by a single character
- *Dialogue:* a conversation between two or more characters

Preparation:

- It is helpful to write the Java Jones scenario and character descriptions up on the board before class begins.

Activities:

Introduction: When the students arrive today, ask them to sit in groups of four. The objective of this exercise is to introduce students to all the essential tools of the playwright through an interactive process. Explain to the students that they are about to participate in an activity that will demonstrate how conflict can inspire dramatic writing and drive interaction between characters.

Conflict (Objective + Obstacle):

Conflict: Unpack the concept of conflict. What is a conflict? Ask the students to think of a conflict they've faced in their lives – could they rest until it was resolved? Ask a volunteer to share an example. Explain that conflict is essential to drama. It is what makes plays interesting because it keeps the audience guessing about what will happen next and allows them the chance to root for one character over another.

Objective and Obstacle: Use one of the students' example conflicts to illustrate the concepts of objective and obstacle. Explain that when a character has a strong objective, but is met with an obstacle, conflict is created. These are the concepts they will explore in their writing today.

Java Jones: Tell the students that they will be exploring the following scenario, "A neighborhood must decide whether to allow a fancy coffee chain, Java Jones, to open in an old building." Within each group of four, assign the following four characters to the students:

The Characters:

- *Developer:* You own the building that Java Jones wants to buy. You will make a lot of money if they are allowed to buy it. You'll also get to drink your favorite fancy coffee!
- *Owner of a Small Mini-Mart:* You fear people will stop buying coffee at your store, even though it's less expensive.

- *Single Parent:* You need a job with flexible hours and health-care benefits for you and your kids. Java Jones will offer both.
- *Resident:* You live in the building that Java Jones wants to take over. You do not own the building and you cannot afford to live anywhere else in the neighborhood. The rent will be too high.

Monologue: Introduce monologue as a playwright's tool. Briefly define the term for the students. Explain that playwrights often use monologues to take a closer look at a character's thoughts and feelings.

Java Jones Monologues: Tell the students that they will be writing monologues for their assigned character. Give them five to ten minutes to write. If you feel that the students could use more structure, give them a starting prompt to begin, such as "I do/do not want Java Jones to move in because..." While the students write, move around the room offering assistance.

Monologue Sharing: After the writing period, ask students to share their monologues with their groups.

Dialogue: Now introduce dialogue as an essential tool of the playwright. Briefly define the term for the students. In a play, dialogue is a primary way characters express themselves and it reveals conflict, themes and actions.

Duet Dialogues: Explain to the students that their next step is to write duet dialogues. Writing a duet dialogue is very similar to passing notes in class. Students must choose a partner within their group whose character disagrees with their own character about Java Jones. Each pair of students will write their duet dialogue on one piece of paper. The first writer begins by writing one line for his or her character. Without speaking, he or she passes the paper to the second writer. The second writer must read his or her partner's line and write his or her character's response. Then he or she passes the paper back to his or her partner. Encourage the students to consider how their characters speak when writing a dialogue with their partners and to be sure to respond to what their partners are writing. The characters should not only be arguing for their own personal objectives but also responding to their partners' points. If at all possible, they can try to work toward a compromise or understanding between the characters. Give the students five minutes to write. (Make sure to cut them off at five minutes. It is important that they not spend too much time on this dialogue so that they don't lose momentum.)

Java Jones Dialogues: Now ask the students to write a dialogue on their own for two characters. They must use their original character and choose any other character with an opposing point of view. Give them ten minutes to write. While they work, move around the room, offering assistance.

Sharing: Allow anyone interested in sharing his or her work to do so. He or she may share his or her duet dialogue or the one he or she wrote independently. After each sharing, discuss the conflict and resolution (if any), characters and character voice. Although there may not be time for all groups to share, you can ask students to share their ideas for compromise or resolution.

Reflection: Review the playwright's tools: character, conflict (objective + obstacle), monologue and dialogue. Ask the students if at any point today they were writing for a character with whom they personally disagreed. What was that like? Did it help them to see the issue from multiple sides?

Using Creative Language

Workshop: Language Lab

Level: Middle School

Common Core State Standards for English Language Arts addressed:

Reading:
- RL.8.3. *Analyze how particular lines of dialogue or incidents in a story or drama propel the action, reveal aspects of a character, or provoke a decision.*
- RL.8.4. *Determine the meaning of words and phrases as they are used in a text, including figurative and connotative meanings; analyze the impact of specific word choices on meaning and tone, including analogies or allusions to other texts.*

Writing:
- W.8.3b. *Use narrative techniques, such as dialogue, pacing, description, and reflection, to develop experiences, events, and/or characters.*

Language:
- L.8.3. *Use knowledge of language and its conventions when writing, speaking, reading, or listening.*
- L.8.5. *Demonstrate understanding of figurative language, word relationships, and nuances in word meanings.*

Vocabulary:
- *Diction:* choice of words especially with regard to correctness, clearness or effectiveness

Preparation:
- For the "Who says THAT?" game, you will need to select ten images of individual people and create one line that each person might say. (For example, an image of a police officer might be paired with the line, "STOP! THIEF!" while an image of a businessman might be paired with the line, "Give me an extra hot no whip half caf skim mochachino and make it quick.") Create enough copies of the images and the lines for every pair of students. The students' task will be to match the lines to the images.

Materials:
- "Who says THAT?" image sheets and lines sheets
- Printed images of people, enough for every student to have one (these will be your "character images")

Activities:

Introduction: Tell the students that they're going to explore how playwrights use language creatively to help tell their stories and create interesting characters. Ask the students to name characters from TV or movies that have a specific way of speaking. What does the character's language tell us about the character? Explain to the students that playwrights choose words and punctuation very carefully to help create these unique ways of speaking. (Some students might suggest that a specific vocal choice, like an accent, is the work of an actor. Let the students know that as writers they can lead actors to make those choices based on what they write.)

Who says THAT? For this exercise students should work in pairs. Explain that they will receive different lines that might be said by a character. They will also receive pictures of characters. In their partnerships, the students should take turns reading the lines out loud. After each line reading, they should work together to guess which picture matches the line. (If you like, you can turn this into a competition: the winning partnership is the one that gets all the correct answers first.) Once all the partnerships have completed the exercise, go over the answers as a class. Ask the students how they were able to identify the character from the text. What does the way the language is written tell us about character?

How Would They Say That? Now tell the students that they are going to practice manipulating language to define a character. Write a couple of generic lines up on the board. (For example, "I want a candy bar. Your Snickers looks good. I wish I had a Snickers. Could I have your Snickers?") Lay out your character images on a table in the classroom. Invite the students to select one image from the table. When they return to their seats, their task is to rewrite the generic text so that it fits the character they see pictured. Give them five minutes to write. As they work, move around the room, offering assistance.

Sharing: Ask for a volunteer playwright to share what he or she has written. For this sharing, the playwright should not read his or her own text. Rather, allow the student to select a volunteer actor from the class. Have the actor perform the line. Then ask the class to guess who is speaking. How old is he or she? Where is he or she from? What else can you tell about the character from the line? Coach the students to look for specific evidence to back up their conclusions. (Have the actor repeat the line as needed.) As this conversation is happening, write the playwright's line on the board exactly as it is written on the page. Now ask the class to offer suggestions to the playwright on ways to revise the line so that the character becomes clearer. Make the changes suggested by the students on the board. (The class should only add or change up to three things.) Have the student actor read the newly revised line. Ask the students to consider the changes they made – is the new line more specific? More fun to hear and watch? Why? Repeat the sharing process with additional student volunteers.

Reflection: Ask the students why it is important to make specific choices regarding word choice and punctuation in their writing. What does language tell us about character?

Workshop: Exploring Language with an Actor

Level: High School

Common Core State Standards for English Language Arts addressed:

Writing:
- *W.11-12.3d. Use precise words and phrases, telling details, and sensory language to convey a vivid picture of the experiences, events, setting, and/or characters.*
- *W.11-12.4. Produce clear and coherent writing in which the development, organization, and style are appropriate to task, purpose, and audience.*
- *W.11-12.10. Write routinely over extended time frames (time for research, reflection, and revision) and shorter time frames (a single sitting or a day or two) for a range of tasks, purposes, and audiences.*

Speaking and Listening:
- *SL.11-12.6. Adapt speech to a variety of contexts and communicative tasks, demonstrating command of formal English when indicated or appropriate.*

Language:
- *L.11-12.3. Apply knowledge of language to understand how language functions in different contexts, to make effective choices for meaning or style, and to comprehend more fully when reading or listening.*
- *L.11-12.3a. Vary syntax for effect, consulting references for guidance as needed; apply an understanding of syntax to the study of complex texts when reading.*
- *L.11-12.5. Demonstrate understanding of figurative language, word relationships, and nuances in word meanings.*
- *L.11-12.5a. Interpret figures of speech (e.g., hyperbole, paradox) in context and analyze their role in the text.*

Vocabulary:
- *Diction:* choice of words especially with regard to correctness, clearness or effectiveness
- *Audience:* the group of spectators at a public event; listeners or viewers collectively, as in attendance at a theater or concert
- *Objective:* the desired goal of a character that motivates action

Materials:
- Copies of four or five unique character outlines, enough for every student. (It's okay for students to use the same outline.) The outlines

should indicate who the character is, who the character is speaking to and the character's objective. Below are some examples:

CHARACTER: a three-year-old child
AUDIENCE: his mother
OBJECTIVE: to get his mother to buy him a toy

CHARACTER: an old woman from the country
AUDIENCE: teenagers
OBJECTIVE: to get some lazy kids off her lawn

CHARACTER: a rapper just starting out in the business
AUDIENCE: dancing crowd at a club
OBJECTIVE: get people to buy his CD

CHARACTER: a military officer
AUDIENCE: new recruits
OBJECTIVE: lead new recruits through rigorous physical training

- If you like, before class begins, you can write the lines that the actor will perform during this workshop on large sheets of paper or on the board (if you have something to cover them until the appropriate moment).

Preparation:
- You will need one actor to help you with this workshop. Before class begins, you should communicate with your actor to explain his or her role in the workshop and ensure the actor has all the materials he or she needs.

Activities:

Introduction: Tell the students that they're going to explore how playwrights use language creatively to help tell their stories. Introduce the guest actor. Explain that the actor is there to help the students explore the connection between word choice, punctuation and character. Explain that a playwright's diction communicates something specific to an audience. Briefly define the term diction for the students.

Multiple Audiences: Now ask the students what an "audience" is. Explain that those watching a play or a movie are the audience for that show, anyone reading something is the audience of that text, and anyone listening to someone talk is the audience of what is being said. Explain that playwrights must consider multiple audiences: the person or people their character is talking to, a reader that picks up their play, a production team (including actors, directors, and designers) that has decided to perform the play and the audience who will sit in the theater to watch the play. In order to communicate clearly with all of these different people, a playwright must be very specific.

Who Says This? Now tell the students that the guest actor is going to perform three different lines. They should pay attention to how the actor's delivery communicates something specific. After the actor performs each line, ask the class to guess who is speaking. How old is the speaker? Where is he or she from? What else can you tell about the character from the line? Coach the students to look for specific evidence to back up their conclusions. (Have the actor repeat the line as needed.)

The Lines:
- "That looks, like, so cute on you. You should, like, totally buy it. You look, like, totally hot."
- "Nah-uh. Y'all ain't gonna get a rise outta me. I ain't gonna pay you no mind. Go on now. Ya hear?"
- "Good mooorning boys and girls. Let's aaall sit criss-cross-apple-sauce on the carpet squares. Now, Timmy, we don't hit our neighbor."

Keep things moving with three or four guesses per line. (Part of the challenge is the speed with which you move through the lines. Immediate impressions are more valuable for this introductory exercise than considered, mulled-over conclusions.)

Discussion: Lead a discussion about this exercise. If it hasn't already been stated, suggest that the assumptions made about the characters were primarily based on the language used by the characters, or the playwright's use of diction. (Some of the students might suggest that they made their guesses based on the vocal and physical attributes the actor applied to the performance. If that happens, engage the actor in the discussion by asking, "What led you to make that particular physical/vocal choice?")

Who Says This? Part Two: Have the actor perform the first line again. Ask the students to listen carefully. Then ask a volunteer to attempt to write the line on the board as he or she thinks it's written on the page. (Have the actor repeat the line as necessary.) When the student finishes writing on the board, reveal the line as written. Discuss the similarities and differences in what the original playwright did and the version developed on the board. Look at the line together and see if you can discover how the actor arrived at his or her performance based on the playwright's word choice and punctuation. Repeat for the other two lines.

Character Outlines: Now explain to the students that you are going to ask them to write one line for a specific character. Assign each student a character outline that indicates a character, a specific audience and an objective. The students should write one line for their characters based on their character outlines. Give them five minutes to develop their lines, encouraging them to use specific words and punctuation. While they write, move around the room, offering assistance.

Sharing: As the writing period winds down, ask a volunteer to give a line to the actor to read (the playwright should not explain anything to the actor, but give the actor a minute to read and "rehearse" the line). Close the writing period and ask the actor to perform this line. After the performance, ask the students what they can determine about the character based on the playwright's line. Who is the character speaking to? What is his or her objective? Encourage the students to look for specific evidence in the playwright's text to back up their conclusions. As this conversation is happening, have the actor write the line down on the board exactly as it is written. Now ask the class to offer suggestions to the playwright on ways to revise the line so that the character becomes clearer. Ask the actor to make the changes suggested by the students on the board. (The class should only add or change up to three things in the interest of time.) Have the actor do a cold reading of the newly revised line. Ask the students to consider the changes they made – is the new line more specific? More fun to hear and watch? Why? Repeat the sharing process with additional student volunteers.

Reflection: Ask the students how a playwright's word choice and punctuation help clarify a character. Why are these choices important to creating a compelling play?

Building Dramatic Structure

Workshop: Structuring a Play

Level: Elementary, Middle and High School

Common Core State Standards for English Language Arts addressed:

Elementary School:
Reading:
- *RL.5.5. Explain how a series of chapters, scenes, or stanzas fits together to provide the overall structure of a particular story, drama, or poem.*

Writing:
- *W.5.3. Write narratives to develop real or imagined experiences or events using effective technique, descriptive details, and clear event sequences.*
- *W.5.4. Produce clear and coherent writing in which the development and organization are appropriate to task, purpose, and audience.*
- *W.5.5. With guidance and support from peers and adults, develop and strengthen writing as needed by planning, revising, editing, rewriting, or trying a new approach.*
- *W.5.10. Write routinely over extended time frames (time for research, reflection, and revision) and shorter time frames (a single sitting or a day or two) for a range of tasks, purposes, and audiences.*

Middle School:
Reading:
- *RL.8.3. Analyze how particular lines of dialogue or incidents in a story or drama propel the action, reveal aspects of a character, or provoke a decision.*

Writing:
- *W.8.3. Write narratives to develop real or imagined experiences or events using effective technique, relevant descriptive details, and well-structured event sequences.*
- *W.8.4. Produce clear and coherent writing in which the development, organization, and style are appropriate to task, purpose, and audience.*
- *W.8.5. With some guidance and support from peers and adults, develop and strengthen writing as needed by planning, revising, editing, rewriting, or trying a new approach, focusing on how well purpose and audience have been addressed.*
- *W.8.10. Write routinely over extended time frames (time for research, reflection, and revision) and shorter time frames (a single sitting or a day or two) for a range of tasks, purposes, and audiences.*

High School:
Reading:
- *RL.11-12.3. Analyze the impact of the author's choices regarding how to develop and relate elements of a story or drama (e.g., where a story is set, how the action is ordered,*

how the characters are introduced and developed.)

- *RL.11-12.5. Analyze how an author's choices concerning how to structure specific parts of a text (e.g., the choice of where to begin or end a story, the choice to provide a comedic or tragic resolution) contribute to its overall structure and meaning as well as its aesthetic impact.*

Writing:

- *W.11-12.3. Write narratives to develop real or imagined experiences or events using effective technique, well-chosen details, and well-structured event sequences.*
- *W.11-12.4. Produce clear and coherent writing in which the development, organization, and style are appropriate to task, purpose, and audience.*
- *W.11-12.5. Develop and strengthen writing as needed by planning, revising, editing, rewriting, or trying a new approach, focusing on addressing what is most significant for a specific purpose and audience.*
- *W.11-12.10. Write routinely over extended time frames (time for research, reflection, and revision) and shorter time frames (a single sitting or a day or two) for a range of tasks, purposes, and audiences.*

Vocabulary:

- *Dramatic Structure:* refers to the parts into which a short story, a novel, a play, a screenplay or a narrative poem can be divided
- *Balanced Situation:* the way things are or were at the beginning of your story – the circumstances that make the conflict possible; it should hint at potential conflict or disturbance
- *Disturbance:* an event that upsets the balanced situation and affects the protagonist; the disturbance jump starts the action of the play
  Conflict/Complications: when characters have a disagreement, a dispute or a collision; the protagonist is met with an obstacle that stops him or her from reaching his or her objective (also referred to as rising action)
- *Climax:* when the disturbance and conflicts are settled; one of the two forces in conflict "wins;" balance or order is re-established
- *Resolution:* how everything ends; the final result; this is when we find out how the play is resolved—whether the protagonist succeeds or fails and how the protagonist (as well as other characters) are affected

Materials:

- Copies of a short play (any play that is age appropriate will do), such as *The Day After Bob Said, Yeah Right* (page 11)

Activities:

Introduction: Tell the students that today you will explore how plays are structured. Briefly define the term dramatic structure. Explain that playwrights use good dramatic structure to make their plays interesting and build suspense for the audience.

Reading: As a class, read a short play together. (There are many good example plays in this book – *The Day After Bob Said, "Yeah, Right"* by Ann Gill (page 11) works especially well in this workshop and is appropriate for all grade levels.)

Dramatic Structure: Now tell the class that you're going to use the play you just read to get a better understanding of dramatic structure. Define the components of dramatic structure for the students, appropriate to grade level. (At the elementary level, we simply use beginning, middle and end. At the high school level, we use balanced situation, disturbance, complications, climax and resolution – these terms are useful because they are specific to drama. You can easily substitute whatever terminology your students are accustomed to, i.e. exposition, rising action, climax, falling action, resolution.) As a class, you're going to plot the structure of the play you just read on the board. Begin by identifying the protagonist and antagonist. What are their objectives? What is the conflict? Then ask the students to identify the different parts of the plot. (If you like, you can work backwards to make it easier for the students to identify each part of the structure.)

Work Period: Now ask the students to use what they've learned to plot the structure of the plays they will write. They can write an outline or, if they are more visual, create a storyboard with images for each step in their plot. Just as you did as a class, they should begin by defining their protagonist, antagonist, their objectives and the conflict. Then they should write the events that take place at each stage in their story. Give them most of the period to write. While they work, move around the room, offering assistance.

Reflection: Ask any student who is willing to tell the class about the play he or she is working on. Allow the students to ask the playwright questions to help the writer think through the plot of his or her play. Now ask the students why a strong structure is important to a play.

Revising a Play

Workshop: The Importance of Revision

Level: Middle and High School

Common Core State Standards for English Language Arts addressed:

Vocabulary:
- *Revision:* to alter something already written or printed, in order to make corrections, improve or update it

Materials:
- Copies of *The Revision Play* (page 322)
- If you like, before class begins, you can make copies of *The Revision Play* idea, or you can write the text on the board (if you have something to cover it until the appropriate moment).

Activities:

Introduction: Begin this workshop by discussing the importance of revision with the students. Briefly define the term. Then explain that professional playwrights spend years revising their work, often with the help of experienced actors and directors, in order to tell the stories they tell in the most compelling way possible. Tell the students that to explore this process, today they will read a play that needs a lot of revision.

The Revision Play: Pass out a copy of *The Revision Play* to every student. Ask two volunteers to perform the play for the class. (You should read stage directions.)

Discussion: Lead a discussion about the play you just read. Ask the students to imagine that they are the playwrights. How would they go about revising this play? On the board, organize the students' ideas into the following categories: big changes, small changes and questions. (Encourage the students to make notes in all three categories: there are small changes like typos, big changes like stage directions that should be turned into dialogue and plenty of things that are unclear that should yield questions.)

The Revision Play Idea: Tell the students that writers sometimes have lots of ideas in their head, but have trouble getting them on paper. Reveal the following information about the playwright's ideas to the students.

The Idea:
- It's the year 3023. Parents can now choose the color of their kids' hair *before* they're born. It's very trendy for people to have green hair – this is considered beautiful in the future. Adults spend a lot of money dying their hair green. Lots of parents choose to have their kids born with green hair so that they will be considered beautiful and so that

they won't have to pay for hair dye. Some parents choose not to change their unborn children's hair color. Some of these parents believe that their kids should have free choice over their hair color. Others believe it is wrong to change children before they are born. Students at Michelle Obama Public Charter School are divided between the majority of kids with green hair, and the minority of kids who have non-green hair. George is a student with green hair. Linda is a student with brown hair. George and Linda both received detention after school today. They are the only two kids in detention, and the teacher has stepped out...

Ask the students how they would have written the scene differently to communicate these ideas. Encourage them to make suggestions with the stage specifically in mind. For example, what could we put onstage to show the audience that it's the future?

Writing Period: Divide the students into pairs. Ask them to work together to rewrite this scene from *The Revision Play*. They can make any changes they like, but they should keep in mind the playwright's original ideas. As they work, move around the room, offering assistance.

Sharing: Ask for volunteers to read their new scenes for the class. After each performance, ask the class to identify the changes made by the playwrights. Did the changes make the scene more compelling?

Reflection: Ask the students why the revision process is important. What can playwrights learn from a reading of their play?

The Revision Play
by YPT

SCENE 1

LINDA: Hi.

GEORGE: Hi.

LINDA: What's up?

GEORGE: Nothign.

LINDA: OK.

GEORGE: I don'tlike you.

LINDA: OK.

GEORGE: I don't like your weird hair.

LINDA: OK.

GEORGE: Quit lookin at me.

LINDA: I wasn't looking at you.

GEORGE: I saw you.

LINDA: Whatever.

George calls Linda stupid. George walks over to Linda's desk. He touches Linda's hair.

LINDA: Hey!

GEORGE: LOL. Uggggggggggly.

LINDA: It's not ugly! It's jst not green!

GEORGE: I can see that! Hairborey! Haaaaaaaaaaaaairbooorrrrey!

LINDA: Don't call me that!

GEORGE: What are you gonna do about it?

LINDA: I don't know.

GEORGE: OK.

LINDA: OK. Just don't call me that again.

GEORGE: Alright. OK.

(LINDA'S DAD comes to the door.)

LINDA'S DAD: Linda, it's time to go now.

(LINDA walks out with her dad. When she gets home LINDA tells her dad what GEORGE said. LINDA cries and her dad promises to help.)

Assessments

The Development of an Assessment Process for the *In-School Playwriting Program*

Barry Oreck, Ph.D.

When I was approached in 2007 to help design a student assessment process for the *In-School Playwriting Program*, the staff of Young Playwrights' Theater (YPT) recognized how challenging that task would be. Designing and implementing a systematic, individual student assessment in schools would require a serious organizational commitment, a critical look at the curriculum and ongoing training for teaching artists. After twelve years of providing the playwriting program to students throughout the DC region, it was clear that the organization was ready to take that next step: to better understand the impact of the program, to evaluate and improve instruction and to be able to communicate to schools, teachers and parents what students were learning through the process. Direct responses and surveys affirmed that students and teachers were excited about the program and students were improving their writing. But how could we investigate the impact of the experience on all students, including those who struggled with written English, those who had been turned off from English class, those who didn't believe they had a story to tell?

YPT works, for the most part, within the language arts classroom, adapting its program to accommodate huge differences in each school's literacy instruction, reading levels, student motivation and a myriad of other local circumstances and challenges. In a time of intense pressure for test-score improvement, the *In-School Playwriting Program* was, for some students, the only creative writing course they would take. How could an outside arts organization, working once a week for twelve weeks in extremely varied DC public schools, hope to assess the impact of the experience on students?

The first step in designing the assessment process was to articulate the central goals of the program. The YPT staff and teaching artists participated in processes to clarify values, to look in detail at the curriculum and progression of lessons and to study student writing from the range of schools and grades YPT serves. The staff identified an overarching value for students: to inspire students to communicate in writing. Finding the "power of the voice" in dramatic form, as the teaching artists put it, empowers students and offers them new tools to express things that matter to them. Some tools addressed character and their settings, motivations and feelings; others focused on storytelling skills involving events and consequences; and other tools supported grammar, punctuation and the conventions of playwriting to allow actors to read and perform the work. All of these central goals and tools directly address Common Core State Standards and local DC Arts Standards for elementary, middle and high school, and the staff was easily able to identify key standards related to each lesson and activity.

Alongside their articulation of large goals and tools for students to work toward them, the team devised assessment criteria and scoring rubrics for writing. The criteria included aspects of creativity, characters and story, as well as form and clarity (i.e. grammar and word choice). Other criteria used to assess students' understanding of these concepts required direct feedback from students and teachers. Issues of motivation, interest and understanding of theater as a vehicle for personal communication and attitudes toward the playwriting experience, writing and English class would be investigated through questionnaires and surveys.

As the assessment criteria began to take shape, we were developing and testing writing activities that could demonstrate learning and growth over time. It was obvious that we could not simply assess the students' final play drafts; too many issues affected the completion of the final product. Instead, we devised a pre-post assessment that would compare students to themselves over the course of the program through an initial writing assignment in session two and a similar but more challenging assignment in session eleven. It was essential that these exercises be engaging and fun for the students, that they offer choices for personal interpretation and that they take an hour or less to complete. They shouldn't seem like "regular" English class assignments or a test. In addition, we redesigned the pre-post surveys for students and teachers to reflect the re-defined criteria.

After five years the process continues to evolve. The results, as you will see, were impressive but realistic. We saw significant – in many cases striking – improvement in many categories, but where we did not see progress was as important as where we did, revealing places for improvement in the curriculum, changes in the process or clarification of the scoring rubrics. Systematic monitoring of student progress and the use of feedback and data to improve instruction are now essential elements of YPT. This model of mixed-methods, pre-post student-level assessment has proved highly useful for the organization and the schools it serves and is one of the most thorough and effective processes I know of used by an arts education organization in the U.S. For that I give tremendous credit to the YPT staff, teaching artists and collaborating schools for their thoughtfulness, diligence and educational understandings in creating and sustaining this process.

*   *   *

Barry Oreck, consultant, researcher, teacher and writer in arts education, received his doctorate in Educational Psychology from the University of Connecticut and is an adjunct professor in Education at Long Island University Brooklyn, and the International Graduate Programs for Educators of SUNY Buffalo. From 1983 to 2001 he directed ArtsConnection's arts-in-education programs in over 150 New York City public schools. Since 2001 he has been a consultant in curriculum, assessment and program development for the Ohio Department of Education, Arizona Commission on the Arts, Shakespeare Theatre Company, Young Playwrights' Theater, Lincoln Center Theater, the Metropolitan Opera Guild, Young Audiences, Educational Testing Service, the Council of Chief State School Officers and the DeWitt-Wallace Readers Digest Fund, among others. He has developed student assessment processes for the Mississippi Department of Education, the Cleveland Municipal School District and the New York City Public Schools. His research on artistic talent, self-regulation and the professional development of classroom teachers and teaching artists has been published as part of the Champions of Change research compendium, Arts Education Policy Review, International Handbook of Research in Arts Education, Journal of Teacher Education, Youth Theatre Journal and Teaching Artist Journal, among other publications.

www.barryoreck.com

Assessment Results

Each year, Young Playwrights' Theater evaluates its *In-School Playwriting Program* using tools that were developed with arts education researcher Dr. Barry Oreck. Students participate in controlled writing exercises during the second and eleventh sessions of the twelve-workshop series. The exercises are designed to measure students' skills in specific areas: creative thinking, developing characters, dramatizing conflict, creative use of language and grammar. YPT conducts these assessments in order to measure student learning in our programs and analyze the impact on students' ability to express themselves clearly and creatively. The following data relate specifically to high school student participants in YPT's *In-School Playwriting Program* during the 2011-2012 school year.

Creative Thinking

During the program, the percentage of students that reached Exemplary or Proficient levels in their ability to convey unique points of view and innovative thinking in their writing rose from 29% to 68%.

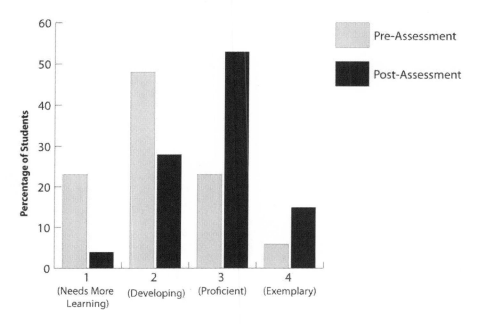

Common Core State Standard addressed: W.11-12.3: Write narratives to develop real or imagined experiences or events using effective technique, well-chosen details, and well-structured event sequences.

"YPT gets anyone and everyone to think creatively and express themselves. I think YPT was valuable because thinking outside the box is very important, because you always have to attack a situation from different angles."

– Rosina, *In-School Playwriting Program* alumna

Character

The percentage of students demonstrating Exemplary or Proficient skill in creating compelling, active and fully formed characters rose from 20% to 76%.

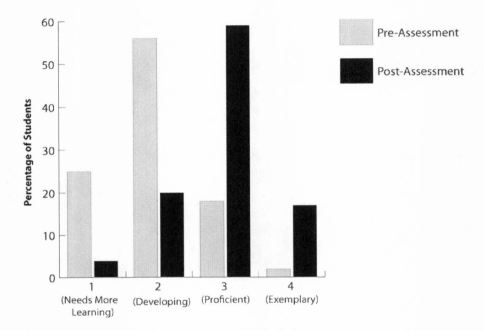

Common Core State Standard addressed: W.11-12.3b: Use narrative techniques, such as dialogue, pacing, description, reflection, and multiple plot lines, to develop experiences, events, and/or characters.

"YPT taught us how different characters might sound using different punctuation and words."
– Jeffrey, *In-School Playwriting Program* alumnus

Conflict

57% of students attained Exemplary or Proficient levels in dramatizing an engaging conflict based on the objectives and obstacles of the characters, as compared to 28% at the beginning of the program.

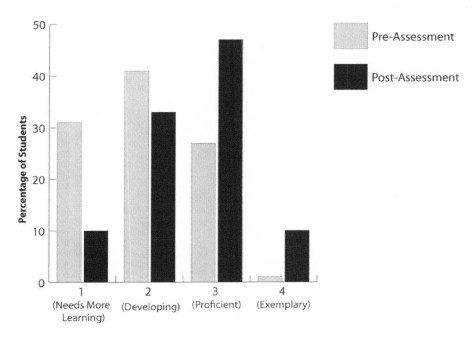

Common Core State Standard addressed: W.11-12 3a: Engage and orient the reader by setting out a problem, situation, or observation and its significance, establishing one or multiple point(s) of view, and introducing a narrator and/or characters; create a smooth progression of experiences or events.

"I think YPT is valuable because it taught me to think, 'Who am I?' and 'How am I viewed in society?'"
– Roxy, *In-School Playwriting Program* alumna

Language

The percentage of students that were able to manipulate language to accurately portray character and situation in their writing rose from 20% to 67%.

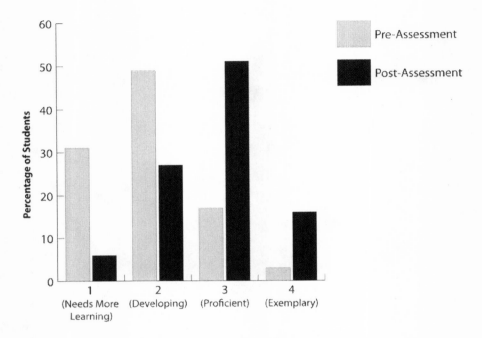

Common Core State Standard addressed: W.11-12.3d: Use precise words and phrases, telling details, and sensory language to convey a vivid picture of the experiences, events, setting, and/or characters.

"YPT taught me how to write in general: how to include details and describe the scenes more."
– Keara, *In-School Playwriting Program* alumna

Grammar

By the eleventh workshop, 64% of students were able to demonstrate Exemplary or Proficient skill in the proper use of grammar, or the intentional misuse of grammar to accurately depict speech communities, as compared to only 30% of students in the second workshop.

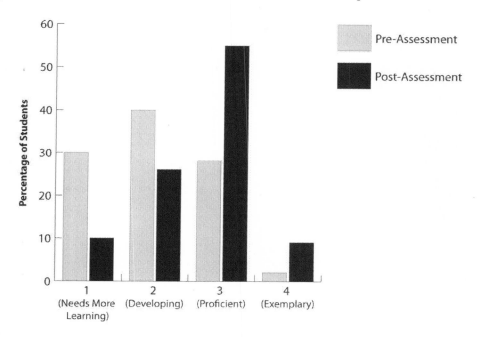

Common Core State Standard addressed: L.11-12.1: Demonstrate command of the conventions of standard English grammar and usage when writing or speaking.

"I would recommend YPT to other students because it helps me practice my English and makes me think of ideas. It was one of most valuable parts of my education because I got a chance to do something that I've never done before and also it was so fun."
– Parichat, *In-School Playwriting Program* alumna, English Language Learner

About YPT

Young Playwrights' Theater (YPT) is the only professional theater in Washington, DC dedicated entirely to arts education. Our mission is to teach students to express themselves clearly and creatively through the art of playwriting. Through interactive in-school and after-school programs, YPT activates student learning and inspires students to understand the power of language and realize their potential as both individuals and artists. By publicly presenting and discussing student-written work, YPT promotes community dialogue and respect for young artists.

YPT's Guiding Principles and Beliefs

Each student has a story worth telling. We believe the stories that our students have to tell are valuable and provide communities with a powerful perspective about the youth experience. The YPT process invites students to share their ideas, dreams and beliefs through the playwright's craft.

The arts are critical to excellence in education. We believe that theater and the art of playwriting are powerful tools in developing creativity and self-expression and in fostering learning across disciplines.

The process is more important than the product. We involve students in an ongoing creative process that enhances their learning and literacy while providing them with appropriate building blocks to construct a play. While we strive for artistic excellence, we believe the effect of the YPT process is ultimately more important than the work produced.

We strive for high standards from all who participate in our programs. The YPT process honors and respects the value of the work of its professional artists, students and partners. YPT expects the same self-discipline and respect from students as it does from the professionals involved in the process.

We meet students where they are. By reaching out to students through organized in-school, after-school and summer programs at neighborhood

337

schools and community centers, YPT provides students of diverse backgrounds with a supportive environment where they can exchange ideas and express themselves freely.

Young Playwrights' Theater
Brigitte Pribnow Moore, Executive Director
Nicole Jost, Artistic Director

2437 15th Street NW
Washington, DC 20009
(202) 387-9173
www.yptdc.org

16990003R00204

Made in the USA
Charleston, SC
20 January 2013